Reading is for Knowing

Literacy Acquisition, Retention, and Usage among the Machiguenga

SIL International
Publications in Language Use and Education

Publication 1

Publications in Language Use and Education is a serial publication of SIL International. The series began as a venue for works covering a broad range of topics in sociolinguistics and has been expanded to include topics in education, including mother-tongue literacy, multilingual education, and nonformal education. While most volumes are authored by members of SIL, suitable works by others will also form part of the series.

Series Editors

Gloria E. Kindell
Graduate Institute
of Applied Linguistics

Stephen L. Walter
Graduate Institute
of Applied Linguistics

Volume Editors

Stephen L. Walter
Marilyn Mayers
Bonnie Brown

Production Staff

Bonnie Brown, Managing Editor
Karoline Fisher, Compositor
Hazel Shorey, Graphic Artist
Patricia Davis, Cover Photo

Reading is for Knowing

Literacy Acquisition, Retention, and Usage among the Machiguenga

Patricia M. Davis

SIL International
Dallas, Texas

© 2004 by SIL International
Library of Congress Catalog No: 2003-109780
ISBN: 1-55671-094-1
ISSN: 1545-0074

Printed in the United States of America

All rights reserved. No part of this publication may be reproduced, stored in a retrieval system, or transmitted in any form or by any means—electronic, mechanical, photocopy, recording, or otherwise—without the express permission of the SIL International. However, short passages, generally understood to be within the limits of fair use, may be quoted without written permission.

Copies of this and other publications of the SIL International may be obtained from

International Academic Bookstore
SIL International
7500 W. Camp Wisdom Road
Dallas, TX 75236-5699

Voice: 972-708-7404
Fax: 972-708-7363
Email: academic_books@sil.org
Internet: http://www.ethnologue.com

Dedication

To the team who made this story possible:

George and Robert McKerihan,
two Canadian brothers whose outreach and prayers
encompassed the globe.

R. W. Nichols and Henry Stuart
—Dallas businessmen, strategic thinkers—
representatives of many who invest in the less fortunate.

Ellen Ross and Wayne and Betty Snell,
who designed the Machiguenga alphabet
and thereby laid the foundation for all that followed.

The Machiguenga bilingual teachers,
true educational pioneers.

Children of different realms, each of these has risen from obscurity
to impact our generation for the better. In the process they have
bequeathed to us sterling examples of faith and perseverance,
hard work, and love.

And to Harold Davis,
who gave his life in pursuit of the dream that one day the story
contained in these pages might become reality.

Contents

List of Tables xv

List of Figures xviii

Preface xix

Acknowledgements xxi

1 The Setting 1
   Introduction 1
   The People 2
   Geography 2
   Social Organization 4
   History 6
   Purpose of the Study 7
   Theoretical Framework 7
   The Problem 9
   The Questions 10
      Sociological questions 10
      Educational questions 11
   Significance of the Study 11
   Definitions and Terms 12
   Organization of the Study 14

2 Literacy in Minority Societies: A Look at the Issues . . . 17
   Introduction 17
   Social Change 18
      Patterns of change 18

	After the shock: Forms of accommodation	19
	Sociological Considerations	20
	Literacy as a basic human right	20
	Uses of literacy	21
	The relation between oracy and literacy	22
	What is it to be literate?	22
	The cognitive effects of literacy	23
	Literacy in society	24
	The importance of mother-tongue literacy	24
	Using a second language as the language of instruction	25
	The relation of literacy to development	26
	The gender gap	27
	Criteria for literacy programs	28
	Critical mass	28
	Predicting acceptance of vernacular literacy	28
	Factors in literacy retention	31
	Literacy acquisition in Amazonia	33
	Educational Considerations	34
	Traditional learning patterns	34
	Minority language students in majority society schools	35
	Chapter Summary	36
3	**Reading: What Is Involved?**	39
	Introduction	39
	Defining Literacy	39
	History of the Discussion	40
	The Reading Process	43
	Mother-Tongue Reading	47
	Evaluation	48
	Testing oral reading	50
	Informal reading inventories	51
	Scoring oral reading tests	53
	Chapter Summary	58
4	**Forty Years in Review**	61
	Introduction	61
	The Beginning of Literacy	62
	Charting Developments	63
	The 1950s	65
	The 1960s	67
	The 1970s	73
	The 1980s and 1990s	81
	Chapter Summary	84

Contents

5 Schools for the Machiguenga 87
Introduction 87
Preparation 87
Teacher Training 89
The Early Schools 90
The Early Textbooks 91
Expansion 92
The Structure of Schools 92
Curriculum Development 95
    Beginning numeracy 95
    Reading 99
School Supervision 100
Educational Reform 102
Author, Print Shop, and Translation Training 106
Textbook Revision 107
Teacher Dedication 110
Chapter Summary 110

6 Developing New Research Methods 111
Introduction 111
Early Preparation 111
    Choosing the sample 112
    Community profiles 114
    Requesting authorization 120
Setting Standards for Machiguenga Readers 122
    Positing minimal levels of skill as criteria for success ... 124
    Levels of difficulty 127
    Criteria for Basic (or functional) skill 127
    Criteria for Intermediate level skill 128
    Criteria for Advanced (full) skill 129
Content of the Evaluation Instruments 129
    The interview form 130
    Reading tests 130
Chapter Summary 134

7 Collecting Data the Cultural Way 135
Introduction 135
Data Collection 135
    The interviews 136
    The reading tests 137
    Writing 138
    Changes made as the result of early testing .. 138
The Population Surveyed 139

Preparation for Analysis. 141
　　　　Transcription of the interviews 141
　　　　Syllable counts 142
　　　　Score charts 142
　　　　Interlinear translations. 142
　　　Coding the Raw Data 142
　　　　The interviews 142
　　　　The Machiguenga reading tests 143
　　　　Recording the reading scores 146
　　　Interrater Reliability 147
　　　　Machiguenga readings 147
　　　　Spanish readings 147
　　　Data Analysis 148
　　　Strengths and Limitations of the Methods 148
　　　　Strengths 148
　　　　Limitations 150
　　　Chapter Summary 152

8　Literacy in Machiguenga Society **155**
　　　Introduction 155
　　　Factors Influencing Literacy Acquisition 155
　　　　Congruence with national policies 156
　　　　Congruence with literacy predictors 156
　　　　A favorable sociological situation 159
　　　　Constructive patterns of accommodation 161
　　　　Productive coping strategies and sense of control 162
　　　　Special challenges 163
　　　How the Machiguenga Define a Literate Person 164
　　　　To read and write is to comprehend print 164
　　　　To read and write is to master a skill 165
　　　　To read and write is to undergo a learning process. . . . 165
　　　　To read and write relates to the self 165
　　　　Reflecting…. 167
　　　Institutionalization of Literacy and Group Custom 167
　　　　The institutionalization of literacy 167
　　　　Group use of literacy 172
　　　　Reflecting…. 173
　　　Chapter Summary 173

9　Personal Perspectives: Attitudes and Usage **177**
　　　Introduction 177
　　　Attitudes Towards Literacy 177
　　　Evidences of Literacy 183

Numeracy	185
The Personal Face of Literacy	186
Attitudes Towards Change	188
Reflecting	189
Factors Influencing Literacy Retention	190
Gender	192
Chapter Summary	193

10 Literacy Levels 195

Introduction	195
Reading Levels Attained	195
The Basic Test	196
Accuracy	196
Fluency	197
Comprehension	199
Rate	202
Number of syllables correct	202
Met preset standards?	204
The Intermediate Test	205
Accuracy	205
Fluency	206
Comprehension	208
Rate	209
Met preset standards?	210
The Advanced Test	210
Accuracy	211
Fluency	211
Comprehension	213
Rate	214
Met Preset Standards?	215
The Spanish Test	216
Accuracy	216
Fluency	217
Comprehension	218
Rate	220
Met preset standards?	220
Community Literacy Levels	221
A Summary of the Results	222
Literates by UNESCO standards	224
Chapter Summary	225

11 Interpreting the Findings 227

Introduction	227

Met Standards—All Tests	227
Critiquing the Scores	230
The accuracy scores	230
The fluency scores	233
The comprehension scores	234
The rate scores	235
Syllable recognition	236
Camisea versus the Other Communities	237
Distribution of Literacy Skills	239
Distribution by Literacy Levels	241
Generalization of the Results	242
Procedural Questions	243
Were the preset minimum reading standards appropriate?	243
Were the assessment instruments appropriate?	244
Reflecting….	244
Were the research procedures feasible under village conditions?	244
Reflecting….	245
Chapter Summary	245

12 Gender, Time in School, and Literacy Retention … 247

Introduction	247
Gender	247
Instruction Time Required for Participants to Reach Each Level of Skill	251
Basic Test	251
Intermediate Test	251
Advanced Test—adults	252
Advanced Test—students	252
Spanish Test	252
Reflecting….	253
Extent to which Basic Literacy Has Been Maintained	253
Adults who met preset standards	253
Adults who had not maintained literacy skills	255
Results from Adult Literacy Classes	258
Chapter Summary	259

13 Lessons and Implications … 263

Strengths and Limitations of the Study	263
The Literacy Rate Compared	264
Lessons and Implications	266
Recommendations	270
Recommendations for policy makers	270

    Recommendations for educators and field workers 273
    Recommendations for future studies 274
  Predictions and Concerns for the Future 276
  A Tribute 277
  Chapter Summary 277

Appendix A: Interview Form 281

Appendix B: Examples of the Reading Tests 287

Appendix C: Reading Score Chart 295

Appendix D: Example of the Comprehension Scale 299

References 303

List of Tables

5.1	Books recommended for the Bilingual Schools—1984.	104
6.1	Reported population of villages.	112
6.2	Random sampling of remote villages	113
6.3	Easy-to-difficult reading material.	127
7.1	The number of students who took the tests	140
7.2	Summary of the Reading Survey	141
8.1	Concepts of literateness	166
9.1	Do you read well?.	178
9.2	Do you read much?	178
9.3	Do you write much	179
9.4	Will you continue reading?.	179
9.5	In which language will you read?.	180
9.6	Who needs to read?	181
9.7	Do women need to read?	181
9.8	Do officials need to read?	182
9.9	Number of types of literacy in evidence.	184
9.10	Can you buy and sell?.	185
9.11	Can you count money?	186
10.1	Basic Test: Fluency	199
10.2	Basic Test: Comprehension.	201
10.3	Basic Test: Number of syllables correct	203
10.4	Basic Test: Met preset standards?.	204
10.5	Intermediate Test: Accuracy	206
10.6	Intermediate Test: Fluency.	207
10.7	Intermediate Test: Comprehension	208

10.8	Intermediate Test: Rate	209
10.9	Intermediate Test: Met preset standards?	210
10.10	Advanced Test: Fluency	212
10.11	Advanced Test: Comprehension.	213
10.12	Advanced Test: Met preset standards	215
10.13	Spanish Test: Fluency	218
10.14	Spanish Test: Comprehension.	219
10.15	Spanish Test: Met preset standards	221
10.16	Community Literacy Levels.	222
11.1	Overall summary	228
11.2	Detailed summary.	230
11.3	Basic Test—Low accuracy compared with low comprehension	231
11.4	Intermediate Test—Low accuracy compared with low comprehension	232
11.5	Advanced Test—Low accuracy compared with low comprehension	232
11.6	Basic Test—Rate related to comprehension	235
11.7	Intermediate Test—Rate related to comprehension	235
11.8	Advanced Test—Rate related to comprehension	235
11.9	Summary of rate and comprehension	236
11.10	Distribution of measured fluency and comprehension skills among the Machiguenga community.	237
11.11	Met standards—Camisea versus other communities.	239
11.12	Met standards—within group.	240
11.13	Camisea	240
11.14	The remote communities.	240
11.15	Spanish Test—Camisea versus remote communities.	241
11.16	Calculations for chi-square goodness of fit tests	242
12.1	Gender of participants.	248
12.2	Literate ranking of females versus males	248
12.3	Goodness of fit—Camisea	249
12.4	Goodness of fit—Camaná	249
12.5	Goodness of fit—all communities	250
12.6	Adults who met preset standards	254
12.7	Adults who met preset standards for the Basic and Intermediate Tests.	254
12.8	Adults who met preset standards for the Advanced Test	255
12.9	Adults unable to meet preset standards	256
12.10	Adults who attended school but did not meet standards on the basic test.	257

12.11	Adults who attended both school and literacy classes but who could not meet standards on the Basic Test	258
12.12	Adult test takers	259
13.1	Literacy rates among certain minority groups in Latin America.	265

List of Figures

10.1	Basic accuracy	197
10.2	Basic fluency	198
10.3	Basic comprehension	200
10.4	Basic rate	202
10.5	Basic syllables	203
10.6	Intermediate accuracy	205
10.7	Intermediate fluency	207
10.8	Intermediate comprehension	208
10.9	Intermediate rate	209
10.10	Advanced accuracy	211
10.11	Advanced fluency	212
10.12	Advanced comprehension	213
10.13	Advanced rate	214
10.14	Spanish accuracy	216
10.15	Spanish fluency	217
10.16	Spanish comprehension	219
10.17	Spanish rate	220
10.18	Literacy level—Machiguenga communities	223
10.19	Literacy level—by UNESCO standards	225

Preface

Literacy among the isolated Machiguenga of the Lower Urubamba River watershed traces its beginnings to 1946 and the commencement of linguistic studies which provided data for the formation of an alphabet. With the help of scores of the original participants, this work describes subsequent events up to 1993. The descriptions and conclusions presented herein are a revision of my Ph.D. dissertation, The University of Texas at Austin, 1994.

The Machiguenga, a comparatively small ethnolinguistic community, deserve respect for the courage and perseverance with which they have met the new challenges. Through literacy they have preserved their cultural heritage and have availed themselves of new knowledge to help them meet the national life and culture. Increasingly, they act as thoughtful, autonomous members of the new society in whose creation they participate—an accomplishment of which both they and their nation can be justly proud.

This is a story which has to be told, yet words can never describe adequately the difficulties, hardships, and disappointments which characterize the saga, or the depth of the joy over any small success. Only those who have lived these years can appreciate the intensity of the struggle. Beyond the bare facts—which, in comparison with certain dismal literacy statistics from other parts of the world, are interesting in themselves—I hope that you will catch a glimpse of the drama surrounding these events, the joy of learning so evident among the Machiguenga, and the thrill of new readers as they develop skills which enable them to cope with their changing world.

Acknowledgements

An unseen host has combined to bring this book to completion. First, appreciation to the Summer Institute of Linguistics (now SIL International) for the grant which made the research possible. I am honored by the confidence.

Gratitude to the Machiguenga leaders and people, who permitted me to crash into their lives and generously shared their knowledge. It has been a precious trust. Gratitude to Professor Edgar Barrientos. His hard work and multifaceted expertise contributed significantly to the depth of the study.

Gratitude to my children and their spouses, Neal Davis and Nancy, and Rosemary and Woody Clayton. Taking turns, they became my travel companions, adopting my project as if it were their own. Gratitude to colleagues in Peru who provided supplies, flights, radio service, treats, and unfailing encouragement.

Gratitude to the members of my doctoral committee each of whom provided unique expertise and enriched my life. Gratitude to Beth McKerihan, Errol Jansen, Randy Boring, and David Harrison for computer aid, to Mary Alice Banker for picture processing; to Hank Bradley, James O. Wroughton, and Merieta Johnson, who read early drafts; to Betty Snell and Elisa Goodson for interrater checks. Gratitude in special measure to statistician Steve Walter, and to administrators, editors, and scores of friends whose support over many years has made them part of the saga. My contribution was small; this incredible host carried me.

Gratitude to the Canadian International Development Agency (CIDA). Many of the school books used in the Machiguenga bilingual schools were generously funded by CIDA. This access to literature contributed significantly to the literary success reported in the present study.

1

The Setting

Long ago I lived in the headwaters and never saw a school, but now we have come to the community and I have learned a little... If I didn't like the school I wouldn't stay here, and if my countrymen didn't like it, do you think they would have moved here? But we came to live in the community. I want my daughters to learn so they can help me. I have only finished a little; there has not been money for me to continue...but my daughter will enter and learn more.
                                             - Father, House 29, Camaná

Introduction

This study investigates the acquisition and retention of literacy among the Machiguenga people of the southern rainforest of Peru. The research was carried out in October through December, 1992, as an attempt to evaluate the results of the first forty years of educational effort in the Lower Urubamba region.[1] No amount of description or statistical data, however, can adequately represent the appreciation for literacy demonstrated by most Machiguenga or the pleasure with which they assert, "Reading is for knowing!" Please add this element to your interpretation of the text as you read on.

---

[1] I am grateful to the Summer Institute of Linguistics (now SIL International) for the grant which underwrote the research project.

The People

The Machiguenga, an ethnolinguistic group of the southern jungle of Peru, belong to the Arawakan language family and are calculated to number between seven and ten thousand. They dwell widely scattered in the rainforest of the eastern foothills of the Andes along the streams which form the Urubamba River watershed in the province of La Convención (state of Cuzco) and on the tributaries of the Manú River in the state of Madre de Dios, a total extension of approximately one hundred fifty by two hundred fifty miles. According to Baksh (1984), the population density is less than one person per square mile, yet the Machiguenga remain one of the most viable aboriginal groups of tropical America (p. 24).

Geography

The Machiguenga homeland falls into three distinct geographical areas. The southern and more mountainous sector, known as the area of the Upper Urubamba River, is separated from the northern Lower Urubamba area by a sharp mountain range and gorge (the *Pongo de Mainique*), which has effectively reduced contact between these two areas of the language group. To the east, a second range, which forms part of the continental divide, separates the Upper and Lower Urubamba people from those in the Manú and Madre de Dios region. Within the three regions, all the rivers are separated from each other by heavily wooded ranges. A few difficult trails connect rivers and/or communities, but most travel is by river—dugout canoe, or, when fuel is available, by motorized dugouts or motorboats. Both the main rivers and the tributaries wind through the jungle in large, horse-shoe curves and are known for their swift current, treacherous whirlpools, and dangerous rapids. At times, during flood season, travel is impossible because of high water. During the dry season, boat travel may also be difficult or impossible because of low water.

As a result of these geographical features, the area has always been remote and difficult to reach. The Lower Urubamba region most easily relates to Pucallpa, the commercial and political center of the adjacent state, which lies 280 air miles—i.e., some 350 naval miles—north of Machiguenga-land. Motorboat travel downstream from the Lower Urubamba area to Pucallpa requires from four to ten days; the return trip upstream requires ten to fourteen days, depending upon the speed of the current. Closer intermediary towns have only partial services. On the Upper Urubamba, beginning at the

Geography

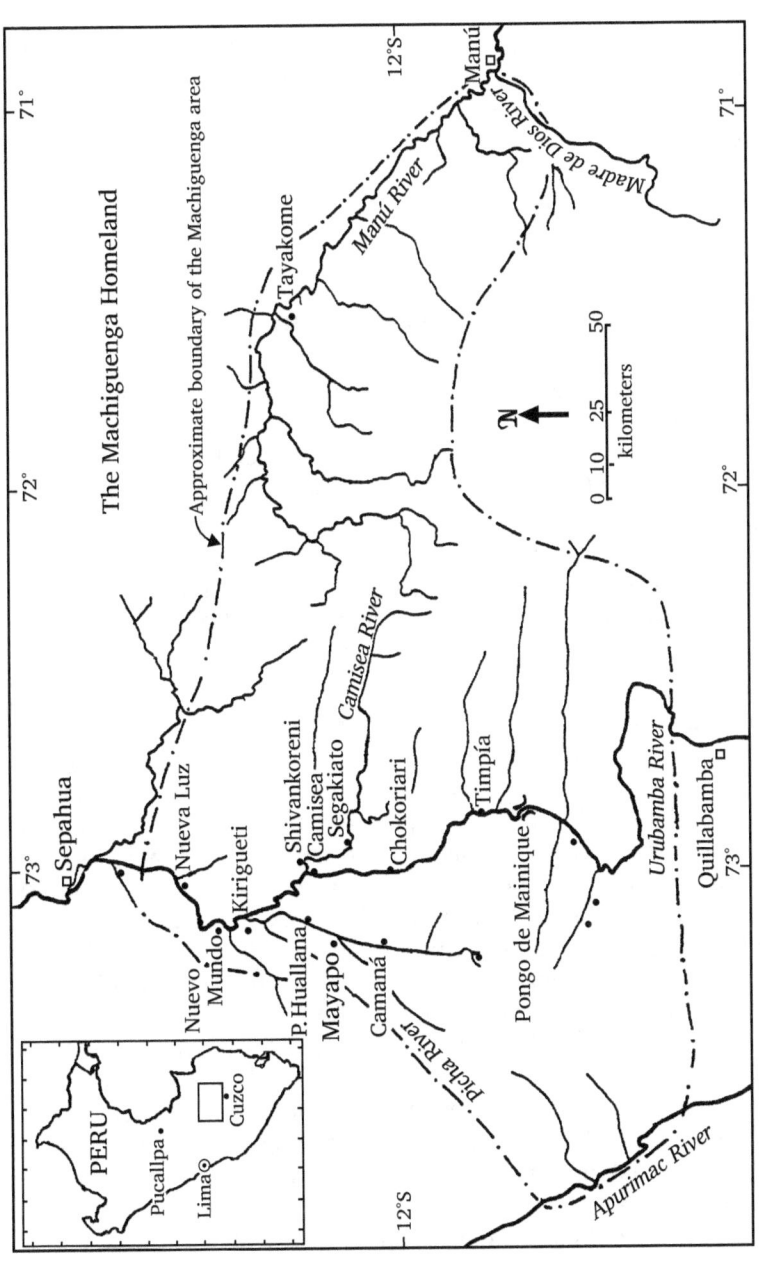

The area currently inhabited by the Machiguenga (Adapted from M. Baksh (1984). Used by permission.)

gorge, approximately five hours' travel upriver with a forty-horsepower outboard motor brings one to the frontier town of Kiteni. From there it is a hard day's journey by truck to the provincial capital of Quillabamba. Another day's journey by train brings one to Cuzco, the capital of the state. These distances, together with the hazards involved, have daunted outsiders; thus the Machiguenga have lived in comparative isolation, particularly in the Lower Urubamba territory. Until recently, no public services were available in the area. There are still very few.

Social Organization

As is typical of isolated Amazonian peoples, the Machiguenga have followed subsistence practices of fishing, hunting, collecting, and slash-and-burn agriculture which, according to their statements, have met their needs quite satisfactorily. Rosengren (1987) describes the society as:

> highly atomistic and amorphous...They do not live in nucleated villages and have no fixed notions of territoriality. They are not divided into clans, lineages or moieties....Their society is loosely structured and they themselves are generally individualistic. People are not arranged in hierarchies of any sort. (p. 3)

Rather, they conform to the classical definition of an egalitarian society "in which there are as many positions of prestige in any given age-sex grade as there are persons capable of filling them" (Fried 1967:33).

Expert in jungle lore, hardworking, and honest, the Machiguenga are, nevertheless, shy people who tend to preserve high levels of intimacy and mutual dependence between husbands and wives and a low level of aggressive or quarrelsome behavior in social relationships (Johnson 1978:285–286). Courtesy is highly valued, and exchange is an important aspect of interpersonal relationships (Baksh 1984:58). A complex set of variables governs the domestic relations relating to exchange (Johnson, 1978, p. 11). Both men and women are skillful in their adaptation to their environment and have well-developed strategies for procuring wild food (Baksh 1984:63–117). The men are also considered to be expert agriculturalists whose agricultural system is efficient and nondestructive (p. 140). In 1992, the skills of weaving, basket making, canoe making, house building, arrow making, and production of string bags were still alive; some people still know how to make clay pots. Rich repertoires of oral literature and knowledge concerning herbal and medicinal plants also exist.

Social Organization 5

A typical village with school and playing field at top left.

At a typical home, coffee and beans are seen drying in the front yard.
(R. Clayton photos, 1992)

History

Western contacts with the Machiguenga can be traced back to centuries-old references in the accounts of the soldiers, priest-missionaries, adventurers, and explorers who first visited Machiguenga territory (Rosengren 1987:36–51). Zarzar (1985:224) cites ancient accounts telling of raids by the neighboring Piro; however, little of certainty is recorded until the mid-1800s. The group evidently was passive and in little evidence as travelers passed through their area after the Spanish conquest, preferring to hide rather than to confront. The bark of the Chinchona tree (the basis of quinine, used to treat malaria and yellow fever) was collected in the area for some decades after the 1850s, but faded in importance with the arrival of the rubber boom, which began in the 1870s. During the rubber boom, the practice of capturing and enslaving the indigenous peoples for forced labor (the tapping of rubber trees) was widespread throughout the jungle. Hundreds, perhaps thousands, of Machiguenga died as a result of mistreatment, epidemics, and hardships; many were taken away as slaves; others fled to remote headwaters in an attempt to avoid contact. In the period following the rubber boom, some haciendas were established in the Machiguenga area, with Machiguenga laborers as the work force.

Dominican missionaries from Spain arrived in the Upper Urubamba portion of Machiguenga territory shortly after the turn of the twentieth century, and, over time, set up four mission stations—Quillabamba, Quellouno, Chirumbia, and Coribeni—with schools which many Machiguenga children attended. Some literacy in Spanish and acculturation to Western society resulted, although, in the mid-1960s, one mission leader voiced to me his disappointment with the low level of retention evidenced. At the present time, only the Quillabamba mission and school remain open.

After 1952, two more Dominican missions—Timpia and Kirigueti—were established in the Lower Urubamba territory. Although the areas surrounding these missions have been strongly influenced by their presence, large sections remained virtually untouched.

Colonization has boomed in the last thirty years, particularly in the Upper Urubamba, as a highway has penetrated from south to north, nearly to the dividing gorge between the Upper and Lower Urubamba territories. Ahead of the highway has come an influx of Quechua and mestizo colonists. Oil exploration during the late 1970s and early 1980s crisscrossed the area of the Lower Urubamba and has resulted in the discovery of a significant deposit of natural gas on the north edge of the dividing range.[2]

Purpose of the Study

The goals of the study were two-fold: (1) to compile a forty-year longitudinal study of literacy and education among the Machiguenga with the hope of reaching an improved understanding of factors which affect literacy acquisition and retention, and (2) to obtain an approximate measure of the success of the program as it was found at the end of 1992. Such knowledge is important both to literacy planners and to Machiguenga educators.

Theoretical Framework

In December of 1993, a summit conference of the leaders of the world's nine most populous countries, meeting in New Delhi under United Nations sponsorship, reaffirmed their commitment to education for all (UNESCO 1994:7). The nations represented at that conference accounted for 70 percent of the world's adult illiterates and more than half of its out-of-school children, the combined total of which was expected to reach 83 million by the year 2000 (UNESCO 1993b:2).

The conference provided additional impetus for literacy workers around the world who are endeavoring to teach reading in newly written languages. Studies such as those conducted by Goody (1968), Scribner and Cole (1981), and Bhola, Muller, and Dijkstra (1983) have provided some information concerning literacy practices in traditional societies. UNESCO (1976) and Bhola (1990a) have accumulated experience in the evaluation of literacy programs. Educators—for example, Laubach (1951), Freire and Macedo (1987), Gudschinsky (1973), and Stringer and Faraclas (1987)—have developed methods for the teaching of reading in preliterate cultures.

For many, literacy is assumed to be a basic human right, as the World Declaration of Education for All reaffirmed (UNESCO 1990:1). Those who belong to this school frequently assume that literacy parallels economic well-being (Wagner 1993:5). Other development workers consider literacy necessary (if not unqualifiedly good) for practical and/or religious reasons, and therefore seek to extend it to all. Some, like Harris (1981), Street (1984),

---

[2]In approximately 1999, an oil company consortium contracted with the Peruvian government to extract the gas.

and Barton (1994), warn of pitfalls. Literacy can be a double-edged sword accelerating cultural disintegration and promoting social discrimination and materialistic values in its unsuspecting "beneficiaries."

Goody (1968:11–17), Walker (1981), and Ong (1982) point out, however, that, in certain societies, reading and writing are not intended for all but are restricted to an elite few, for example priests or appointed individuals. In these societies, the chosen are the only ones permitted access to the institutions which teach literacy skills. In other cultures, multiple literacies exist: The Vai of northwestern Liberia were found to use three scripts, each in a different and unrelated domain (Scribner and Cole 1981). The Tuareg of the Sahara, the Cham of Vietnam, the Yi of China, and the Cherokee of North America have (or have had) a script which was known to many but which has fallen into disuse. In contrast, the Quiché of Guatemala (Henne 1985) and the Quechua of Peru (Weber 1994) have—in the main—rejected literacy in their own language. The sociological factors which engender such a diverse array of attitudes towards literacy acquisition are obviously situation specific, but do underlying patterns exist, and, if they do, how well do we understand them?

Then there is the matter of literacy retention. Heath (1986a) asserts that having reason to speak about the content of written material is one factor which helps to preserve literacy in a society: "Research...gives...evidence that...the establishment of institutions in which talk about written sources takes place is important for retaining and explaining literacy" (p. 227). Giesecke and Elwert (1982) and Thomas (1974) also support this proposition. Talk about the *content* of written sources appears to be more significant in the maintenance of literacy skills than does classroom-type talk about the actual *processes* involved in reading. The Adult Performance Level Reports (U.S. Office of Education 1977) indicate that even in literate societies, few people—least of all marginal literates—converse much about reading processes. Wagner (1993) notes, however, that "The vast majority of studies of human learning have focused on the acquisition of various skills and abilities. Relatively few have looked at the retention and loss of complex skilled behavior" (p. 219), even though retention of literacy ability has been a key concern in developing countries (p. 220) and to educational planners (p. 221).

In addition to sociological factors, literacy programs must address pedagogical issues. Researchers have succeeded in developing a large body of knowledge with reference to many aspects of reading. The following are but a few examples: definitions of literacy (de Castell et al. 1986), reading methods and approaches (Chall 1967, 1983; Guszak 1985; Goodman 1986; Stahl and Miller 1989; Juel 1991), eye movements (Huey 1968; Stanovich 1991), reading instruction (Aulls 1982; Barr and Johnson,

1991; Sticht and McDonald 1992), individual differences (Stanovich 1986), comprehension (Pearson and Fielding 1991), fluency (Hoffman and Isaacs 1991), reading diagnosis (Barr et al. 1990), and reading evaluation (Bhola 1990a; Anthony et al. 1991; Calfee and Hiebert 1991), adult and workplace literacy (Taylor and Draper 1989; Soifer et al. 1990; Mikulecky and Drew 1991; Sticht 1991; Rogers 1992). Nevertheless, this body of knowledge is based on English, and except for Scribner and Cole's (1981) and Wagner's (1993) extensive work, few studies have directed attention to reading evaluation in minority societies. Wagner observes that international education policy is hampered by a lack of understanding of literacy among youth in developing countries (1993:12).

The Problem

As the above discussion indicates, knowledge is still scanty as regards the sociological patterns underlying the acceptance or rejection of literacy, the types of support which must be provided to assure the continuance of literacy, and educational issues related to the teaching and evaluation of reading in languages which do not belong to the Indo-European family. Ferguson (1987:234) noted that authors "offer relatively little on the actual processes of literacy instruction." Heath (1987) requested that evidence be collected from minority societies. Wagner (1993) comments that many literacy-related questions still remain without definitive answers and without empirical data on which to base educational judgments. He cites the need for basic and applied research, along with effective program evaluation, to provide "critical information that will lead...to greater efficiency in particular educational programs...[and to] a broader understanding of the complex reality in which literacy, culture and development are interconnected" (p. 267).

The present study seeks to contribute to accumulated understandings by providing detailed descriptive information about a program which appears to have been relatively successful from the standpoint of the Machiguenga people and by criteria of acquisition, retention, and gender equality. As knowledge grows, an educational data base can be built, making possible correlational and comparative studies which eventually may answer our broader questions.

The Questions

If, as Heath suggests, "institutionalized support" for literacy permeates a literate society, it should be possible, by observation, to identify some of the factors which constitute support, even though cause and effect can seldom be established with certainty in situations so complex. The history of literacy acquisition among the Machiguenga is therefore reviewed, tracing community development projects, the educational process, and other events which originated outside the Machiguenga homeland but which significantly impacted Machiguenga education.

Several subsidiary purposes arose:

1. to explore the Machiguengas' concept of what it is to be literate;
2. to gain information regarding the number of readers produced by the Machiguenga reading program and their levels of skill;
3. to determine the average length of time required for individuals to reach basic, intermediate, and advanced fluency levels, and the lengths of time that literacy skills have been retained[3]; and
4. to ascertain whether attitudes point to the long-term preservation of reading in the society and whether literacy opportunities are equally distributed among the sexes.

The following questions served to guide the research design. They are grouped to reflect chronological order and the dual aspects of the study.

Sociological questions

1. What factors have contributed to the present state of literacy acquisition?
2. How do the Machiguenga define a literate person?
3. Have factors which support literacy become institutionalized, or part of group custom? If so, in what domains do these factors operate?
4. Do the attitudes expressed indicate that literacy will be maintained?
5. What factors have influenced the retention of literacy skills?

---

[3]School instruction is not always a key factor in literacy acquisition. However, the Machiguenga of the Lower Urubamba had not developed any tradition of reading or writing such as Foster and Purves (1991) describe for Pre-Moghul of India, and they had no other forms of academic instruction of the Western genre. For them, schools have been the principal source of literacy and in this study must be reflected as such.

Educational questions

6. What percentage of the population surveyed is literate at a basic, or functional, level?
7. What percentage of the population surveyed has reached an intermediate level of skill?
8. What percentage of the population surveyed is literate at an advanced, or full, level of skill?
9. How much instruction has been required for participants to reach each level?
10. To what extent has basic literacy been maintained?
11. Are reading levels uniform among communities?

At the same time that the main research was being carried out, informal evaluation was also ongoing: Did the preset minimum reading standards prove appropriate for the Machiguenga language and Machiguenga readers? Did the assessment instruments access the core data in culturally appropriate ways? Did the assessment procedures prove feasible under village conditions?

Significance of the Study

This study is significant for the following reasons:

- Among the Machiguenga, favorable attitudes towards literacy and a comparatively high literacy rate have developed in an isolated, formerly monolingual area of the jungle where government schools (the first in history) have been established only since 1954.
- All primary-level instruction has been carried out by Machiguenga teachers. At first, most were themselves barely literate. They continued their education in summer sessions and shared their knowledge with their pupils year by year as they advanced through the grades. By 1992 primary teachers possessed at least a high school diploma, and three high schools existed, staffed both by Spanish-speaking teachers and Machiguenga personnel with tertiary education.

- For nearly ten years, the Machiguenga elementary school program has been overseen at the local level entirely by Machiguenga supervisors.
- Many literacy programs fail once the initiators leave the scene. This one has increased in strength. The factors producing this phenomenon merit investigation.
- Rarely is it possible to document a minority society program of forty years' duration with the aid of hundreds of participant-observers who have known the program since its inception. A research colleague who belonged to the language group but who is also a trained and brilliant educator made possible an insider's perspective on many occasions. The researcher's prior acquaintance with the people and the language also contributed to reduce tension for the shy Machiguenga. This rare and fortuitous combination has yielded data which otherwise would have been very difficult to procure.

The study is offered as a contribution to general knowledge of literacy endeavors in minority language groups and with the hope that it may provide data for scholars, a historical record for the Machiguenga people, and information useful to Machiguenga school administrators.

Definitions and Terms

Based on the writings of authorities in the field, the following working definitions are employed for the purposes of this study:

Nonliterate: A person who does not know how to read or write and has had no literacy instruction of any kind.

Semiliterate: A person who has acquired some notions of reading but who, on an easy story about everyday events, could not meet the following preset minimum standards: 92 percent accuracy, a score of 2 in fluency (on a scale of 1 to 5), a score of 3- in comprehension (on a scale of 1 to 5), and a rate of 80 words per minute.

Literate (by Machiguenga standards): The Machiguenga definition of a literate person could not be determined in advance. It had to be worked out empirically. As individuals described their concept of what it is to read during house-to-house interviews, definitions emerged which are discussed in chapter 8.

Definitions and Terms

Literacy levels

Basic, or functional, level: Able to read material familiar in daily experience and language genre which, potentially, employs all of the syllables of the language, while meeting at least the following minimum standards: 92 percent accuracy, a score of 2 for fluency (on a scale of 1 to 5), a score of 3- for comprehension (on a scale of 1 to 5), and a rate of 80 syllables per minute.

Intermediate level: Able to read material unrestricted as to vocabulary and syllable patterning but moderately sophisticated in language genre and partially unknown in content, while meeting at least the minimum standards listed above.

Advanced level, or full literate: Able to read texts of formal genre which contain new information and abstract concepts, while meeting at least the minimum standards listed above.

Fluent: Able to read with the prosody and expression of natural speech.

Institution: An organized body such as the school, church, community General Assembly, or Machiguenga *Central* in which reading and writing play an integral part.

Group custom: Well-established traditions, like letter writing, which promote use of and talk about written sources.

Literacy retention: The maintenance of reading skill.

Literacy assessment: The testing of reading skills.

Reading, writing, school, literacy: Reading, writing, and school are terms which the Machiguenga understand to be different but are so closely linked in their minds that they are sometimes used almost synonymously with each other and with the concept of literacy. This usage may be noticed in some of the quotations cited.

When writing a book of this nature, the question arises as to what terms may appropriately be employed to refer to the ethnolinguistic groups of Amazonia, especially since, over the years, terms considered appropriate in one era have been labeled derogatory in another. In this paper, taking note of the references made by indigenous groups to themselves, I use the terms indigenous, native, and aboriginal interchangeably, and always with respect. The term mestizo is a cultural designation used in South America to indicate individuals of mixed Spanish-Indian heritage, as differentiated from those of purely Spanish heritage or of purely indigenous descent.

I have also adopted the Spanish use of *Professor* to refer to the Machiguenga teachers. This term of respect for teachers was in use among the Machiguenga at the time of my 1992 visit.

Organization of the Study

Chapter 1 introduces the Machiguenga setting and the goals of the study. Chapters 2 and 3 review the literature and the theoretical background upon which the research was based. Chapters 4 and 5 trace the evolution of the community development and educational programs. Chapters 6 and 7 describe the research design and execution, including the interview and evaluation procedures which were culturally adapted for use in a group-oriented society. Chapter 8 discusses the institutionalization of literacy among the Machiguenga and chapter 9 personal attitudes towards literacy. Chapters 10 and 11 report the results of the reading tests and comment on the findings. Chapter 12 investigates the factors contributing to literacy retention. Chapter 13 draws lessons and makes recommendations—for policy makers, educators, and for future studies. Examples of the questions, test instruments, and school statistics are included in the appendices. Photographs and maps of the communities are scattered throughout the text.

Organization of the Study

Machiguengas continue to preserve traditional arts and teach them in school.

Above: Spinning – Nueva Luz, c. 1972.

Left: Flautists – Pto. Huallana, 1976.
(P. Davis photos)

2

Literacy in Minority Societies
A Look at the Issues

Long ago, headmen were different. They lived in the headwaters and made people work. They knew how to organize people to work and to accustom them so that they would not run away, but they were often mean and angry. Then their people would run off and hide in the jungle; they couldn't get accustomed [to that treatment]. Now the [village] president cares about the people, and we like living in the community. He learns paper so that he can defend his fellow villagers.   - Father, House 18, Mayapo

Introduction

Comparatively little has been written about literacy development in isolated, minority societies; however, in the literature which does exist at least three major themes recur: social change, sociological conditions which promote or discourage reading and writing, and educational considerations.

   This chapter reviews literature concerning social change and some of the sociological considerations related to literacy. The discussion then turns to literacy programs—criteria, predictors of acceptance, factors affecting literacy retention, and variables related to learning.

Social Change

Patterns of change

Centuries of sporadic contact with the Western world notwithstanding, in the early 1950s the Machiguenga of the Lower Urubamba had retreated into an unusually pristine environment, the like of which is now to be found in few places on earth. A number of models have been proposed to describe the processes of culture change set in motion when isolated societies come into heavy contact with majority societies. Those most useful for the purposes of this study are listed below.

Wallace (1956:268–275) postulated a uniform process which occurs when societies face major cultural-system innovation and weather it successfully. It can be diagrammed thus:

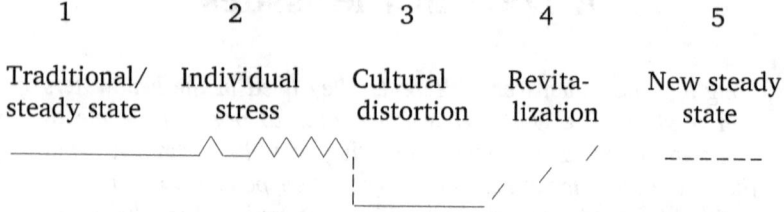

1	2	3	4	5
Traditional/ steady state	Individual stress	Cultural distortion	Revita- lization	New steady state

According to Wallace, the traditional state, which in pre-contact days is relatively stable (barring unusual catastrophic changes), begins to suffer impingement under prolonged exposure to change agents. Every culture has a certain degree of elasticity, but, eventually, when the flexibility of individuals is overtaxed, signs of stress appear. Discomfort may be alleviated, if stress-reduction techniques can be found or the impingement ceases, but appears again with recurrence of the stressor. When impingement becomes relentless and/or violent and traditional coping techniques fail, increasingly severe symptoms are evident which vary with the person. Flexible individuals tend to try out systematic adaptive changes, but rigid individuals prefer to tolerate high levels of chronic stress rather than face the threat of admitting their system is inadequate and a major change is necessary.

Nida (in a 1964 lecture at Yarinacocha, Peru) noted that at this point there may be a resurgence of traditional religion (e.g., the ghost dances of the American West), in hopes that the gods will be moved to deliver the faithful from impending doom. (See also Nida 1954 and Turner 1966.) If all means fail, at least some persons turn to what Wallace (1956:259) calls "psychodynamically regressive innovations," which include "alcoholism, extreme passivity and indolence, highly ambivalent dependency relationships, intragroup violence, disregard of kinship and sexual mores, irresponsibility in public officials, states of depression and self-reproach, and probably a variety of psychosomatic and neurotic disorders. Some of these...become, in effect, new cultural patterns." Guilt may be evident as well as anxiety about the loss of the culture, disillusionment with traditional systems, and apathy towards the future.

Wallace asserts (1956:270) what we have observed: "this process of deterioration can, if not checked, lead to the death of the society." However, he also maintains that native groups have often prevented or postponed extinction through revitalization movements in which the people themselves consciously determined to organize and "construct a more satisfying culture" (pp. 265 and 279). Revitalization movements may include nativistic movements, cargo cults, messianic movements, social movements, and reform movements but often are religious in character. The effect is to reformulate the cultural system and provide more satisfactory ways of dealing with the stress agents.

If the new cultural system proves workable and becomes established as a group norm, a new steady state comes into existence. My observation is that certain people groups develop coping strategies which are more satisfactory to them than do other groups; thus, there are different levels of accommodation.

All anthropologists do not view culture change from Wallace's point of view. Presently, a popular theory understands demoralization to be generated by impingement from a majority society which leaves members of the minority group fewer and fewer options for problem resolution (Gram Vikas and Pradan 1990:105–107; Varese 1985:201–216).

After the shock: Forms of accommodation

Spindler and Spindler (1971) from their experience among the Menomini of the United States felt that reactions in situations of culture change were highly individual but that the following patterns were salient.

1. Traditionalist: Seeking to preserve a way of life that is dying (p. 92).

2. Syncretistic: Seeking to reconcile two divergent cultural systems of beliefs and behavior through a mixture of Peyotism and Christian elements in an effort to reduce self-doubt and provide an acceptable identity for "those who have lost their way" (p. 140).

3. Transitional: Exhibiting acute identity problems. These "In-betweeners" have separated themselves from aspects of both their native culture and

white culture, although they have had some identification with and experience in each.

4. Elite acculturated: Having become psychologically White (p. 191).

Foster (1973, quoted in Hill 1990, personal communication) identifies six stages which can be expected in cases of rapid acculturation:

1. Recipient antagonism
2. Increasing acceptance
3. Rejection of much of the indigenous culture
4. A headlong rush to acquire foreign culture
5. A period of disillusionment
6. An increased feeling of threat and insecurity leading to demoralization/ depopulation or nationalistic nativism

Paulston (1980) indicates that three stages can be expected in the life of an aboriginal society as it becomes a recognized entity within a majority culture:

1. A period of oblivion during which contact with and recognition by the majority is nil or minimal.
2. A period during which the native people acquire education and become aware of their marginalized status. During this time, a strong desire for acceptance may result in rejection of the native language and culture.
3. A period of politicalization during which they strive for equality. They may also give new value to their culture, striving to regain traditional knowledge lost during the second era.

The culture change patterns listed above have been evident in Amazonia, although not equally in all situations, and almost all can be observed to some degree among the Machiguenga.

Sociological Considerations

Literacy as a basic human right

"More than 40 years ago, the nations of the world, speaking through the Universal Declaration of Human Rights, asserted that 'everyone has a right to education'" (UNESCO 1990:1). In 1985 the International Conference on Adult Education, meeting in Paris, adopted a declaration of the "Right to learn":

Sociological Considerations

> The right to learn is:
> - the right to read and write;
> - the right to question and analyze;
> - the right to imagine and create;
> - the right to read one's own world and to write history;
> - the right to have access to educational resources;
> - the right to develop individual and collective skills.
>
> (Bhola 1989a:176)

By 1990, however, more than 960 million adults, two-thirds of them women, were still illiterate. Concerned, participants in the World Conference on Education for All assembled in Jomtien, Thailand, in March of 1990 reaffirmed the right of all people to education and adopted resolutions intended to make basic education universal and accessible to all (UNESCO 1990:3–10).

Uses of literacy

Goody, one of the best known students of literacy in traditional societies, has considered the implications of the graphic representation of language for cognitive processing (1977). Tracing the long-term effects of writing on the organization of society (1986), he points out that writing develops around the core social needs of religion, economics, administration, and law. A thirteen-country survey by Greaney and Neuman (1990) mostly in majority societies, revealed that reading was used for three main purposes—utility, enjoyment, and escape. Heath's research (1983, 1986b) further identified uses for reading in the home.

- Instrumental (for daily life—e.g., price tags, checks, street signs)
- Social interactional (e.g., greeting cards, letters, bumper stickers)
- News related (e.g., newspapers, political fliers)
- Memory-supportive (e.g., notes on appointment calendars, grocery lists, address books, notes on telephone pads)
- Substitutes for oral messages (e.g., messages left by parents for children, notes from parent to teachers)
- Provision of permanent record (e.g., birth certificates, tax forms)
- Confirmation (e.g., directions for putting items together, advertisements, the Bible)
- Critical, aesthetic, organizational, and recreational uses

(1986b:21, 22)

The relation between oracy and literacy

Ong (1982) makes the point that speech is primary. It existed long before writing systems and continues to be primary. Many functional and complex societies have existed, and still exist, without literacy. Thus we have PRIMARY ORACY in groups where there is no literacy and SECONDARY ORACY in societies in which oracy is supported with written materials. Ong sees them as interactive. Literacy per se is not necessarily well understood (Harris 1986) or good, as Harris (1981), Street (1984, 1993), and Barton (1994) point out. Like speech, it can empower by opening the door to new knowledge, but it can also open the door to exploitation or manipulation. Commitment to literacy teaching should be balanced by sober understanding of its limitations and the realization that speech is still primary.

What is it to be literate?

To Heath (1991), the "sense of being literate" is a whole which is much greater than the sum of its literacy skills components. It derives "from the ability to exhibit literate behaviors" (p. 3), which are defined as the ability to "compare, sequence, argue with, interpret and create extended chunks of spoken and written language in response to a written text" (p. 3). Literateness has been erroneously associated with learning to read, rather than reading and writing to learn (p. 5). Few realize that core language behaviors, *with the social relations and cultural practices which support them* (italics mine), form the basis for true literateness (p. 6).

Purves (1987) writes in the same vein, "Literacy, then, must be seen as a complex of various forms of cultural knowledge, which individuals must acquire and put into practice when they read and write. As people become literate, they join a larger cultural community as well as specialized communities" (p. 229).

Stubbs (1980), who observed that "people use different reading skills under different conditions" (p. 10), argued, "written and spoken language are complementary to each other by being used, by and large, for different purposes in different situations" (p. 17). His position was supported by data from the Vai people of Liberia (Scribner and Cole 1981), who employ three writing systems, each in a different domain. Cook-Gumperz (1986), and Cook-Gumperz and Keller-Cohen (1993:283–287) are representative of many who now support the concept of multiple literacies. Note, however, that separation of domains can occur only in societies where uses for literacy have already developed.

The cognitive effects of literacy

Related to the above discussion is another debate as to the cognitive consequences of literacy and whether intellectual/cognitive differences are dependent on schooling. Langer (1987:7), cites Vygotsky (1962, 1978) and Bruner et al. (1966) to argue that "literacy learning grows out of...communicative relationships, and that these joint learning activities support higher levels of cognitive development." As such, "Intellectual differences are a function of the ways in which particular literacy activities are used within a culture; it is the particular uses of literacy rather than schooling per se that makes a difference in cognition" (Langer 1987:6).

Street (1984), however, representing a different school of thought, objected to claims for the cognitive benefits of literacy, feeling rather that they reflected the egocentric bias of the researcher (p. 2). The findings of Scribner and Cole (1981), who studied literacy among the Vai of Liberia, also failed to support claims that literacy led directly to context-independent, abstract thought" (Malone 1994:43).

Herriman (1986:159–160) feels that the emergence of literacy produces the ability to think objectively about the form and function of language (metalinguistic awareness). This leads to the ability to "realize this power of text, to exercise it to both convey and extend his or her capability for logical thought" (p. 170). As a result, the individual is able to employ language to greater advantage in the educational process and to attain a higher general standard of literacy (p. 172). For Wagner (1993, who cites Inkeles and Smith 1974), the new information and changes of attitudes develop new cognitive abilities and "social behaviors needed in a modern industrialized society" (p. 5) and so belong to the school of thought which sees literacy as a means to economic advancement.

A different aspect of the discussion is presented by Cummins (1979), who made a strong claim that "a cognitively and academically beneficial form of bilingualism can be achieved only on the basis of adequately developed first language skills" (p. 222). He asserted that in order to avoid cognitive disadvantages and to benefit academically, the bilingual must attain linguistic competence in both languages (pp. 227–238). Since success in school is dependent on reading skills, Cummins recommended that reading instruction begin in the mother tongue to facilitate literacy acquisition, especially if the child has not been reared in a literate environment (pp. 239–240).[4]

---

[4]See also Baker, C. 1997. *Foundations of Bilingual Education and Bilingualism*, 148–160. Bristol, Pa.: Multilingual Matters.

Literacy in society

Clammer (1976), Trudell (1993), Goody (1968, 1986), and others have documented societal changes brought about through literacy. However, some societies also reject literacy (e.g., Henne 1985; Schieffelin and Cochran-Smith 1984), or lose it through disuse (Gray 1961:27). Langer (1987) cites Cressey (1983), who attributes literacy rejection to "push-pull" conditions in the society which cause individuals to perceive literacy as unnecessary or unproductive.

> Push factors are the external ideological or political forces that attempt to influence people, while the pull factors are utilitarian, internal concerns. Some balance of internal and external factors seems to be needed to make a difference in the development of literacy within a culture. (Langer 1987:5)

Langer (1987) also notes that while literacy creates initial changes within a culture, it also enables literate individuals in the society to make further modifications, according to their desires. "In this way, literacy can change across time within a particular culture, and it can change differentially at the same time across different cultures. Both of these processes need to be addressed when considering issues of literacy in society" (p. 5).

The importance of mother-tongue literacy

Literacy in the mother tongue has an importance even beyond the skills and cultural knowledge involved. As Guiora recognized, the use of the mother tongue in school, "entails cognitive and affective benefits for the reason that the mother tongue is the very life blood of human self awareness, the carrier of identity, the safe repository of a vast array of affective and cognitive templates making up the total web of personality" (1984:10).

"Since the mother tongue is so deeply intertwined with personality, it is not possible to forbid its use without harming the person" (Harris 1987).[5] This point of view is also sustained by Matshazi (1987) and Kashoki (1989). Thus for psychological health as much as for educational reasons UNESCO (1953a) educators recommended, "A child should first learn to read and write in the language spoken in his home....When this foundation has been laid he can acquire a full command of his own and, if necessary, of other languages; without it, there is danger that he will never achieve a thorough command of any language" (p. 67).

Nida (1949), a widely-experienced sociolinguist, agreed.

---

[5]Dr. Ben Harris, professor and international educational consultant, the University of Texas at Austin, class lecture Spring 1987.

> It is impossible to overemphasize the psychological importance of the first step in learning to read...the grasping of this essential value of symbolization is infinitely more easily taught if the symbolism reflects [the student's] own language rather than one which is unfamiliar, or perhaps only partially familiar to him. (p. 19)

Matshazi (1987), an African educator who himself had been required to study in a second language, pled for mother-tongue literacy on the basis that, "Learning to talk in your mother tongue is an arduous task. Learning to read and write in that language is even more difficult. But learning to read and write in a language other than your own is an experience that requires an enormous capacity for endurance" (p. 52).

Presently, the discussion is also framed in terms of minority society rights. The final report from the 1992 International Conference on Education (Geneva) included a statement concerning "the right of individuals and various ethnic groups to preserve their cultural identity, of which their language is one of the most important vehicles" (ICE 1992:4). The International Reading Association Position Statement on Second-Language Literacy Instruction (IRA 2001) supports this right.

Using a second language as the language of instruction

Strenuous objections to the use of mother-tongue instruction (for example, Bull 1955) tend to center around the cost of producing materials in many languages, the need of indigenous peoples to be prepared to cope with the outside world, and the limited educational opportunity available to those who know only minority languages. Modiano's (1968, 1973) research in Mexico, however, indicated that indigenous children taught academic concepts in their mother tongue first, performed better on all other tasks, including their acquisition of Spanish, than did monolingual minority children studying in classrooms where Spanish was the language of instruction. Critics of mother-tongue education, however, cite the Lambert (1978) experiment in which both French and English-speaking students were immersed in a second language (without any transition) and were highly successful. Research commissioned by the World Bank (Dutcher 1982, 1995) strikes a balance, concluding that instruction in the second language may be right for an additive language situation, when students already speak the second language and are adding to their prestige by improving their skills in it. However, in subtractive situations, in which children are monolingual, the minority language is not appreciated, and children are in danger of losing their mother tongue, it is important both psychologically and educationally for students to begin instruction in their first language.

Educator Paulo Freire (Freire and Macedo 1987) argued earnestly for mother-tongue education. In his view, literacy programs in Guinea-Bisseau, if conducted only in Portuguese, the language of the conquerors, would assure that only the elite could succeed, since minority-language children would then have difficulty competing. As a result, access to economic and political success for the masses would be greatly limited (pp. 162–165).

The relation of literacy to development

How closely is literacy linked to economic success? In 1965 the World Conference of Ministers of Education, which met in Tehran, Iran, identified literacy as an essential component whereby economic problems might be solved. As a result, UNESCO and the United Nations Development Program sponsored the huge Experimental World Literacy Program, ten intense years in which over a million illiterates from special groups, such as farmers and factory workers, were enrolled for job-specific training and reading classes. This new approach, known as FUNCTIONAL LITERACY, based reading lessons on occupational vocabulary (Gillette 1977:601–602). (An example of a functional-type program from Gambia is found in Anzalone and McLaughlin 1983). Functional literacy programs cost about $266 per new literate—the cost of an entire seven-year primary education in some countries (Gillette 1977:603), but they failed to raise levels of national prosperity. A study of formal education in a village of south India (Rao 1985) has also drawn similar conclusions and added, further, that formal education may but reinforce existing socioeconomic differences.

John Cairns, former Director of the Experimental World Literacy Program, summarized the conclusion arrived at after years of effort: "In general, literacy is an essential, but insufficient component for development [nevertheless] if we ignore it, we have great difficulty solving other development issues" (Cairns 1985).

This point of view was also expressed by Gough (1968):

> Literacy is...an enabling rather than a causal factor, making possible the development of complex political structures, syllogistic reasoning, scientific enquiry, linear conceptions....Whether, and to what extent, these will in fact develop depends apparently on concomitant factors of ecology, intersocietal relations, and internal ideological and social structural responses... (p. 153)

As for empowering the weak, Freire and Macedo (1987) argue that

> Literacy by itself [should] never be understood as the triggering of social emancipation of the subordinate classes. Literacy leads to and participates in a series of triggering mechanisms that need to be

activated for the indispensable transformation of a society whose unjust reality destroys the majority of people. (p. 106)

Bhola (1989b:64; 1990b:140) points out that literate citizens are able to contribute to their world and to take more charge of their own lives. Supporting this view of literacy's relation to development, Eberle and Robinson of the Vermont Adult Basic Education program (in Ardery 1988) comment, "Perhaps what becoming more literate *can* do is give a person the opportunity to make more choices, rather than waiting in anxiety for someone else's decisions" (p. 61).

Years before, Galtung (1976) had questioned what would happen if the whole world were to become literate. His answer:

> Not so very much, for the world is...structured in such a way that it is capable of absorbing the impact. But if the world consisted of literate, autonomous, critical, constructive people, capable of translating ideas into action, individually or collectively—the world would change. (p. 93, quoted in Graff 1986:82)

If, as Galtung suggests, thinking people can change the world, with or without literacy, then educators should direct as much effort towards teaching thinking skills as they do towards teaching syllables.

The gender gap

In 1980, according to UNESCO program specialists Gillette and Ryan (1983), there were 824 million illiterates fifteen years of age and above in the world (p. 19), 60 percent of whom were women (p. 37). In 1990 UNESCO estimated the number of illiterate adults to be 948 million, nearly two-thirds of whom continued to be women (UNESCO 1993a:7). Women composed 34 percent of the illiterates in East Asia and Oceania, 68 percent of those in South Asia, 64 percent of those in Sub-Saharan Africa, and 17 percent of the illiterates in Latin America and the Caribbean (p. 9). Of the 20 percent of the world's school-age population who do not attend school, most are girls (p. 10). One example, Johnson (1993 citing Stromquist 1989), reported that the education of rural women in Papua New Guinea reflected a level of education "lower than that of males in either rural or urban areas and also lower than that of women in urban areas" (p. 198). This pattern is common in the developing world (Johnson 1993:198; Stromquist 1990:95).

Criteria for literacy programs

Certain basic considerations must be taken into account when planning any literacy program. Goodman et al. (1978:9–10) list the most important as follows:

1. Consideration of linguistic realities—e.g., number of languages? is there a literate tradition? attitudes towards language? towards literacy?
2. Congruence with political, economic, and cultural realities—e.g., national policies towards literacy? support for literacy? religious, ethnic, cultural patterns?
3. Realistic relationship to existing and potential educational programs—e.g., who controls schools? supports schools? supports the status quo? desires change?

These issues become even more crucial if bilingual programs are under consideration.

Critical mass

For a time it was thought that in preliterate societies, a certain proportion of the population must accept the concept of literacy and learn to read before literacy could gain enough momentum to become a permanent part of the culture. Street (1984:2) cites Anderson, who wrote in 1966 that a society requires a 40 percent literacy rate for economic "take off." These suppositions have been challenged by Graff (1986), who writes, "More important than high rates or 'threshold levels' of literacy...have been the educational levels and power relations of key persons; ...capital accumulation, cultural capital...," and similar factors, including consumer demands (p. 76). He asserts, "the history of literacy clearly shows that there is no one route to universal literacy...no one path destined to succeed in the achievement of mass literacy" (p. 77). He notes, however, that mass levels of ability to use literacy have typically lagged behind literacy rates (p. 81).

Predicting acceptance of vernacular literacy

Motivation is a key factor in the acceptance of literacy of any type. United Nations educators have found that "it is more or less futile to try to promote literacy...until keen interest in learning to read and write has been awakened" (Gray 1961:23). Interestingly, Brown and Fernandez (1991) suggest that millennial beliefs (the conviction that goods and wealth might accrue to them through the white man) may have influenced the Campa (or Asháninka) of Peru in their acceptance of outside influences and of education. The Campa are closely related to the Machiguenga, and the Machiguenga do have origin stories telling how God taught them to use fire, provided them with manioc and other necessities, and then left in anger when his good counsel went unheeded. Some say that he went to the land of the white men, who now possess advanced technology as a result. However, to my knowledge, none of the linguists or anthropologists who have studied among the Machiguenga have sensed that their high motivation to acquire knowledge is attributable to such beliefs.

Other factors are at work, however. Walker (1987) attempted to identify them and to develop a model for predicting the acceptance of vernacular literacy by minority-language groups. Of his thirty-eight predictors he found the most important to be the desire to purchase vernacular language materials, and the desire to read Scripture. Close proximity to a town where the national language is spoken, economic pressure for national language proficiency, domination of religious services in the national language, lack of community involvement in the literacy program, and a vernacular language orthography that is very difficult and/or very different from the national language all proved to be hindering factors. Walker's conclusions coincide with findings by Heath (1984) that

> Literacy as a factor in change—economic, social or individual—is highly dependent upon numerous other factors such as distance from urban centers, family size, regional economic growth and community institutional support in matters related to oral and written language uses. (p. 51)

Spolsky et al. (1983) postulated five necessary conditions if the introduction of vernacular literacy is to be successful in traditional societies and, subsequently, if literacy is to be maintained:

1. The group (or at least its influential members) must see value in literacy.
2. Native uses for literacy must be developed.
3. The language must be widely spoken.
4. Those who introduce literacy must support mother-tongue literacy.
5. Literacy is supported by a school system over which the people themselves have some control.

A study of literacy in Samoa has supported these hypotheses (Huebner 1987).

Further, the linguistic choices made by those who reduce the language to writing, i.e., the writing system chosen, the dialect used as the basis for the alphabet, and the teaching materials prepared for reading, strongly affect the "taking hold" of literacy (Ferguson 1987:232). For Ferguson, "taking hold" meant that literacy "becomes a part of the shared cultural resources of the society and is not merely a marginal phenomenon activated only by direct involvement with an impinging, alien culture" (p. 224).

Ferguson (1987) also hypothesized

> The...introduction of a new technological complex such as writing and its associated behaviors and values will succeed best when it 1) builds on an existing pattern in the host society, 2) meets some apparent needs in the society, or 3) is closely connected with another complex that is being successfully introduced. (p. 232)

He suspected that, consciously or unconsciously, agents of change operate with hypotheses of this type in mind.

Case studies

To illustrate, Ferguson (1987:230–233) relates that missionary-linguists arrived in 1824 among the Aleut of Alaska and in 1838 among the Diyari of Australia. In each case, these missionaries, who stayed at least ten years, used reading and writing constantly in daily life, thus providing a model. They were committed to the use of the local language and learned to speak and write it with fluency; they produced books in the language, as well as a grammar and a dictionary. They were fascinated with the local culture and studied it seriously. Ferguson feels that all of these factors contributed to the spread of literacy among the Aleut and the Diyari. The missionaries then established schools in which the native peoples learned to read and write in their own language.

Interestingly, despite the foreign nature of literacy, both the Aleut and the Diyari valued it and maintained it as long as possible. In the case of the Diyari, mother-tongue literacy continued until the language became extinct. In the case of the Aleut, vernacular literacy was still alive in 1986, but English is now reluctantly learned because of the pressure of English-language schools and of society in general. As a result, many of the younger generation no longer speak their ancestral tongue.

Clammer (1976) has presented a detailed case study of the "literate revolution" which took place in Fiji from 1835 to 1874. His conclusion:

> Literacy made possible the acquisition of information, introduced new knowledge, created new wants, led to the possibility of religious, social, and economic revolution, and allowed the individual

Fijian to embark on a personal voyage of self-education....the Fijian could reformulate the organization of and perception of his society and culture... (p. 201)

In 1987, over one hundred years after the initial Fijian literacy program, the two weekly newspapers in the Fijian language had a circulation of 17,000 (Mangubhai 1987:191), evidence that literacy skills have been retained on a large scale.

Factors in literacy retention

Just as important as the initial acceptance of literacy are the factors which promote literacy retention. One key ingredient is sufficient practice. Wagner (1993), in a study of literacy in Morocco, concluded that "the important [factor] in the development of literacy is its actual use by children" (p. 137).

United Nations educator, William S. Gray (1961:20–21), recounts experiences in which—because of budgetary and time limitations—only rudimentary reading and writing skills were taught with a series of about twenty-four lessons in one to three primers. Ability to sound out the words of an easy passage and to write one's name (or a simple message) were the only goals. If training was discontinued before students could read and write with ease, they made little or no attempt to use their skills once they had graduated from a class and received their literacy certificate. Without continued practice, they soon lost the skills they had acquired. "Reading skills disintegrate through disuse" (p. 27). Dr. John Cairns, former Director of the Experimental World Literacy Program (cited by Watters 1990), suggests that initially nonliterate students require 500 to 600 contact hours with printed material before they can be considered literate and to have entered the postliteracy phase (p. 53).

Gray (1961) also recognized that "as a community becomes more literate, its reading matter usually becomes more varied and difficult. Hence a level of achievement that was suitable at the outset soon proves inadequate" (p. 27). He recommended, therefore, that a reading program be organized in stages. The goals of the first stage should be low enough and simple enough that students can reach them quickly. As that stage is being completed, motivation can be developed for the next stage. This plan proved effective in the Gold Coast, Africa, where literacy campaigns issued both preliminary and final literacy certificates (p. 27).

Heath (1987, July) in a discussion paper presented to a Vernacular Literacy Conference held on the campus of Stanford University tentatively postulated the following as favorable predictors of literacy retention.

1. Members of the minority language think and talk about language. They make distinctions between saying and meaning, and in some way notice segments. This may include use of puns and awareness of dialectical differences.

2. Kinship and naming practices are not intertwined with land holding, status/leadership distinctions, or other symbolic systems which legitimatize power. (Kinship and naming practices are intertwined with land holding and power structures among the Australian Aborigines, and this has had an adverse influence upon literacy, which is seen as a competitive way of symbolizing property and capital, and hence power.)

3. Opportunities exist to talk about information from written materials in institutions other than the family and the school.

4. Collective sociopolitical discussions take place as an established practice—i.e., the people take part in decision making rather than only a select group of elders.

5. At least some of the following features occur:

    - It is acceptable to borrow vocabulary from other languages, and mechanisms exist for doing so.
    - The society has a broad range of oral narrative types.
    - Speakers do not hold unusually strong valuations of their language as being either bad or good.
    - Speakers have at least some opportunity to explicate the scope and sequence of tasks during the process of activities.

6. There is opportunity for interactive (not merely one-sided) exposure to the outside world.

7. As minority group members adjust to the outside world, a diversity of skills is promoted and rewarded. (When formal schooling is the only source of literacy, everyone tends to develop the same skills, and the delicate balances of the society may be upset. One result may be the exodus of youth to urban areas.)

8. Membership in a modern religious group, IF:

    - The group has frequent meetings to discuss religious texts.
    - There is organizational provision for involvement for both genders and across generations.

- Membership rites are assigned considerable significance.
- Members are encouraged to share their faith actively.

Davis (1988) considered all of the favorable factors listed by Spolsky et al. and by Heath to be true of the Machiguenga; however, in 1992 the situation merited reevaluation in the light of increased pressure from and contacts with the outside world and the absence of much outside support for literacy.

A needed warning concerning retention was sounded by Winchester (1990): "Literacy is not self-maintaining and self-propagating. A perpetual 'campaign' is required if high literacy levels are to be maintained" (p. 37).

Literacy acquisition in Amazonia

Trudell (1993) examined historical, ethnic identity-related, and educational program-related factors which have affected literacy acquisition in the mother tongue and in Spanish among ten indigenous ethnolinguistic groups of the Peruvian jungle, including the Machiguenga. She concluded that for those groups the following positive and negative factors had affected the acquisition of vernacular literacy.

Category	Positive Factors
Historical	Isolation: historical or present History of domination over other Indian groups Control over own economic development
Ethnicity-related	Sense of control over life and future Ethnic and economic self-sufficiency High sentimental attachment to mother tongue Little attempt made at assimilation to national culture Viability of traditional customs Strong domain(s) for vernacular literacy
Education	High regard for learning Willingness to live in larger communities for the sake of bilingual schooling Strong bilingual education program Perceived purpose for learning and education Vernacular literacy instruction available Family "habit" of vernacular literacy The educational reform leading to greater indigenous control in schools

Category	Negative factors
Historical	High degree of contact with the outside world
Ethnicity	Lack of sense of control over destiny Decreased sentimental or instrumental attachment to mother tongue Failed attempts at assimilation to national culture Lapse in use of customs and traditional leadership
Education	Desire for education only in Spanish No bilingual school or a poorly functioning one No adult vernacular literacy promotion The educational reform damaged bilingual school system.

(Trudell 1993:143–144)

Educational Considerations

Traditional learning patterns

A number of authors have described learning patterns prevalent in traditional societies. Among them we find:

- Observation and imitation, personal trial and error, close relationships with instructors, cooperation; difficulty with hypothetical and rhetorical questions (Harris 1982).
- Personalization of instruction, global structure of lessons, and explicit presentation of principles (Ramírez and Castañeda 1974).
- Measured responses, great respect for individuals, indirect commands (Lipka 1991).
- Flexible punctuality, permissive atmosphere (Flinn 1992).

Culture affects the process of learning to be literate (Langer 1987:7). Students socialized into a traditional culture have acquired many skills which promote learning, but their expectations frequently clash with Western educational procedures (Davis et al. 1990; Davis 1991; Heath 1991:3). If traditional learning patterns, categorization patterns, and world view are disregarded instead of used as building blocks, reading and other instructional programs can bewilder the student and make learning more difficult.

Unconsciously, teachers may demand verbal and thinking skills rewarded in mainstream schools. These skills include weighing information, questioning, defending one's point with evidence in socially acceptable ways, imagining, labeling, categorizing, explaining the steps of processes, identifying likes and differences, and relating learned information to real life (Heath 1982, 1983, 1986a, 1986b, and 1991). Heath's list identifies skills which must be acquired by minority-language students if they are to be successful in Western-type schools. Usually, these must be overtly taught as second-culture acquisition, taking care not to disparage traditional patterns.

Minority language students in majority society schools

Studies from colonial countries (e.g., Nkemnji 1989—Cameroon; Dorsey 1989—Zimbabwe) often highlight the inappropriate design of school systems imported from a colonizing country and describe attempts by new republics to improve the quality of education. Another body of literature reports on the lot of involuntary minorities in majority society school systems, especially in the United States (e.g., Ogbu 1978, 1987, 1991; Giroux 1983; Solomon 1992). These studies often report adversarial relationships in which students perceive that in school their inferior status is reinforced; in addition, they may see little relationship between their classes and the work world. Other research describes the dissonance created for minority students who are faced in school with values vastly different from those of their own culture: Leap (1991)—Northern Ute; Fordham (1993)—black women students; Henze and Vanett (1993)—Yup'ik Eskimo. Student reactions to these types of negative perceptions may include passive resistance in the classroom and the formation of tightly-knit minority-group peer groups in which oppositional tactics are affirmed. Unfortunately, by these actions and attitudes victims contribute to their own victimization (Ogbu 1991). In contrast, Foley (1990, 1991) recognizes the existence of adversarial trends but affirms that minority peoples are not entirely passive victims; as they maneuver to control their circumstances they freely make choices leading to positive or negative consequences (1991:83).

Leap (1991) describes a number of cultural adaptations made to facilitate Northern Ute learners' acquisition of reading skills, while still allowing students freedom to decide how much use to make of the information. These techniques include expecting the learner to take the responsibility for learning and for participation (rather than the teacher); linking each phase of literacy training to concrete, immediately obtainable, highly personalized goals; including literacy components within other vocational and adult programs already established; subject matter discussions which show strong links between literacy tecnhniques and the skills used in real life; and use of oral and visual teaching techniques (pp. 34–37).

Even more refreshing is a study by Mehan et al. (1994) describing a program which places students from low-income ethnic and linguistic-minority backgrounds in college prep classes along with high-achieving peers from the majority society. The Advancement Via Individual Determination (AVID) program developed by the San Diego, California, City Schools system aims to prepare underachieving students from minority groups to perform well in high school and to seek a college education. Those students, whose parents guarantee to support their children's participation, enroll as soon as they begin high school, and take an elective class which emphasizes writing, inquiry, and collaboration in addition to their regular course load. As a result of this program, 60 percent of three-year AVID students from families who earned less than $20,000 per year enrolled in college. The authors conclude that "AVID teaches a version of achievement ideology, telling students they can be successful (which AVID defines as going to college) if they are motivated and study hard" (Mehan et al. 1994:101). AVID students, although they are aware of the structures of discrimination, feel they have developed methods for coping with them. They therefore continue to affirm their ethnic heritage and expect—through effort—to achieve academic and occupational success. Mehan and his colleagues refer to this ideology as "accommodation without assimilation," following the terminology of Gibson (1988:105).

Chapter Summary

This chapter contains a review of theoretical and practical issues relating to social change and reading, with particular application to minority societies. Patterns of social change described by Wallace, Spindler and Spindler, Foster, and Paulston inform us of attitudes and trends which may be expected as societies meet inexhorable change.

Sociologically, literacy, now viewed as a basic human right (UNESCO 1990:1), is recognized to be a catalyst for many profound changes in traditional societies. Goody, Heath, and Ong detail some of these. Some researchers suggest that literacy enhances cognitive skills; others, however, regard the correlation as tenuous. Numerous authors plead for the need to begin the teaching of reading in the mother tongue.

Turning to educational considerations, Spolsky, Engelbrecht, and Ortiz postulated five necessary sociolinguistic conditions as predictors of literacy acceptance. To these Ferguson added the linguistic choices made when the alphabet is first formed. Gray, Cairns, Heath, and Trudell

Chapter Summary 37

outlined factors which affect literacy acquisition and retention both positively and negatively. Other researchers (e.g., Ogbu, Foley, Henze and Vanett, Leap; Mehan, Hubbard, and Villanueva) have described minority language students' difficulties in majority society school systems.

School children's writing practice
was found on a prickly pear cactus.
(Woody Clayton photo, Mayapo, 1992)

3

Reading: What Is Involved?

I look [at the paper]. Depending on what is written, I understand it in my head. I know I am not mistaken about what I have understood in my head. I think about what I am reading. The person who does not know how to read does not understand what he is looking at, and so he babbles. He cannot read alone [without being told what the words are], and he does not know how to write.
— Father, Camisea, House 31

Introduction

Reading is central to literacy and to success in Western school systems, but much discussion has been evoked and, over the years, many changes have taken place as regards its definition, standards, and evaluation procedures. A brief discussion is therefore in order.

Defining Literacy

Finding a satisfactory definition of what it means to be literate is not a simple matter (Keller-Cohen 1993; Venezky 1990; de Castell, Luke, and MacLennan 1986; Heath 1986b; Wagner 1986, 1987:xii; Stubbs 1980). This is partly because of changing theoretical assumptions and partly because of rising expectations regarding the levels of literacy needed. In the United States, literacy has been a moving target; criteria for literateness have risen as technology has advanced (Miller 1988:1293). Thus Venezky (1990) mentions conventional literacy, functional literacy, survival literacy, and functional adult literacy (p. 4). Keller-Cohen (1993) traces a progression of understandings from the 1700s to the present—reading, reading and writing, decoding written language, use of printed information to function in society; a bank of knowledge, such as math literacy, science literacy, computer literacy, cultural literacy (pp. 291–295)—and comments that literacy today is differentiated along many continua (p. 294).

In the purely pedagogical realm definitions have also varied. Commenting on this diversity, the renowned educator William S. Gray (1984) states that reading has variously been described as (1) a mechanical process of recognizing and decoding printed symbols, (2) a fusion of words into meanings, i.e., a blend of rate and comprehension, (3) a process which includes reflection on the meanings (pp. 17–18). His working definition is "A person is functionally literate when he has acquired the knowledge and skills in reading and writing which enable him to engage effectively in all those activities in which literacy is normally assumed in his culture or group" (p. 24). A less inclusive definition (UNESCO 1958, cited in UNESCO 1983) stated: a literate is "a person who can with understanding both read and write a short, simple text on his everyday life" (p. 3). This latter definition, however, excludes persons who can read but not write, as the UNESCO Statistical Yearbook points out (1971:31).

History of the Discussion

More than seventy years ago, Thorndike (1917) described reading as "a very elaborate procedure involving a weighing of each of many elements in a sentence, their organization in the proper relation one to another, the selection of certain of their connotations and the rejection of others, and the cooperation of many forces to produce the final response" (p. 323).

For many years, attention focused on decoding aspects: "In order to read alphabetic writing one must have an ingrained habit of producing the phonemes of one's language when one sees the written marks which conventionally represent these phonemes" (Bloomfield and Barnhart 1961:10).

By 1972, Gough was positing a strictly serial, bottom-up process: "...the Reader is not a guesser. From the outside, he appears to go from print to meaning as if by magic. But I have contended that this is an illusion, that he really plods through the sentence, letter by letter, word by word" (p. 354).

At nearly the same time top-down theorists were contending that reading was a process of bringing meaning to print, not extracting meaning from print: "It is only by understanding what you read that you can read aloud or to yourself....The sound must come last and can be dispensed with altogether" (Smith 1975:180).

By the 1980s, interactive models of reading were gaining acceptance. Goodman (1981) assumed that "the goal of reading is constructing meaning in response to text....It requires interactive use of grapho-phonic, syntactic, and semantic cues to construct meaning" (p. 477).

Thus Kennedy (1981) combines decoding and meaning construction, describing reading as "the ability of an individual to recognize a visual form, associate the form with a sound and/or meaning acquired in the past, and, on the basis of past experience, understand and interpret its meaning (p. 5). The prestigious Commission on Reading (Anderson et al. 1985) defined reading as a "process of constructing meaning from written texts. It is a complex skill requiring the coordination of a number of interrelated sources of information" (p. 7).

Seeking to explain the process, schema theorists analyzed reading as the "activation, focusing, maintaining, and refining of ideas toward developing interpretations (models) that are plausible, interconnected, and complete" (Tierney and Pearson 1981:11). Barr and Johnson (1991) speak of reading as a relationship between comprehension, prior knowledge, and skill with print. Skill with print must be developed for the process to function smoothly. Prior knowledge and vocabulary underlie the smooth functioning of the comprehension process. Comprehension is the goal (pp. 16–17).

By the 1990s, Klein, Peterson, and Simington, observed, "most of the contemporary definitions of reading include the following: (1) reading is a process, (2) reading is strategic, (3) reading is interactive, (4) reading instruction requires orchestration" (1991:6). Two examples:

> Reading is a thinking, linguistic, and cultural/social process that is interrelated with and supportive of the other communication processes—listening, speaking, reading and writing. (Hittleman 1988:2)

> Reading is an interaction between the author and the reader. For this interaction to occur, the reader must perceive, interpret, hypothesize, and evaluate printed text. These interactive processes occur in varying degrees, depending on the reader's prior experiences and familiarity with the language, structure, and concepts of the text. (Lapp and Flood 1992:6)

Lapp and Flood point out that although educators disagree as to the exact definition of reading, most do concur that the reading process includes:

1. A strong sense of language.
2. Letter and word perception and recognition.
3. Comprehension of the concepts conveyed by the printed word(s).
4. Reaction to and assimilation of the new knowledge with the reader's prior knowledge and experiences.
5. Understanding of the text's structure. (p. 6)

Following Vygotsky (1978), who asserted that learning took place through social interaction, other reading theorists focus on the construction of meaning as the reader interacts with the author's message, his own understandings, and his experiences with others. "Reading entails both reconstructing an author's message and constructing one's own meaning using the print on the page" (Hittleman 1988:2). As a result, the interpretation an individual reader constructs from a text may—within certain limits—be different from the author's expectation and different from the interpretations of others, and yet be legitimate (Rosenblatt 1989:155–163).

Certain educators, however, have gone beyond the internal processes of reading to include elements of functional literacy (usage).

UNESCO (1953b and 1957) expanded the definition to include writing and numeracy (language not specified), and a level of ability high enough to assure that the skill would not be lost: "[A person] is literate when he has acquired the essential knowledge and skills which enable him to engage in all those activities in which literacy is required for effective functioning in his group and community, and whose attainments in reading, writing and arithmetic make it possible for him to continue to use these skills."

The World Conference of Ministers of Education on the Eradication of Illiteracy, which met in Tehran in 1965, concluded that

> Adult education (and literacy in particular) should not be confined to elementary reading, writing and arithmetic, but should also include both general cultural subjects and a vocational preparation in which account is taken of the opportunities for employment and the better use of local natural resources and which would lead to a higher standard of living. (UNESCO 1965)

Gudschinsky (1973) included mother-tongue reading and writing: "That person is literate who, in a language that he speaks, can read and understand anything he would have understood if it had been spoken to him; and who can write, so that it can be read, anything that he can say" (p. 5).

More recently, literacy is perceived—in the metaphors of Scribner (1988)—as adaptation (survival skills), power (ability to mobilize for fundamental social changes), and as a state of grace (endowment with culture and virtues). Thus, as Venezky observes, most writers now consider that literacy implies a continuum of skills, which include not only the mechanics of reading and writing (1990:4), but are applied in a social context—the logical outworking of the ideas operationalized by UNESCO in the 1950s (Gray 1956; UNESCO 1957).

The Reading Process

The complex facets of the reading process are addressed by several bodies of research. Extensive investigation of readers' eye motions published by Huey in 1908 established the concept of a visual field, the center of which is called the *fovea*. The eye moves along a line of print in jumps called *saccades*, stopping briefly to fixate upon small sections (Carpenter and Just 1977:110). Six to eight letters are clearly perceived as the *fovea* comes to rest on a line of print (Huey 1968:67; Rayner 1981:146). Fixations are more frequent (Stanovich 1991a), and longer on grammatical elements and on ambiguous or infrequent words (Rayner 1981:146–147; Downing and Leong 1982:145). "Most studies...have found that eye movement patterns are determined directly by the difficulty of the material being read" (Downing and Leong 1982:144). A reader also gathers some information (such as the shape of the next word) from the less-clear periphery (Huey 1968:67; Rayner and McConkie 1977:198; LaBerge and Brown 1986). With reference to the total perceptual span, Rayner and McConkie (1977) assert that "no more than 15 to 17 letter positions can be taken as the normal area from which a reader identifies words...it is seldom that a text unit as large as a phrase will lie completely within this region" (p. 199).

This discussion is relevant to the teaching of reading in polysynthetic languages characterized by series of morpheme sequences longer than the normal perceptual span. Whereas in English, entire words—and even as many as two or three words—can usually be perceived by foveal vision, readers of agglutinative languages are able to perceive few entire words, even with the aid of peripheral vision.

Coupled with visual limitations is the limitation of short term memory which is restricted to the number of items or "chunks" of information it can hold at one time. Normal limits are about nine binary digits, seven letters of the alphabet, or five monosyllabic English words—a rule of thumb later referred to as *seven, plus or minus two* (Miller 1956:131; 1967:14).

Unrelated bits of information difficult to remember in isolation (for example, 9, 1, 4, 9, 8, 4) become manageable when organized into meaningful wholes (such as, 8/4/1994). These wholes can come to represent large amounts of information (p. 136). Miller reiterated his findings in 1967. He recognized that the units defined by the reader and the span of immediate memory severely limit the amount of information that we are able to receive, process, and remember. "By organizing the stimulus input simultaneously into several dimensions and successively into a sequence of chunks, we manage to break (or at least stretch) this informational bottleneck" (pp. 42–43). Weaver (1977, pp. 35–36) understands Miller's application to be the organizing of letters into words, and then words into phrases which allows the reader to perceive, learn, and process material in chunks much larger than single letters.

When the reader uses a perceptual span which is too narrow, however, and focuses only on small units such as the letter and syllable, reading comprehension suffers (Downing and Leong 1982:143). Reading researcher Kenneth Goodman (1982b) describes this phenomenon: "I have encountered many youngsters who are so busy matching letters to sounds and naming word shapes that they have no sense of the meaning of what they are reading" (p. 66). These readers also miss important syntactic and semantic clues (1982a:90). Goodman's experience leads him to believe that psycholinguistic universals are such that "the reading process will be much the same for all languages with minor variations to accommodate the specific characteristics of the orthography used and the grammatical structure of the language" (1982b:67). See also Alegría and Morales (1991) and Gough and Juel (1991).

Research abounds to the effect that the word is the unit of reading (Stanovich 1991a, Morris 1992). According to the above discussion, however, the concept that words bounded by space are the basic units of reading appears to be based upon English and European languages and is not as appropriate for the long sequences of polysynthetic languages. Rather, the syllable unit is more generally held to be salient in the perception and production of speech and is common to a wide range of writing systems. Word delimitation tends to be found only in alphabetic writing, in contrast to oral language where word boundaries are not systematically indicated by phonetic features (Henderson 1984:19; Gleitman and Rozin 1977:48).

In polysynthetic languages, many syllables may also be one-syllable morphemes. Pierce (c. 1960) cited the need to list morphemes, rather than words, in a word list compiled for Turkish since "verb and noun stems rarely occur without some sort of inflection or derivation, and the counting of each...as a different item would make a word list meaningless" (p. 6). To a lesser extent, this has also been true for Machiguenga.

Although most of the English language research fails to discuss morpheme recognition apart from the word, comprehension in polysynthetic languages is dependent upon recognizing single syllables as either a syllable, a morpheme, or (infrequently) a word, depending on the context.

Describing how the reading process takes place for speakers of the Guahibo language of Colombia, field linguist and reading specialist Riena Kondo (personal correspondence, September 1994) advises that when literacy teaching was first begun she suspected long words in Guahibo might need extra teaching. Thus length was controlled while beginning students learned that two letters together (a syllable) can represent a sound, and two syllables pronounced together can have meaning (a word). Thereafter, length of words was not found to be a serious problem. Kondo writes:

> I believe this is because they read by morphemes. That is, they read a new word by syllables to a point where something makes sense (perhaps a one-syllable prefix plus a root); then they read to a place where more meaning has been added (another morpheme or two) and adjust their understanding of the word. This they do morpheme by recognizable morpheme until the end of the word, without needing to pause, since their brain processes each added bit of information and adjusts the perceived meaning instantly....
>
> More fluent readers read by morphemes in another sense. They sight-read morphemes or clusters of morphemes and therefore read words in chunks like *bajara-powa-jawabelia* 'to that woman (north, south, or unknown direction)', which contains seven morphemes, three chunks. There is no doubt that reading practice helps with reading long words more fluently, as readers learn to read more chunks by sight.

Kondo tried breaking long words, thinking it might facilitate reading, but testing showed readers, particularly slow readers, were confused by spaces which fell in the wrong places. In the end, only one modification proved helpful: hyphens are now written to distinguish the syllable/morpheme boundaries in vowel clusters, which potentially could be isolated syllables, diphthongs, or—occasionally—triphthongs (e.g., *naca-eweta* 'they are waiting for us').

Linguist Gloria Kindell (personal conversation, October 1994) cites experience from an agglutinative language in Brazil in which perturbation reduces and changes morphemes so that the root morpheme is unrecognizable. In such a case, the reader must use contextual cues as well as information from the syllables in order to construct meaning, and may have to read and reread before the word is understood.

Field linguists and reading specialists of SIL, who teach reading in agglutinative languages, have found that beginning readers tend to bog down in long sequences and that for them to achieve mastery the learning process may be longer than for short-word languages. In polysynthetic languages, readers must learn to group morphemes into chunks large enough so that long sequences can be spanned before the capacity of short-term memory is exhausted. To shorten the spans primer makers for the Piro (Peru) and Choctaw (North America) have separated clitics with hyphens (personal conversations).

Another model, suggested by Burns (1984), uses flip charts for teaching Quechua readers. "Without separating the suffixes from the context of the word of which it is a constituent, the flip section subtly indicates the morpheme divisions which native reaction indicates are internalized by the Quechua speaker" (p. 13). The flip section makes it possible to teach or review at least twice as many suffixes, strings of suffixes and combinations of stems plus suffixes than would otherwise be possible. The following is an example:

(1)

Contrasting stems	Same suffixes	Same stems	Contrasting suffixes and strings of suffixes
pichana	ta	nina	chu
tipina	ta	nina	ta
nina	ta	nina	tachu
Ana	ta	nina	pichu

(Burns 1984:13)

Davis (1981c) developed different chunking exercises, which were used after the syllables of the word were known to Machiguenga students. The "chunks" used in drills of this type were either morphemes or were particles which frequently occur together, and the arrangement of the drill was intended to show how known parts can be combined into a new word.

(2)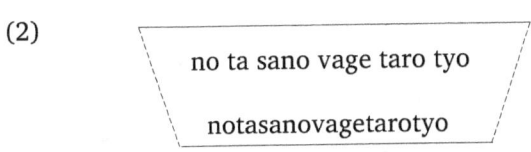

(3) samani   korempi   ikemake
    osamanitake   korempitake   ikemavakero
    osamanitanake   korempivagetake   ikemapaakero
    osamanivagetanakera korempivagetankitsi ikemavetakaro

Mother-Tongue Reading

Reports focusing on mother-tongue reading instruction in traditional societies are difficult to find in United States libraries, although they undoubtedly exist in libraries in India, Africa, and the South Pacific. Neijs (1961), UNESCO (1963a), Pierce (c. 1960), Laubach (1951), Gudschinsky (1973), the International Reading Association (1986), and Stringer and Faraclas (1987) have published guides for primer construction.

A few case studies exist, however. Mangubhai (1987) reported that in the South Pacific literacy took root quickly in monolingual countries but was held back in multilingual countries where education had to be presented in a trade language (p. 186). He also found that flooding classrooms with well-illustrated, high-interest books appreciably increased reading skills and interest when students were allowed thirty minutes per day for sustained silent reading.

Au and Kawakami (1986) taught reading in the mother tongue to at-risk children of Polynesian descent in Hawaii's Kamehameha School. They found that comprehension and participation increased when the students were allowed to discuss the context of the text in traditional *talk story* form (everyone speaking at once). Thereafter, the teacher would ask leading questions, occasionally calling upon an individual to reply. Finally, questions would be asked which would require students to look back at the text in order to find answers.

In another study, Lingenfelter and Gray (1981) described the process of preparing primers for the Bulsa of Ghana, who experienced great difficulty in breaking words into syllables. The primer makers accommodated by teaching whole words first. When words first began to be divided, only words whose parts had meaning were introduced. Slow progression coupled with adequate practice finally enabled students to be successful.

In Davis 1981c, d, I recounted the challenge of designing effective reading texts for a long-word language and illustrated the methods chosen to: introduce open and closed syllables, present the concept of syllable families, give practice in chunking, establish word-building skills, teach capital letters and punctuation marks, and develop comprehension.

Although still comparatively small, the body of literature which describes literacy programs in developing countries is growing. For example, *Reading Today,* published by the International Reading Association, describes IRA cooperation with literacy initiatives in developing countries. *Read Magazine* (Ukarumpa, Papua New Guinea, published by SIL twice yearly) represents reading programs in the South Pacific area. *Notes on Literacy* (published by SIL through 2002) presents a spectrum of articles from a variety of reading programs around the world.

Evaluation

Although many cross-cultural studies have been carried out and information does exist concerning assessment in large literacy programs (e.g., Couvert 1979; Bhola 1990a), the literature is almost silent on the subject of testing reading in minority societies. Authors agree, however, that cross-cultural testing is fraught with multiple hazards. Gray (1961:25) offered the following guidelines:

1. The best way to measure functional literacy is to ask students to engage in literacy activities—such as reading and understanding short notices posted in the village or reading and writing a letter. Readings from the types of materials most familiar (songs, sacred literature, newspapers, etc.) are recommended.

2. The greater and more varied the demands made on the reader, the more difficult are the tests.

3. Reading tests should be developed to measure all aspects of reading—word recognition, word meaning, sentence and paragraph meaning, and rate of

reading. Each test should include graduated exercises that range from simple to very difficult.
4. If possible, the exam should be tested with other members of the community before being administered to the class in question.

When defining a satisfactory criterion for literacy, Gray (1961) felt that "It is essential to adopt a relatively high standard, for there is very little printed matter related to adult needs and interests which can be read by anyone who has not acquired the reading ability normally attained by children who have had four,...or even seven years of schooling" (p. 26).

With reference to evaluation, Klich and Davidson (1984:169–171), expressed dissatisfaction with many of the studies carried out in Australia. Among their concerns:

- Language barriers. Most tests had been administered in English to subjects whose English competence was limited and whose mother-tongue lexicon did not contain certain abstract terms used in the testing.
- The hazards implicit when subjects in one culture are required to respond to stimuli and procedures designed by researchers from another culture.
- Unfamiliar testing situations.

Klich and Davidson's rigorous and culturally-oriented testing procedures included:

- Instructions in the vernacular language.
- Administration of tests by the regular Aboriginal teacher either to groups, or within sight and hearing of other Aboriginals.
- Practice items to assure comprehension of each procedure.
- Opportunity for the child tested to nominate the next person to take the test in order to give back a little control to the test taker.
- Refinement of the test instruments based on previous testing.

Anthony et al. (1991) pinpoint other areas of importance:

- Evaluations should be based on natural language (authentic texts), which are contextually grounded (p. 77) and therefore facilitate comprehension.
  "If children are confronted with inauthentic or peculiar language, then their capacity for applying what they know is reduced and their behavior is unlike the behavior they exhibit in normal language use" (p. 69).

- Tests, as well as texts, should be interesting. "The behavior observed in a test situation will be much more revealing if the procedure sets the child an interesting problem to solve" (p. 70).
- Assessments of reading may not be accurate if the students are seeing the material for the first time. "We were struck by the huge discrepancy between the joyful way in which children read their rehearsed texts and the halting manner in which they read the basal-like language of the unfamiliar passages" (p. 78).
- When assessing comprehension ask, "Does the reader have a reasonable interpretation of the passage?" Even through it may not be the teacher's interpretation, an interpretation may be reasonable if it can be supported with relevant information from the text and from prior knowledge (p. 83).

Testing oral reading

All school reading was done orally before 1910 (Miller 1978:53). However, in North America and Europe teachers began to realize that oral reading alone did not reflect the needs of the typical adult reader, and so the teaching emphasis shifted to silent reading. Silent reading continues to receive primary emphasis today.

Experts disagree, however, as to how closely oral reading skill represents silent reading capabilities. In 1978, May and Eliot stated, "Research has demonstrated a rather high relationship between silent reading comprehension and accuracy of word recognition in oral reading" (p. 144). However, Rae and Potter, writing in 1981, felt "oral reading tests do not reflect the child's ability to read and comprehend silently. Great gaps can occur between oral and silent reading" (pp. 10–11).

Miller (1978) lists some of the differences: Eye movements are different. Oral readers usually try to pronounce each word accurately, whereas in silent reading unimportant words are skipped. A major purpose in silent reading is comprehension, while in oral reading it may be word pronunciation (p. 54).

However, Miller (1978), while advocating that teaching emphasis be devoted to silent reading—since that is what students beyond primary level will need most—also lists reasons why oral reading is important. Among them: From oral reading students come to know that they are really reading. Oral reading can be used to confirm information to others. It is useful in performance situations, the reading of plays, poems, story dialogues, or for tape recording. It is also valuable as a diagnostic tool (pp. 54–55).

Evaluation

Today's reading specialists advocate much caution in the testing of oral reading: "The information acquired...should be gathered as systematically as possible, and it must be interpreted and used with caution" (Bond et al. 1989:128). They also warn that a thorough diagnosis cannot be made from only one sample of oral reading (Ekwall and Shanker 1988:423).

Despite the controversies and hazards, the use of oral reading in assessment can be defended because, as Aulls (1982) observes, "In determining a student's reading problems, the teacher can only identify **observable** behaviors that describe reading tasks which can or cannot be performed" (p. 171). Ekwall and Shanker (1988) state:

> It is true that oral reading may present a slightly distorted view of a student's reading ability. Unfortunately, however, there is no way of analyzing directly a student's decoding skills when the student is reading silently. Therefore, we feel that closely observing oral reading behavior is the most accurate barometer of a student's ability **in the act of reading**. (p. 416)

Informal reading inventories

In English, standardized tests are normally used to test reading. However, in the absence of standardized tests, it is possible to turn to an Informal Reading Inventory (IRI) format. The IRI is a method of reading assessment developed by Emmet Betts (1946, 1954). Since the criteria and constructs he established have been widely accepted, it has become a "basic assessment device which teachers and reading specialists have been using for over fifty years" (Aulls 1982:602, citing Monroe 1932 and Killgallon 1942). Its purpose is to gather information concerning a reader's level of proficiency by observing the number and kinds of mistakes made during an oral reading and the percentage of comprehension questions over the passage which are answered correctly.

Taylor et al. (1988) describe typical usage:

> IRIs are collections of short reading passages...one of which is to be read orally...and one to be read silently....[the] procedure...involves having a student first orally read one of the two passages...as the teacher records word recognition errors. The student then answers the comprehension questions. (p. 117)

The second passage is read silently, and again the student answers comprehension questions. This process continues through passages of increasing difficulty until a frustration level is reached and the test is stopped. The teacher is then able to determine an appropriate instructional level for the student.

Experts recommend using selections of different length and successive levels of difficulty for differing age groups. Portions of between 100 to 200 words were recommended by May and Eliot (1978:143), texts of 100 to 150 words by Bond et al. (1989). Ekwall and Shanker (1988) advocate passages of 25 to 100 words for students in grades 1 or 2, and 100 to 200 words for students at grade 3 or above (p. 411).

IRIs, because they are teacher made and cannot be as closely controlled as standardized reading tests, are recognized as having certain inherent problems: First, one test may not be enough for accurate assessment; a number of passages, usually four or five, are better (May and Eliot 1978:144). This requires considerable time expenditure—a problem both in a busy classroom and in individual testing. Second, results are not necessarily uniform since they "depend on the experience of the observer, the number of observations, the degree to which the observations are unbiased, and the relevance of the information to the understanding of the child's reading difficulties" (Bond et al. 1989:128).

Disagreement has existed among reading experts and across IRIs as to what should be counted as a word recognition error (Taylor et al. 1988:117). To clarify the matter, these experts suggest:

> The following should be counted: substitutions, omissions, insertions, and unknown words pronounced by the teacher. The following should not be counted as word recognition errors: repetitions, self-corrections, hesitations, "mispronunciations" due to dialect, missed punctuation marks. (p. 117)

Comprehension scores are at best somewhat tentative, thus it may be necessary to give more weight to the word recognition score than the comprehension score, especially in cases of discrepancy between them (May and Eliot 1978:144; Bond et al. 1989:118). "The criteria for judging instructional and frustration levels are arbitrary and must be considered as guidelines needing 'generous' interpretation" (Taylor et al. 1988:118). Furthermore, Ekwall and Shanker (1988) warn, "one of the difficulties in constructing questions when using informal reading inventories is to be sure that the questions are passage-dependent...[i.e.,] to eliminate questions that the student might answer correctly without reading the passage" (p. 407).

Nevertheless, IRIs do have high content validity, can be very reliable when properly employed, and can be relatively easy for teachers to develop (Taylor et al. 1988:107). They are a useful tool in the diagnosis of specific reading abilities (Ekwall and Shanker 1988:395–396).

Evaluation

Scoring oral reading tests

Issues related to the scoring of reading tests have to do with the test components and the standards set.

The test components

A fairly high degree of consensus exists among the experts as to the essential components of the reading process. Barr et al. (1990) identify these elements as print skill (composed of print awareness and print knowledge), integration and fluency, vocabulary knowledge (which includes understanding both word meanings and the context of the passage), and comprehension strategies, all of which lead to comprehension, the end goal of reading (pp. 9–10). Check lists for teachers and reading diagnosticians elaborate on these categories. For example,

1. Print awareness includes: Directionality, visual discrimination, visual memory, letter forms, and picture-word associations (Guszak 1985:191). These aspects of reading are normally taught in kindergarten and reading readiness classes.

2. Print knowledge includes: sound-symbol relationships, word recognition (Guzak 1985:191); consonant blends, vowel patterns, and syllabification (Aulls 1978:174–175, 178). These aspects are taught in beginning reading classes. See also Liberman and Shankweller (1991).

3. Integration and fluency include: connected reading with reasonable accuracy and speed (Guszak 1985:192), phrasing and correct use of punctuation (Aulls 1978:179, 280), and natural expression (Taylor et al. 1988:123). These aspects, although taught from the beginning, become a major focus at about grade 3 level (Aulls 1978:177). See also Samuels and LaBerge (1983) and Samuels et al. (1992).

4. Comprehension strategies include: predicting, locating, organizing, remembering, and evaluating (Guszak 1985:192). These become the focus about grade 4 level: "...Once a student has obtained the word attack, word recognition, and phrasing competencies to read material of fourth grade difficulty with seventy to eighty percent literal comprehension, the major factors of instructional importance become vocabulary, reasoning skills, and reading rate (Aulls 1978:180). See also Pearson et al. (1992), and Ouane (1989).[6]

---

[6]Stanovich (1991b), Olson et al. (1985), and Rieben and Perfetti (1991) also address these issues.

The standards set

Over the years, standards have been developed for each of the major aspects of reading: rate, accuracy, comprehension, and fluency.

Rate

A massive five-year, fifty-state study called The National Assessment of Educational Progress undertaken by the Education Commission of the [United] States (1972) established the median rates for silent reading as follows:

> 9-year-olds   117 words per minute (wpm)
> 13-year-olds   173 wpm
> 17-year-olds   195 wpm
> Young adults   188 wpm   (pp. 4, 53, 98)

Oral reading tends to be considerably slower, however. Guszak's (1985) experience has led him to set the following minimum oral rates:

> Grade 1 (all books)   60 wpm
> Grade 2   70 wpm
> Grade 3   80 wpm
> Grade 4 and above   90 wpm   (p. 64)

McCracken (1967) had already set 150 wpm—the rate at which people normally speak—as the maximum oral rate at which good readers are likely to read with naturalness and comprehension. The Gilmore Oral Reading Test of 1968 (cited in Barr et al. 1990:71 and Miller 1978:72–75) set an average range of rates, beginning with 30–54 wpm. for grade level 1.8 and reaching 136–167 wpm at grade 8.8.

Accuracy and comprehension

Emmet Betts (1946, 1954) suggested levels of reading performance differentiated on the basis of accuracy and comprehension.

Reading Level	Words decoded without error	Questions answered without error
Independent	99% accuracy	90% or greater accuracy
Instructional	95% accuracy	75–89% accuracy
Frustration	90% accuracy or less	Less than 50% accuracy
Capacity		75% accuracy or better

(Adapted from Betts 1946:449–453)

According to Betts' criteria,

> At the independent or free reading level the student can function adequately without the teacher's help.
>
> At the instructional level the student can function adequately with guidance yet still be challenged to improve.
>
> At the frustration level the student cannot function adequately and often shows signs of tension and discomfort. (Ekwall 1989:4)

These main categories remain today, although some specialists have altered Betts' percentages slightly (e.g., May and Eliot 1978:144). When either the accuracy or the comprehension score is in the frustration level, it is normally impossible for the student to be at any other level" (Ekwall and Shanker 1988:405).

To evaluate accuracy, readings are coded for errors, which are next summarized in checklists. Accuracy can then be calculated as a percentage—total number of words (or syllables) correct as compared to the total number of words (or syllables) in the passage. Barr et al. (1990:73), and Ekwall and Shanker (1988:416–429) describe the coding system traditionally used to mark omissions, insertions, substitutions or mispronunciations, repetitions, corrections, reversals, pauses, and punctuation.

Reading comprehension is the acquisition of information from printed material (Lapp and Flood 1992:117). It requires a set of interactive skills which take place concurrently. These range "from the lower-level processes that recognize the printed words and encode contextually appropriate meanings for them to the higher-level processes that assemble and integrate the underlying propositions and relate them to previously acquired knowledge" (Daneman 1991:532). Accordingly, "comprehension can refer both to the processes whereby the component sentences are understood and to the way in which the message itself is understood" (Sanford and Garrod 1981:4).

Comprehension is recognized to be a product both of what the reader brings to a text and what the author has brought to it (Guszak 1985:101; Schallert and Vaughan 1979:51). Thus readers call upon prior experiences and already-established schemata as they strive to construct meaning from an author's words (Lapp and Flood 1992:120; Sanford and Garrod 1981:5).

Guszak (1985) names five major skill areas in reading comprehension: predicting, locating, organizing, remembering, and evaluating (p. 108). There are three levels of comprehension: text explicit comprehension, text implicit comprehension, and world knowledge (Lapp and Flood 1992:121). From these are derived the categories of literal comprehension, inferential comprehension, and critical comprehension (p. 124), although Lapp and Flood warn that it is inappropriate to think of these categories as mutually exclusive or as a rigid hierarchical progression (p. 121).

Teachers who need to assess the degree of comprehension achieved by students are taught to ask questions and to orchestrate activities which will prompt learners to give facts (showing literal comprehension of the text), make predictions or draw inferences, and to evaluate the information given (Aulls 1978:285–290; Guszak 1985:108–115; May and Eliot 1978:248–255; Santeusanio 1983:5, 297; Lapp and Flood 1992:129–162). Asking students to retell the story, either individually or as a group, is another way to evaluate comprehension (Guszak 1985:103; May and Eliot 1978:249; Santeusiano 1983:300; Lapp and Flood 1992:153). The number of questions correctly answered, or the number of facts correctly retold can form the basis for a comprehension score, which may be recorded in percentages or on a scale (Santeusiano 1983:300–301). Educators such as Goodman (1969) and Goodman and Burke (1972) prefer to advocate miscue analysis when assessing comprehension. In cross-cultural studies, however, miscue analysis must be used with great caution since miscues are easily misinterpreted when either the test administrator or the test taker are working in a second language.

Comprehension assessment is recognized to be imprecise, for it is never possible for any person to know exactly what has taken place in another's mind. Some learners do not know how to express what they have understood; others are too nervous to speak, although they know the answers. Yet others may recall and relate what they have read but have failed to understand the passage (Farr and Carey 1986:39). Thus, teachers are warned to exercise much caution when drawing conclusions from comprehension scores, giving more weight to the accuracy score than to the comprehension score, especially in cases of discrepancy between them (May and Eliot 1978:144; Bond et al. 1989:118).

Fluency

Although all reading specialists recognize a component of reading called fluency, they differ in its definition. One school of thought considers it to be the skill and rapidity with which sounds are blended. "Cognitive psychologists who study reading conceive of reading fluency as the ability to recognize words rapidly and accurately" (Nathan and Stanovich 1991:176, citing La Berge and Samuels 1974; Perfetti 1985; Rayner and Pollatsek 1989; Stanovich 1980, 1986).

Another school conceives fluency as having to do with prosody. Until just after 1900, elocution (interpretive performance of texts) was an important part of the school curriculum, but then attention turned to silent reading (Stayter and Allington 1991:143). Some reading specialists (e.g., May and Eliot 1978:245–248) still mentioned reading with expression. However, as Dowhower (1991) has observed,

> Reading researchers usually have investigated fluency by quantifying rate (words per minute) and accuracy (number of words correctly identified) and have left the third bedfellow of fluency called prosody unattended....Prosody is...a general linguistic term to describe rhythmic and tonal features of speech...also called suprasegmental features. (pp. 165, 166)

Dowhower (1987) lists inappropriate hesitations, length of the phrases read, inappropriate phrasing, appropriate pitch changes, and appropriate stress as indicators of a student's mastery of prosody. Hoffman and Isaacs (1991) exhort teachers that "students must be taught that no longer is it a case of getting through the story and on to the next one. Rather, the focus is on achieving fluency with the stories, a fluency that is demonstrated through expressive, interpretive reading" (p. 192).

Seeking to find a way to evaluate fluency, Aulls (1978) established a seven-point rating scale which began with word by word reading, and ended with "reads in phrases, preserves all punctuation and uses acceptable expression" (p. 280). Wiederholt and Bryant (1987) mention word-by-word reading, poor phrasing, lack of expression, pitch too high or low, voice too soft or strained, poor enunciation, disregard of punctuation (p. 13). Ekwall and Shanker (1988) list disregard for punctuation, unnatural voice tones, poor enunciation, word-by-word reading, poor phrasing, lack of expression, pauses (pp. 528–529).

Zutell and Rasinski (1991:214) prefer a four-point scale:

1. Clearly labored and disfluent (slow, word-by-word, pauses, sound-outs, repetitions, lack of expression).

2. Slow and choppy (60–80 wpm), two- and three-word phrases, many pauses, sound-outs, repetitions.
3. Poor phrasing and intonation but reasonable pace. Fewer sound-outs, repetitions, etc.
4. Fairly fluent—good pace (more than 110 wpm), longer phrases, good sense of expression and intonation.

Chapter Summary

The chapter reviews definitions of literacy and the history of reading theory. It describes the reading process, then turns to evaluation, which poses special hazards in cross-cultural situations. Gray, Klich, and Davidson, and Anthony, Johnson, Mickelson, and Preece have offered guidelines for assessment. Miller warns of the difficulties of testing oral reading. Informal Reading Inventories, developed by Betts and discussed by many authors, prove useful for diagnostic testing. Scoring often follows Betts' criteria, elaborated by Ekwall and Shanker, in which reading performance is differentiated on the basis of accuracy and comprehension. Fluency—researched by educators such as Aulls, Dowhower, Hoffman and Isaacs, Zutell and Rasinski—and rate—discussed by reading specialists like McCracken, Guszak, and Miller—are also considered important components of reading evaluation.

Chapter Summary

Above: School books are transported on turbulent rivers by canoe, which sometimes must be pushed through treacherous spots. Picha River, 1992.

Below: Teacher Venturo Cruz takes the school inventory. Mantaro, c. 1970. (P. Davis photos)

4

Forty Years in Review

The Cruel One was the henchman of a patrón...He lived in the area; that is how he managed to capture my father. He was an angry man who kidnapped people. He went out hunting them, and he brought them to the patrón [at gun point]. As he was capturing them, he beat them...then he would tie them together and march them away from their homes to the patrón...He went to the headwaters of the Mantaro Chico and of the Picha...and made my people suffer enormously. He even killed some. If women were [slowed down because of] carrying babies in arms, he would take their babies away and throw them in the river. While he was alive there was great suffering. - Account from Mantaro Chico, 1968

Long ago I did not live here; I lived in the headwaters. Now it is different. Long ago they used to plot to sell us. Now that has ended...I am not afraid; we do not have to flee to the jungle when a White person comes.
- Grandmother, House 13, Shivankoreni, 1992

Introduction

The purpose of this chapter is to trace the unfolding of events in the Machiguenga educational program, data for which is drawn from Davis et al. (1992). A historical chronology is presented, for literacy programs cannot be understood apart from the context in which they take place. At first perusal, this chronology will appear to be merely a record of community development efforts. Nevertheless, the projects undertaken in hopes of providing coping mechanisms for the Machiguenga are now thought to have played a large part in creating uses for the printed word and so have formed an important base for literacy development. A second part of the chapter traces literacy and educational endeavors. The account brings us to 1993.

The Beginning of Literacy

In 1946 field linguists of SIL commenced studies of jungle languages under an agreement signed with the Peruvian Ministry of Education. Two women—Ellen Ross and Lulu Reber—completed a tentative orthography of the Machiguenga language and began grammar analysis. When they were unable to continue, they were followed, in 1952, by Wayne and Betty Snell. In that era, most of what is now known about community development principles had not yet been formulated; thus the knowledge available today was not at their disposal. However, the young linguists soon found themselves face to face with an ethical dilemma: Here was a group which was for the most part monolingual but whose isolation would not be maintained much longer. Although their culture was rich and complex and they were highly skilled in it, they lacked the technical knowledge and skills, knowledge of Spanish, and orientation to the ways of the outside world which would enable them to survive Western diseases and to cope with the inexorable onslaught of cultural change about to engulf them. To put their Western knowledge of the majority society and its systems at the disposal of the ethnolinguistic group, acting as catalysts and mentors in an effort to help them prepare to meet the outside world would precipitate great struggles for all. For the people, it would initiate far-reaching changes, not all of which would necessarily be positive. For the Snells, it would add huge responsibilities and leave them open to much criticism. To do nothing was to leave the Machiguenga vulnerable to gross exploitation.

The linguists began to do what they could to ameliorate the situation. Teaching adults to count money—something that could be done with minimal knowledge of the language—was one first step. However, it is important to understand that their underlying motivation was not ethnocentric devaluation of the Machiguenga culture or a desire to "Westernize" or "modernize." Neither was it subtractive—to eradicate native customs in order to "civilize." The intent of their action was additive—to help the Machiguenga gain skills with which to relate successfully to the majority society and to take part in the administration of their own affairs. The Snells did not have the option of choosing whether—or how—to introduce literacy. Within months of their beginning to study the language, the government made the decision to begin bilingual schools. However, to the best of their ability, in both education and community development endeavors, SIL workers presented alternatives and encouraged the people to make the choices. That which followed was the outworking of those choices.

The Snells were concerned that the culture be preserved and made it evident by the interest they took in the language, customs, legends, and crafts. When SIL members were asked by the Ministry of Education to help prepare textbooks for the new bilingual schools, they worked as quickly as possible to finalize a sociolinguistically-based alphabet. Then, as local legends were recorded, some were used in primers and advanced reading material. Machiguenga teachers were then prepared in Ministry of Education training courses. Slowly, as their students became literate, new skills such as grafting, primary health care, mechanics, storekeeping, sawmill operation, and carpentry could also be taught. Little by little, almost everyone learned about Western organizational systems of the Peruvian genre.

But the newcomers of SIL were learners as well, dependent upon their patient hosts and instructors for knowledge about the language, courtesies, beliefs, survival skills, the uses of medicinal and edible plants, and all the other lore necessary to function in their new community. Over the years strong bonds were forged and learning was ever a reciprocal affair.

Charting Developments

These teaching-learning processes have, in the case of the Machiguenga, taken place over forty years and have included a predictable number of trials and errors. At first, because of the people's lack of knowledge of the outside world, projects tended to be initiated by the SIL workers, either in response to government decrees or because of obvious needs (such as health care) in line with the people's desires. Increasingly, however, the Machiguenga were consulted and trained until the end goal was realized—both initiation and administration became their responsibility. Then the team slowly withdrew. Ten years later, it is still too early to report all the long-term results with confidence, but some observations can be made.

Literacy does not exist in a vacuum; it exists in a multi-faceted society where it has been found to serve useful purposes. It is affected by attitudes towards language, by government legislation, by the peoples' felt needs, by geography, and by ideologies. Reading programs, therefore, cannot be understood apart from their history and their complex ties to the sociological and political environment of their day. As early as 1935, Richards recognized that

> Any culture can only be fully understood in its historical context, and when the culture under consideration has undergone revolutionary changes within a generation the relative importance of the historical context is very much greater than when the culture has been comparatively static. (p. 21)

Continuous interaction between indigenous cultures and the outside world leads to pragmatic adaptation, chiefly on the part of the minority group, and a mix of new and old practices which may include the maintenance of different literacies used for different purposes.

> It is not...a simple choice between "freezing" traditional values...or of crude "modernism"....Rather the issue is that of sensitivity to indigenous cultures and recognition of the dynamic process of their interaction with dominant cultures and literacies. The reality...is of pragmatic adaptation...to the new skills, conventions and ideologies being introduced.... (Street 1987:61–62)

Street exhorts those involved in practical, grass-roots literacy campaigns to "abandon outdated and ethnocentric models of literacy that can only distort practical efforts" (p. 62).

This chapter cannot be exhaustive; it will trace only the events deemed most important. (A more complete time line is posted on the SIL website [www.sil.org/silewp] entitled "A Chronology of Education and Development among the Machiguenga Bilingual School Communities of the Lower Urubamba, 1946 to 1993.") However, it is necessary to recognize that many other complex occurrences less easy to identify also have played significant roles in both enhancing and inhibiting Machiguenga reading development. One negative factor, for example—a phenomenon rooted in the attitudes of Spanish and Portuguese conquerors and common to South American countries—has been the general opposition of the majority society to equality for indigenous peoples, despite the passage of favorable laws. A positive event has been the modeling and encouragement of key Peruvian educators, who have greatly influenced the Machiguenga.

The following sequence of events, reconstructed with the aid of participant observers, is as accurate as human frailty permits.

The 1950s

1952

In 1952, the Minister of Education signed a decree instituting a training course for teachers from the ethnolinguistic groups of the jungle. SIL members, because of their presence in isolated minority groups and knowledge of the language, were requested to write primers in the indigenous languages and to help select teacher candidates. The Snells, after only six months of language study, began to prepare material to teach reading.

1954

Education

For eleven weeks the first Machiguenga teacher candidates, some of whom were barely literate, received rudimentary instruction in teaching methods. Immediately after the course, the first Machiguenga bilingual schools were opened in the villages of Etariato and Pangoa. Slowly, the quality of the training and the number of teachers and schools increased, until in 1990 the majority of the first generation of Machiguenga teachers had retired and had been replaced by thirty new teachers, most of whom had completed high school.

Health

The Machiguenga were wise in their understanding of medicinal herbs but suffered acutely from maladies the herbs could not cure. The Snells treated patients without charge, promising to help the people economically so that at a future date they could buy medicines. This served to establish friendship, provide medical services which were much needed, and introduce the people to Western medical procedures. Preventive measures, such as boiling water and covering food from flies, were also taught both verbally and by example.

By the end of the 1950s, teacher trainees were provided instruction in first-aid at the summer teacher-training courses. Thus rudimentary care, along with preventive health lessons, became available in school communities. Later, primary health workers were trained for each community through SIL and Swiss Indian Mission (SIM) programs.

Community building

As word about the schools spread, the Machiguenga people, who do not traditionally live in villages and towns but rather in extended family groups, became interested in the protection they perceived school knowledge could provide. Knowledge of reading, writing, and arithmetic would protect them from exploitation by unscrupulous traders. Knowledge of Spanish would enable them to communicate with visitors and with the outside world. As teachers were trained and offered their services, people began to move together in order to acquire education for their children. Originally, the Ministry of Education required twenty-five school-age children to be registered in a community before a school and a teacher were authorized. Later that number was raised to forty students.

Community living unavoidably engendered stresses the people had not previously encountered (Davis 1981:199–227; Baksh 1984). My recommendation now would be that, whenever possible, education begin with the adults and that—if it becomes necessary for people who are not used to living together to form communities—measures be taken to alleviate pressure, such as maintaining some distance (and jungle) between houses. However, people did the best they knew at the time, and it was the Machiguenga, not the consultants, who decided upon the Peruvian settlement pattern, laying out their villages in a line along the river or, in later years, flanking the airstrip. The Machiguenga also chose the names for their communities. Many were named for the rivers or streams on which they were located; others were given Spanish names. During weekends and vacations community members tended to scatter in order to relieve tensions, visit more distant garden plots, hunt, fish, and gather food in the jungle. However, after teachers, as part of their training, were instructed in first aid and were equipped with basic medicines, the people noted that in school communities deaths no longer occurred as frequently as they had in their isolated settlements. Machiguengas began to cite this fact, along with the opportunity for education, as reason to stay in the community more permanently.

Examples are in order: An early survey carried out by the Snells produced the finding that the average woman could be expected to bear ten children, of whom seven would die. Twenty years later, after the advent of antibiotics, medicine for malaria, and treatment for tuberculosis, the situation was reversed. Seven out of ten babies lived. Now young adults, both male and female, often marry later because of their desire to attend high school and also because of their new sense of independence. Families want fewer children because of the cost of providing food and education for them. Nevertheless, because fewer children die, the population is increasing.

Wayne Snell also relates that in the late 1960s, the village of Shivankoreni was feeling the pressure of community living, and at a town meeting several agitated for dispersing once again to the jungle "where they wouldn't suffer." Village President Abram Italiano spoke for others when he replied, "You go if you want, but my family and I are staying. We suffered so much from sickness and death [before we moved here]; now we have medicine and a school—my children won't suffer like we used to." No one moved out.

One matter of grave concern to the SIL workers was the manner in which teachers formed a community. Harrowing stories were told—not all of which were necessarily accurate—describing how representatives of other entities tore children from their homes by force, or bought them with trade goods, to intern them in boarding schools. Machiguenga bilingual teachers with whom SIL members had contact were strictly charged not to use force nor to "buy" community participation with trade goods. In a culture in which reciprocal gift-giving is part and parcel of establishing friendship, team members will never know if, or when, the lines were blurred in the teachers' presentations to headwaters dwellers. However, they tried to make it perfectly clear to all villagers that although a certain number must live in communal proximity if there were to be enough children for the government to pay a teacher, individually they were free to stay or to go.

The 1960s

1964

The Davis family (my husband, children, and I) was assigned to the Machiguenga project. Harold Davis was a dynamic teacher of many skills; both he and I had received basic training in linguistics and anthropology and spoke Spanish. We spent a major portion of the first year in language learning and orientation. During the year, Harold prepared model garden plots in each community visited, bequeathed the harvest to a responsible person who was to share it with others, and distributed seeds. The people seemed to enjoy the tomatoes, green beans, and other garden vegetables, but the next year when we returned to the village, the seeds were gone, and no one had replanted the varieties demonstrated. It was forthwith decided that Western-type garden vegetables were not a felt need among the Machiguenga of the Lower Urubamba and Madre de Dios, since their diet was already varied and fairly adequate. Furthermore, since garden vegetables require more intensive cultivation of the soil and protection from insects than do the crops normally planted in Machiguenga fields, the people's reluctance to undertake vegetable production was understandable. Chickens and ducks, introduced several times by both Snell and Davis as protein sources, proved susceptible to predators and disease and were only partially successful even as late as 1984 (Baksh 1984:273–278).

Health concerns were an entirely different matter. In every village, the team was saddened to see the large number of distended stomachs, cases of severe anemia, and persons reported to be eating earth (all signs of heavy parasite infestation), as well as the high proportion of malaria sufferers. The people were eager to gain relief from these and other maladies, even willing, for the most part, to take the Epsom salts which, in those days, accompanied the worm treatment.

1965

The Davises began an annual circuit of community visits. For the next seven years, in cooperation with the Snells and the Friedlis, our schedule would include the following activities. The complexity of each project varied with the length of time a project had been underway and with the degree of technology successfully transferred to the Machiguenga:

School book production

Textbooks were needed for all the subjects of the curriculum. Design and production of these materials required a large block of time yearly.

Health care

Parasite treatments; attending epidemics (in 1965 ten percent of the population of two villages died in a measles epidemic, despite day and night care and three charter flights of medicines); immunization coverage for everyone of the appropriate age (measles, yellow fever, T.B., polio, a series of three DPT immunizations; small pox vaccination was carried out separately by the Ministry of Health); daily medical work; arranging for emergency medical flights; caring for patients in our home. (We once had five pneumonia cases and an eye surgery case simultaneously. A stream of other patients required from weeks to months of care; the team shared in attending them.)

Census work

Harold Davis shouldered the responsibility of establishing first names, father's surname, and mother's surname for the approximately 2,000 people living in the Machiguenga communities contacted by SIL at that time. The

Machiguenga traditionally used kinship terms rather than personal names, but complete names were obligatory for school registers and for land papers. Unused to the ways of the outside world, teachers had been assigning different Spanish surnames to siblings as they enrolled them in school. As a result, blood lines were in imminent danger of being obscured and lost, and Machiguenga heritage was not being reflected in the naming practices. At a series of community meetings, family heads discussed alternatives and chose names satisfactory to them. Teachers and leaders learned the importance of preserving the same surnames for all the members of a family.

An explanation is in order here. Smith (1950:61) and Murdock (1960:132 and 1946:124) postulated the universality of personal names. However, the Snells' investigations over thirty years have uncovered no evidence that names (with the exception of the occasional nickname, usually derogatory) form part of traditional Machiguenga culture. (See Snell 1964.) My inquiries into the subject have yielded the same information. In approximately 1967, Harold Davis visited a remote village in the headwaters area of the Manú River. Upon his return to the community of Tayakome, one of the men who had moved from that headwaters village to Tayakome the previous year visited my husband obviously concerned for the health of his aged father. Was he alive? Had Harold seen him? Had he sent any message for his son? The next fifteen minutes were an exercise in utter frustration, for as earnestly as Harold wished to reassure him, our Machiguenga friend had no way to identify his father beyond the fact that he was elderly, had dark hair, wore a cushma, and was related to other men and women, all with similar characteristics. They never were able to establish that Harold had seen the father in question, although our visitor did everything he knew to describe him to us. The incident convinced me that traditional Machiguengas did not use personal names.

Since names were not used commonly, people found it difficult to remember the names which they had adopted. We were often visited by puzzled villagers, asking, "What is my name?" or "What name did we give my baby?" Certain individuals who had adopted the practice of assuming and then changing names frequently also had difficulty accepting the idea that, once chosen, a name should be permanent.

Adult education

Adults were taught to understand the proportionate values of the bills and coins used in Peruvian currency, also the fair market value of their goods and products.

Economic development

Income generation entailed seeking sources of revenue for the people—encouraging crop production, and encouraging the production and sale of artifacts. (Attempts to speed up weaving with a spinning wheel failed because we could not find one suitable for cotton that the women could operate while seated on the floor—as they are accustomed—rather than on a chair.) It also involved finding markets and training village storekeepers.

Training

The training role included identifying and recruiting suitable trainees for courses in agriculture, store keeping, carpentry, lumbering, mechanics, public health, and teacher training, and then supplying, supervising, and encouraging these trainees as they took up employment in their villages. On location, it was necessary to troubleshoot and to further their knowledge of bookkeeping. The first trainees were chosen by SIL workers, but by the mid-1970s candidates for courses were chosen by the village council, which also was asked to provide some financial support and an official letter of recommendation for each student sent to training courses.

In the villages, most of the follow up of formal training was carried out on an informal apprenticeship basis whenever team members visited the community. Much of this training might have appeared so casual as to seem almost insignificant were one not aware that very new concepts can be internalized only gradually and need considerable reinforcement. The advantage of training, Machiguenga-style, is that one seldom does anything in private. A crowd of interested observers always gathers around. This provided opportunity to spread the knowledge among many, even though only one might be responsible for actually performing the task.

Teaching at training courses

Guides were written for the teacher training courses. Formal training sessions were held in Machiguenga communities. In-service supervision and logistical support for each teacher yearly was provided in response to a Ministry of Education request. This included making arrangements for flights and the transport of school and medical supplies.

Making arrangements for land reservations

By law, ten hectares (24.7 acres) per person over the age of five could be requested by the native peoples as a permanent community reservation.

Charting Developments

Although this was not enough to support their seminomadic lifestyle permanently, in view of the influx of colonists expected, it was imperative for the Machiguenga communities to move quickly to request land. The paperwork required for the submission of a land request, however, was daunting, yea impossible, for isolated, virtually monolingual communities to accomplish without substantial help and financing. The requirements included a complete census, two visits (flights) to each community by a government surveyor to measure and establish boundaries, properly prepared applications in Spanish on special forms, and maps written in Spanish. Harold Davis expended a great deal of energy and money from his own pocket before, in 1971, he was able to submit completed applications for all the Machiguenga communities served by SIL which had not previously been allotted a land grant.

Changes in laws caused additional difficulties for the Machiguenga people in preserving title to their homeland. I am told that the communities of Camisea and Shivankoreni received land twice but lost their titles through changes in agricultural laws. They were granted a third title under the agricultural reform of the revolutionary government of 1968–1978.

Airstrip building

Schools had to be supplied by airplane, and the wheel planes required airstrips; thus one evidence of a community's willingness to support a school was willingness to build an airstrip. Leveling three hundred meters of jungle by hand is a backbreaking task. Davis and Snell bought and borrowed as many axes, machetes, pick axes, shovels, and wheel barrows as possible for each project, leaving a number of them behind for maintenance purposes when the project ended. Counting from the beginning of the Snells' allocation, seventeen airstrip projects were carried out with much expenditure of effort on the part of both SIL workers and the Machiguenga. In the early 1970s, Wayne Snell and a Peruvian school teacher developed a set of wheels and a mower blade which could be attached to the Briggs-Stratton motor used on canoes. SIL pilot George Woodward, a civil engineer, later redesigned this mower so that it could be produced in quantity. Thereafter, villagers were spared the drudgery of cutting airstrips by machete.

1966

Werner and Vreni Friedli, members of the Swiss Indian Mission (SIM), were assigned to language learning and church development among the Machiguenga. At their mission's central campus near Pucallpa, a Bible

Institute was developed, and later a cattle herd for teaching purposes and shops for mechanical and carpentry instruction. Over the years several score of Machiguenga received training in these programs.

Team Impact

All members of the Machiguenga team were active in community development. In addition to his linguistic and translation programs, Wayne Snell sought funding, helped with airstrip building, and took primary responsibility for the sawmills and the cattle projects which developed in a number of communities. Introduction of cattle was seen as necessary for protein in the future, and as a product which would bring a good price in the Peruvian market, although at the time the Machiguenga neither ate nor milked them, and also experienced difficulties as they learned to manage them (Baksh 1984:267–273).

One of Wayne Snell's major contributions was to lay the groundwork for the Machiguengas' understanding of formal political organization—the election process, the responsibilities of elected officials, and ways communities could work together. The Snells also organized a sewing course for women, attended innumerable patients, gave time to help develop, check, and proofread school books, and assumed most of the responsibility for the research and trial of new ideas. Some of the latter, like a speed boat for fast transport between communities and an electric light plant for one village, proved not to be feasible because of high operating costs. Even so, the light plant provided intangible benefits. Wayne recalls that after having set the plant up and assuring himself that it was operating properly, he turned to one of the village headmen and said, "Now it is yours."

"What do you mean," Arturo replied cynically, evidently expecting strings to be attached. "You can throw it in the river tomorrow, if you want," Wayne replied, "but this is your light plant, to use as you wish."

A quiet awakening chased across the men's faces and after that made itself evident in their attitudes: Machiguengas could own something of value, like other Peruvians. They could be somebody. It was preparation for a later day when they became owners of a twenty-ton barge, of which Arturo was the captain.

Werner and Vreni Friedli also carried heavy responsibilities in the community development program. They saw to the teaching of health workers and cattlemen, helped them with in-service training and the restocking of supplies, and handled many mechanical repairs. Werner helped the Machiguenga leaders design the two high school dormitories and encouraged the people to cut lumber for them, then arranged for SIM personnel to help supervise the construction. Their counsel and encouragement was always available to community storekeepers, carpenters, and mechanics. They cared for many patients in their home.

Team members were scarcely ever in the same village at the same time, but since their work required itineration, they were able constantly to follow up on projects, place supply orders, and troubleshoot as necessary. Frequent planning sessions and two-way radios made close communication possible among team members. Despite occasional glitches, this working format proved helpful both to the team and to the Machiguenga. Team members could maintain consistency in their approach. Without becoming dependent on a resident foreigner, trainees and villagers could receive help and reinforcement every time any team member arrived in the community.

The 1970s

At the end of 1971, Harold Davis died in a commercial airline crash as he returned from submitting land requests for all of the bilingual school communities. This loss was a major blow not only to his family and to the team but to the Machiguengas and to the community development program, which was just beginning to gain momentum. I—left with two young children—was able to continue only with school supervision and teacher training. For lack of personnel, support to two remote communities was virtually suspended; precious time was lost in other projects as well. However, after some months, Gerald and Eunice Hamill were assigned to continue the programs already underway. Jerry was a versatile technician who had worked in research and development with the U.S. aerospace program. Eunice had background in bookkeeping and education. They had already served several years in Peru, although they did not yet know the Machiguenga language. Under the Hamills' direction, health, airstrip, and economic development programs were continued. Logistical support was provided to the schools. A transportation system (motorized dugout canoe) initiated by Wayne Snell was carried forward, and a crew was trained to sell produce in the downriver city of Pucallpa and to purchase goods for the village storekeepers. This transportation system was an important step in economic independence, for it freed the Machiguenga from dependence on middlemen and enabled them to take charge of their own buying and selling.

The maiden voyage of the motorized dugout from Pucallpa to Machiguenga land was made in April of 1972. Abel Choronto, an expert among Machiguenga motorists, was navigator and captain. This canoe was powered with a twelve horsepower Briggs-Stratton motor and by local standards was large—wide enough to load 55-gallon barrels of gasoline crosswise—but could carry only one ton of produce. Quickly, it proved to be too small.

Leadership and citizenship training

Harold Davis had been greatly concerned about the need for the Machiguenga to have educated leaders who could represent their people to the outside world and had helped sponsor and mentor three of the first Machiguenga students to attend secondary school. After his death, funds given in his memory were used to provide scholarships for other students, with the understanding that when they graduated, they would, in turn, help others. From this little group, key leaders have developed, leaders who continue to pass on their knowledge and skills to others.

Throughout the time of the SIL presence, efforts were made to put the Machiguenga in touch with the far-away government offices of their region, particularly those to which the people most commonly need to relate—agriculture, forestry, education, and documentation.

In 1973 a special excursion organized by the Hamills enabled ten Machiguenga and two Piro teachers—for the first time—to fly over the dividing gorge and visit provincial educational, agricultural, and legal offices in Quillabamba, their district capital. They also visited the historic ruins of Machu Picchu and their state capital, Cuzco. In Cuzco, the delegation called on the Head of the Supreme Court of the state, petitioning registers for births and deaths. The kind reception which they were granted by the officials noticeably reduced their fear of approaching government offices, and since that time they have made many trips on their own to these capital cities on official business, even though the journey is expensive, difficult, and dangerous.

Over the years, with the help of the team and Peruvian officials, scores of Machiguengas have obtained birth certificates, certificates of military inscription, and their voter registration. As they have done so, they have accepted the responsibilities of citizenship with pride and have learned the procedures which must be followed when contacting different offices.

The agricultural cooperative

In the 1970s, the government instituted new regulations whereby petitions from native communities would be honored in public offices only if the group were formally organized and submitted their requests in the name of the community as a whole. In view of this policy, Wayne Snell spent considerable time teaching Machiguenga community members how to hold elections, and how elected officials should function in order to act within the guidelines established. The outcome, over a period of years, was the formation of a Machiguenga agricultural cooperative. Eventually the cooperative boasted an executive body and committees which oversaw:

- Warehousing of agricultural produce, which was gathered from the nine participating communities, into a central warehouse and then shipped to market in Pucallpa.
- The barge and crew which transported the produce and supplies.
- The central store, which supplied all the smaller community stores.
- Other services, such as the central medical supply, the central gasoline supply, the central repair and parts department, and the central schoolbook and supply depot.

Members of the cooperative built a complex of buildings at Nueva Luz to house these central services. Werner Friedli assisted them in the procurement of cement and the pouring of a large concrete slab needed to dry beans and coffee.

Math lessons taught in the bilingual school were put into practice as the Machiguenga weighed beans and other produce for market. (P. Davis photo, c. 1974)

Bookkeeping

In the beginning, Wayne Snell trained village storekeepers, who had minimal education, to keep two notebooks. In one the storekeeper maintained a record of his inventory and what it had cost him. In the other, he kept a record of what he had sold. No effort was made to balance the books, but when the lists were totaled it was possible for both the storekeeper and the visiting supervisor to see at a glance where he stood. Until his death, Harold Davis continued on-location apprenticeships in sales, inventory, markup, and bookkeeping for the storekeepers.

The cooperative grew to a multi-million *sol* business. In approximately 1978, the school teacher from Segakiato reported (personal conversation) that 12,000 kilograms of produce had been shipped that season from his community alone. With an operation of that magnitude, bookkeeping became a crucial area of concern, and it was necessary to move into a formal bookkeeping system. The central bookkeeping system was decentralized so that each person involved—i.e., the administrators of the central supply depots and each village storekeeper, health worker, and motor repairman—became responsible to account for the area designated to him. About 1982, the capable manager-in-training, José Pereyra—one of the early high school students now returned to his people—began teaching short courses in bookkeeping to others associated with the cooperative. Guillermo Ríos, one of his students, became so expert that he was soon coaching others who were having difficulty. A purser was trained to receive produce, sell it, make purchases in the city, and to keep the accounts.

The Princess of the Urubamba

Courtesy of the Peruvian navy, a crew—pilots, navigator, and engineer—was trained in the naval school in Iquitos. These men then trained two more crews so that eventually the three crews served on a rotation basis and no one was required to be absent from his home and garden plot so long as to cause hardship.

A barge was procured through a grant from the German government. Jerry Hamill's mechanical experience and knowledge of drafting made possible the presentation of an acceptable design—a one-engine vessel, approximately ten tons in capacity, open cargo deck (except for the pilot house), flat-bottomed so as to draw no more than three and one-half feet of water. These specifications would make it possible for the craft to traverse the Urubamba year-round, in both high and low water. During construction, however, specifications were changed for reasons beyond the Machiguenga team's control, and the resulting vessel carried twenty tons, drew four and one-half to five feet of water, and required two engines. Deck space was also allotted for cabins. As a result, this boat became more expensive to operate than had originally been envisioned and could only navigate the river during high-water season.

Despite this disappointment, a dramatic christening ceremony was held at which the Machiguenga received ownership papers. The boat was named *La Princesa del Urubamba* (The Princess of the Urubamba), and morale soared. José Pereyra became administrator and bookkeeper for the central warehouse. He checked the books kept by the crew as they arrived back at the central depot after each trip. Wayne Snell went over the books with them as they arrived in Pucallpa with cargo. In this way, help and supervision was available at both ends of the route. At first, the novice crew sheared several propellors because of lack of knowledge of the channel depths—tricky business in rivers which constantly change course. However, as they gained expertise this problem was overcome, and we came to admire the professional skill of both the pilots and the diesel mechanics. The *Princesa* began to serve all the communities along the route, carrying gasoline and cargo for private businesses, government institutions, and Catholic missions, as well as for two other language groups, Asháninka and Piro.

The executive committee of the Machiguenga Cooperative presented budget reports at the annual General Assembly. (Betty Snell photo, c. 1980)

The Princess of the Urubamba in port at Nueva Luz.
(Werner Friedli photo, c. 1980)

The prestige produced in the Peruvian community by these accomplishments and the self-confidence engendered within the Machiguenga community cannot be measured. On one occasion, the *Princesa* crew, which was equipped with a two-way radio, was even called upon to help government guards recapture prisoners who had escaped from the jungle penal colony of Sepa.

During the time that the *Princesa* was in operation, the men of the team spent a great deal of time supervising, training the network of participants involved in the project, and helping the crew develop maintenance skills. SIM also provided considerable mechanical aid, while Jerry Hamill gave advisory support to village storekeepers, health workers, and mechanics.

Contrary to our fears, the operation proved profitable, partly due to the fact that in the jungle fuel was subsidized by the government and therefore operational costs could be kept low. Volume operation made it possible to charge lower rates per kilo than other commercial transport. When government subsidy ceased, however, gasoline prices jumped from one to two dollars (or more) per gallon, and the operation became unprofitable. Prices received for most agricultural produce were no longer high enough to cover transportation; thus few people could afford to ship cargo. The *Princesa* made fewer trips, and on two occasions was rented to other entities.

Political change

In the mid-1970s the revolutionary government of Peru requested the withdrawal from the country of United States-owned businesses and then the SIL organization. Nine months' notice was given. Supervision of the Machiguenga schools was taken over by Professor José Pereyra K., who, in addition to his administrative duties with the cooperative, was now an experienced teacher. Supervision of the cooperative was taken over by the cooperative executive committee, with the backup of Werner Friedli. In neither case was training complete, but everything possible was done in the amount of time available to smooth the transition. Although in the end, SIL never did have to leave the country, restrictions thereafter prevented SIL members from assisting in the schools.

The Machiguenga church

Machiguenga team members believed that it is not possible to help marginated people successfully unless the work is built on the universal principles outlined in the Christian Scriptures. Nonsectarian and nondenominational in stance, they nevertheless maintain that in the chaos of cultural change, the teachings of the Bible provide spiritual hope and ethics for living. The main goal of the Snells, therefore, was—in cooperation with mother-tongue speakers—to provide an accurate translation of the New Testament in idiomatic Machiguenga so that all could have the option of knowing its message. In 1976, after twenty-four years of labor, the published New Testament was presented to the people. SIM workers dedicated themselves to seeing that the message was understood as relevant to daily life and to teaching those Machiguenga who wished to increase their knowledge of the Scriptures. The organization of an indigenous church in 1975 was one of the outcomes.

In 1976 the Machiguenga church leaders set up a two-month Bible Institute. Although initially team members were called upon for advice, subsequently the Institute has been conducted annually upon the initiative of the Machiguenga administration and staff. By 1993, at least 86 students had attended the four-term general course. One of the important functions of the Bible school has been to provide equal training for women. The church also holds general conferences annually; representatives (male and female) attend from thirteen or fourteen communities. Six itinerant evangelists are sponsored by the church, as well as pastors or lay pastors in each community. Church leaders serve voluntarily, and maintain their own gardens, although congregations also contribute as they are able to recompense them for travel expenses and for time spent in sermon preparation and counseling.

The church also organizes special campaigns, trains women as Sunday school and Bible teachers, and conducts other activities, all without outside initiation or supervision, although input may be requested from outside entities. In 1993, the president of the Machiguenga church association was a dedicated and enthusiastic leader who had graduated from both high school and a Bible institute in Lima. Twice he has served as president of the Association of Native Churches of the Jungle; he has traveled to a number of other language groups to speak at their invitation; and in 1990 he represented the ethnolinguistic groups of the jungle at an international conference on evangelism held in Manila, the Philippines.

As with any other institution, the church has struggles and is an imperfect organization. Numerically, its members are in the minority; yet it serves as a recognizable factor in present-day social cohesion. Measured by expressions of caring for others, concern for what is right, and cooperation, positive attitudes tend to be more in evidence among church members than among the general populace.

Church members desire education because they wish to be able to read Scripture. Morality as taught in the Scripture is seen as bringing about more harmonious relationships than did the traditional drinking festivals of several days' duration, which often precipitated infidelity, hard feelings, and fights. Unity is promoted in that it is frequently the church attendees who are most willing to work on community projects, to help those in need, and to bear patiently with others.

Interestingly, the New Testament has become a prestigious piece of literature—at least partly, it appears, because of the satisfaction the Machiguenga feel at having a large book in their own language. In the Lower Urubamba villages almost every Machiguenga household owns one New Testament, whether or not the members of that household are church attendees; some households own more than one. In the evenings, as one walks through villages one sees families gathered around the fire, each member reading from his or her own copy of the New Testament (Cowan, 1986). Valuing literacy and developing skill in it for religious reasons also pays dividends for communities as a whole in that, increasingly, individuals are able to handle the reading tasks related to civic affairs. In such a situation, it becomes difficult to separate the religious from the secular.

The 1980s and 1990s

Development continued in several important aspects between 1980 and 1993, when this study concluded.

The joint high school

In 1982 the Ministry of Education established an agricultural secondary school in the Lower Urubamba region. For some time the Snells had seen the need for further education for students who wished to continue beyond the elementary grades offered in their communities. (Finding suitable housing and funding for secondary school students in distant cities had proved both difficult and unsatisfactory.) This high school was intended to serve both the Machiguenga and Piro language groups, and one of its goals was to provide students skills which would enable them to make a living in the community rather than having to emigrate to the cities—a trend which has not been very extensive thus far but which is expected to increase. It was to teach the normal secondary school curriculum, and the language of instruction was to be Spanish.

Like other projects, the venture precipitated stresses and difficulties—the problem of finding competent Peruvian staff willing to live in the village, work under the direction of the Machiguenga and Piro administrators, and respect the indigenous culture; the tensions caused by a mix of students from two language groups; the drain on the host community and the surrounding ecological resources. Nevertheless, the Machiguenga have valued the opportunity to have high school training, and young people have willingly left their home communities to study at the secondary school.

By 1992, fifty-three male and thirty-nine female students had graduated. Of these ninety-two graduates:

- 30 had become bilingual teachers or adult literacy teachers
- 2 were attending university (one in Cuzco studying Agricultural Science, one in Lima studying Business Administration)
- 6 were studying in pedagogical institutes
- 1 was in nursing school.

Most of the remaining graduates were working in their home communities, and a number had been elected to their community Executive Committees. It appears that few secondary school graduates have emigrated from their linguistic community to work for mestizo lumber workers and land owners. Rather, those who are considered permanently lost to the community are school dropouts, some from the upper levels of primary school and some from the second and third years of secondary.

A double-edged problem is faced by the secondary school. One problem is the lack of facilities common in developing nations. A second problem is that, at secondary level, students are competing on the terms set by the majority society. By those more urbane (and frequently prejudiced) standards they are often judged to be below par, culturally and scholastically.

Continued development

By 1980 the revolutionary government had been replaced through the electoral process, and SIL was again being requested by Peruvian officials to continue school and community development programs in specifically agreed-upon areas, with special emphasis on transfer of technology to nationals. However, by this time the members of the SIL Machiguenga team had been given other responsibilities and were free only to act as trainers and consultants on a sporadic basis. Only Betty Snell continued with the preparation of school books, translation of selected Old Testament portions, and a lengthy dictionary and grammar description. The Machiguenga leaders continued mostly on their own.

In 1983, sheep were introduced to the Machiguenga area, and by 1984 or 1985 a course in shepherding became part of the high school curriculum. Those who took the training were to receive animals to start a herd. According to reports received by Wayne Snell, the flock increased rapidly; the people enjoyed the meat and were glad for a new protein source. (Wild game—once plentiful—is becoming scarcer around villages which have been in existence for some time, although it has not been depleted as completely as we had feared it might be.) Herd owners have difficulty obtaining the medication needed to control worms, but at least one high school graduate has begun a flock in a community other than the high school location.

Learning to eat mutton was made easier for the Machiguenga by a special event held to celebrate the granting of a land title to the community of Nueva Luz. Professor Tapia, a much-loved and respected Peruvian educator/development worker who had arrived for the presentation of the documents, worked with the leaders of the event showing them how to butcher and roast a sheep just as it is done by the Quechuas of the mountains and sharing his excitement because the result would be especially delicious. By the time the feast was ready, Professor Tapia's enthusiasm had broken down the reticence which could normally have been expected, and the team had had a lesson in how important the modeling of a prestigious person can be.

The situation in 1993

Towards the end of the 1980s, the economic situation of Peru became chaotic, and subversive political movements began to control areas on the main rivers of Amazonia. Travel became unsafe, and operating costs for the large barge became untenable. It was sold, and the money was deposited in a bank. At the present time, following trends elsewhere (Perez-Crespo 1986:262–263), the Machiguenga cooperative has changed its role to that of a central organizing body and is known as the Machiguenga *Central*. It serves to give the people self-administration, representation to government agencies, and a political voice. Annual conferences continue, but the organization possesses little agricultural or purchasing capacity.

The central warehouses and village stores went out of business when inflation escalated so rapidly that storekeepers (who had no way to know that prices had changed) consistently sold goods for less money than required to replace the stock. A contract signed by the Machiguenga with the Ministry of Health in the provincial capital, Quillabamba, guaranteed validation for their trained health workers, medicines, and medical supplies. However, because of the national economic crisis, the Health Department has not been able to fulfill many of its commitments; as a result, the health posts have lacked medicines. In case of emergency, the Machiguenga travel to Catholic missions or a government health post out of the ethnolinguistic area, where there may or may not be sufficient supplies and expertise to meet their need. Without barge transportation to market, the Machiguenga have again become largely dependent on Peruvian traders and middlemen.

Perhaps even more serious is the fact that some Machiguenga still do not understand the majority society well enough to know why it is important for them to band together despite differences of opinion (something foreign to their traditional culture). Consequently, the organizations and leaders which do exist and which are working for independence and cooperative self-administration may be criticized by their fellow Machiguengas rather than supported.

On the positive side, the Machiguenga have had the experience of managing successful organizations, which many recognize as having appreciably bettered their lot—socially and spiritually, healthwise and materially—even though they have personally borne the brunt of the strains. They have learned to deal with outsiders in such a way that they receive a much higher degree of respect than formerly. (For example, with formally organized communities and justices of the peace, villagers are now able to take legal disciplinary action if visitors exploit their women.)

When the highway reaches their area—as it will—they will have the expertise to reinstate their cooperative. Bilingual young people are available who can be trained as truck drivers. Now they also have a significant number of Spanish speakers, high school graduates, graduates of pedagogical institutes, several with credentials in bilingual education, and others who are enrolled in tertiary education of different types. The cattle projects continue.

The Machiguenga language is still strong enough to be viable for the foreseeable future, and so the Snells are reviewing the New Testament translation in preparation for the publication of a much-requested second edition. Despite heavy social pressure from the Western world, and noticeable language and cultural impingement from the outside, with accompanying stress symptoms, in 1992 much of the traditional belief system and practice still remained.

Chapter Summary

This chapter traces community development efforts among the Machiguenga by decades from the time the study of the language began in 1946, until 1992–1993, when this research was carried out. It was during this period that members of SIL and Swiss Indian Mission worked both to preserve the culture and to teach skills which would enable the Machiguenga to cope with the Western world. From very small beginnings, despite many hardships and setbacks, the program grew until trained artisans, community leaders, and medical services had all been developed and the Machiguenga were themselves staffing and administering three rather large and complex institutions—a school system, a church organization, and an agricultural cooperative. In addition, communities have received land reservations, and scores of individuals are taking their place in the national life as documented citizens.

The community development efforts are described here because, although originally they were not conceived with literacy in mind, we now realize that their existence created uses for literacy which have contributed to its maintenance. Success can be partially measured by the comments of Peruvian officials who have expressed surprise and pleasure upon visiting personally and seeing for themselves the orderly manner in which some of the projects have been carried out. One supervising doctor remarked to Wayne Snell, after finding a perfect health post inventory and up-to-date accounting, "This is better than we are doing at my hospital!"

Chapter Summary

Rice huller and sawmill are operated by Machiguenga technicians.
(P. Davis photos Camisea, 1992)

5

Schools for the Machiguenga

I have sent all my sons and daughters to school. They should know how to read and write and to defend me. I say to them, "Learn to read. Don't be like me. If you don't know how, how will you manage later?" - Father, House 12, Puerto Huallana

Introduction

Simultaneous with community development, the Machiguenga schools were growing. Except for the fact that, slowly, the schools were producing better-trained candidates for specialized training options, the two programs were not thought of as related, for at that time the concept of functional literacy was not well known. Time, however, has revealed unanticipated results. To understand them, we must now trace the development of the school program.

Preparation

Literacy requires a written language. The Snells, who had been trained in principles of descriptive linguistics—after an initial period of language learning and cultural orientation—turned their attention to completing the analysis of the Machiguenga sound system, checking the practical alphabet prepared by their predecessors, and describing the grammar (word, sentence, paragraph, and discourse structure). The formation of the alphabet was guided by five principles established by Smalley (1963:31–52):

1. Maximum representation of speech. One symbol per sound unit.

2. Maximum motivation for the people to want to read. No symbols to which the people objected.

3. Maximum ease of learning. No symbols which the people found confusing or difficult.

4. Maximum ease of transfer to the national language. Under existing guidelines, alphabets were to look as much like Spanish as possible in order to facilitate transition from the mother tongue to the second language, but because certain combinations of sounds were potentially confusing, the Machiguenga workers received permission to use the letter *k* (instead of *c* and *qu*).

5. Maximum ease of reproduction on typewriters and presses.

The Machiguenga alphabet as it was finally approved consisted of 22 letters: *a, ch, e, g, i, j, k, ky, m, n, ñ, o, p, r, s, sh, t, ts, ty, u, v,* and *y*.

Only six months after the Snells had begun language study, the government initiated bilingual schools and requested the help of all field linguists in the preparation of school materials and the training of teachers. Although, humanly speaking, it was too early in their program, the Snells did the best they could, drafting the first two reading books to be prepared in the Machiguenga language. These books, published in trial form in 1953, with Ministry of Education approval, were simple sight word books. Above the key words, line drawings illustrated items from daily life—items such as father, mother, a clay pot, a woven basket, and a nutria.[7]

Downstream from the Snells' isolated and monolingual location, three literate men were found who spoke Machiguenga—Morán Zumaeta Bastín, Abelino Manuel Salas, and Silverio Pérez Ganta. They had lived among the adjacent Piro and had had opportunity to attend school for a short period. These men were concerned for the Machiguenga, who were generally considered to be abandoned and devoid of services, and so they were contacted to see if they were willing to attend the government's 1954 bilingual teacher training course, with the understanding that subsequently they might have opportunity to teach in Machiguenga communities.

---

[7]The nutria is a large, beaver-like South American rodent valued for its fur.

Despite the good intentions of the government, however, no school could be initiated without the approval of the Machiguenga themselves. Wayne Snell tells of making a long trip by dugout canoe in 1953, accompanied by Morán Zumaeta Bastín, to speak with the heads of families of the area where the Snells had begun language study. The group gathered in a circle, whereupon—in typical Machiguenga fashion—the men turned their backs on each other and spoke into the air simultaneously. For three hours the conversation swirled past the neophyte field worker in the machine-gun-like staccato of formal conversation as Mr. Zumaeta explained the government's offer, described the functions of a school, who could attend, the advantages of education, and the responsibilities a school incurs (such as the construction of a school building and sending children regularly). These were new concepts; the men asked questions, commented, discussed. After three hours as the conversation drew to a close, Wayne, who had understood very little of the discussion, inquired, "Well, what did they say?" Morán's answer was as enigmatic as the conversation, "They say they are going hunting tomorrow."

Later, when they were alone, Morán explained. The men wanted time to discuss the proposal among themselves; then they would communicate their decision. True to their word, the answer was received in due time. The Machiguenga had chosen to have a school and to accept Morán Zumaeta as their first teacher. He would train Abelino Manuel Salas as his replacement.

Teacher Training

With this groundwork in place, Morán Zumaeta Bastín and Abelino Manuel Salas joined Silverio Pérez Ganta and three daughters of an influential Machiguenga-mestizo at the government teacher training course in January to March of 1954. The three young women had attended a Spanish-speaking boarding school on the Alto Urubamba and had then been chosen by their father as possible teachers for a school in his community. Some of these teacher candidates had very rudimentary literacy skills and none had ever read the Machiguenga language before. They learned to read Machiguenga as they learned the steps for teaching the new Machiguenga primers. They improved their handwriting as they practiced, and secured their numeracy knowledge as they learned the steps for teaching elementary counting, addition, and subtraction. They learned to teach Spanish as a second language through oral drills and flash cards, and they learned how to construct a classroom and to manage school records. Because several ethnolinguistic groups were represented at the training course, lessons were first presented in

Spanish. Then the group was divided by language groups, and the field linguist who spoke the language reviewed the lesson in the mother tongue. Teaching steps were practiced over and over in the mother tongue until students knew both the progression and the teaching script (the explanation) by heart. The field linguist also served as mentor and coach for other homework assignments. (See Shell 1981:87–108, for a more complete description of the training of bilingual teachers.)

Early teacher candidates with very limited exposure to school models struggled to understand all of these new concepts in Spanish, their second language. Mentally it was exhausting. However, by the end of the training course they were equipped to teach one school year of material to a class of beginning students, and those who passed the course returned to their communities armed with textbooks, a blackboard, chalk, pencils, and notebooks.

Year by year, the teachers returned to learn how to teach the next grade. Slowly, as the government increased the offerings at teacher training courses, many bilingual teachers finished primary education, and then high school. For individuals brought up in the most remote corners of the jungle, it has been a saga of admirable perseverance and courage.

The Early Schools

As the school year began in April of 1954, with her father's backing, Antonina Pereyra Baca opened a simple school for the Machiguenga children of her home community, Pangoa, which lay just upriver from the gorge of Mainique.

Below the gorge, at Timpía, teacher Morán Zumaeta gathered the first group of students on the floor of the Snells' house, which was empty at the time. Within weeks, the community moved upriver to the mouth of the Etariato stream, and a more permanent school building was constructed. These children had never before seen pencils or paper, knew nothing about holding books, and did not understand any of the concepts underlying reading or arithmetic. They were also very shy. Nevertheless, they loved to learn. At least six bilingual teachers eventually developed out of this small and tenuous beginning.

In the first Machiguenga bilingual school, classes were held on the floor until desks and benches could be built. (Wayne Snell photo, April 1954)

The Early Textbooks

The Snells' next task was now to prepare the next year's textbooks. Primers 3 and 4, which introduced syllables and the reading of story material, were drafted and published in 1954 (with revised editions in 1957, 1958, and 1961). Advanced primers 5 and 6 were published in 1959. Meanwhile, in 1957 and 1958 bilingual arithmetic books 4, 5, 6, and 7 were published in Machiguenga and Spanish. (Arithmetic books 1–3 contained only numbers and so could be used for all languages.) A simple bilingual natural and social science textbook was also published in 1958 with Machiguenga and Spanish text on facing pages. The oral Spanish course for beginners used flash cards and charts with pictures of familiar objects. Later, simple dialogues, which were acted out, taught greetings, the terms for buying and selling, and other survival-type vocabulary. Spanish reading was not introduced until *Segundo Año* (grade 3) after the concept of reading was fairly well established in the mother tongue. At that point, reading skills could be transferred quickly from one language to the other once the pronunciation of the Spanish letters was known. In every case, Ministry of Education representatives were involved in planning, reviewed the textbook manuscripts, and granted approval for publication.

Expansion

In 1956, Abelino Manuel Salas, who had apprenticed under Morán in Etariato, moved to the Picha River, where his services were needed to open a school. By 1958, graduates of the teacher training course had traveled to the Manu River and to the upriver Camisea to offer schools to those Machiguenga who were interested. In remote areas where contact with the outside was infrequent, the people often found it difficult to envision the world their children would face and to understand the need to prepare for it. "If the government has to have children to put them in school," they would query, "why doesn't it have children of its own instead of taking ours?" Some declined the opportunity to move to a school community. Others, however, had had sufficient exposure to understand their vulnerability to exploiters and to disease. They indicated their willingness to gather so that their children might learn the skills a school could teach. As they gathered, the teacher became the mentor and contact with the outside world; however, in most cases, the teacher's success was dependent upon the help and goodwill of the headmen and heads of families, and so leadership was shared.

An older, respected man from the community usually convened formal and informal meetings when the need arose to allocate space for houses and fields, decide schedules, organize community work projects, or discuss any aspect of community life. Teachers might ask for meetings when school matters needed to be addressed. As life became more complex, communities organized formally. They now have legal charters, formal membership, executive committees, and statutes which regulate community activities and discipline.

Today, most of the school communities have moved one or more times as the people have sought locations which—for one reason or another—they deemed more favorable, but the model established early on has served well. Over the years, some have become disgruntled and have left the school communities; however, by far the largest trend has been the arrival of families from the headwaters who have heard good reports from the schools and who have wanted their children to benefit from the opportunity to learn in their own language.

The Structure of Schools

The government's original agreement with the jungle peoples was that if they would construct the school and playing field and maintain them, the

Ministry of Education would train, allocate, and pay teachers and provide school materials. The building of an airstrip was also part of the bargain wherever the only reasonable means of school supply was via small plane. The Machiguenga people are hard workers, and those who wanted a school not only agreed to shoulder these tasks but carried them out faithfully. Schools were built of cane or palm wood, with packed earth floors and palm thatched roofs. Temporary desks and benches made of cane were soon replaced with boards salvaged from old hand-hewn canoes.

Government regulations required the enrollment of children six years of age and up. However, in Machiguenga-land, no one knew his age. Teachers learned to calculate children's ages by testing the length of their arms and looking at their teeth. Children who could reach over their heads with their right arm and touch their left ear were approximately six years of age but often proved too immature to enjoy school. Children who had changed all four front teeth were approximately eight years old and normally studied with pleasure. As a further complication, most of the children had no personal names. Teachers required to list their students in an official school register met the demand by assigning a name to each child. Later, they learned the importance of assigning each person the same name each year and of using the same surname for all the members of a family.

The bilingual school curriculum was based upon the standard Peruvian curriculum for elementary schools (a traditional curriculum of the 50s and 60s), but was culturally adapted for the jungle peoples. Quickly it was realized that beginning students who lack all the readiness orientation which surrounds children in Western societies, required more time to become accustomed to the school culture and to assimilate the new concepts. The first year of the Peruvian school system, which at that time was called *Transition*, was therefore divided into three years—*Transition 1, Transition 2,* and *Transition 3*. The second year of the Peruvian curriculum, called First Year, was also divided into two—*First Year* and *First Year Advanced.*

Patiently, teachers explained in language the children could understand what they were going to do and how to go about it. Since students were unused to sitting still for long, lessons could be shortened and recesses lengthened as necessary. Additional material was prepared to give adequate practice of new concepts. All texts used culturally-adapted illustrations. At first, eighty to ninety per cent of the teaching was in Machiguenga, and oral Spanish was taught with second language methodology for one period of the day. Each year the amount of Spanish was increased until at *Second Year* level (the sixth year of school) students were expected to use the Spanish textbooks of the regular Peruvian curriculum.

Students listened as teacher Arturo Aradino Italiano taught from one of the first books written in the Machiguenga language. Camisea's first school building was temporarily constructed with cane walls. Older students and young children all began *Transition 1* together.
(Don Hesse photo, Camisea, 1959)

The Machiguenga chose the hours of 7:00 a.m. to 1:00 p.m. for their school day in order to leave time for fishing and other work in the afternoons. The schedule included an hour each of reading, math, writing, and oral Spanish, with recesses interspersed, and then a fifth hour which varied on alternate days and included science, physical education, music, art, and vocational training. The teaching of traditional arts and crafts was encouraged during these periods. Subjects such as Spanish reading, history, and geography, were added as pupils advanced through the grades, The schedule varied somewhat with different Ministry of Education decrees; however, there were few fundamental changes until the educational reform movement of 1972. The stability of these first eighteen years of the program greatly benefited beginning teachers and communities and enabled the Machiguenga people to internalize many educational principles. (See Davis 1981b, for a more detailed description of the Peruvian bilingual schools.)

Curriculum Development

Early in the 1960s, after the assignment to the Machiguenga project of Harold Davis, who was a trained elementary teacher and reading specialist, the team began to evaluate existing school materials and to develop new ones. The first handwriting guides, which I prepared, were published in 1966 and 1967. Harold Davis teamed with Betty Snell to revise the upper-level math series. But major problems encountered in both beginning math and beginning reading required some years to resolve and merit explanation.

Beginning numeracy

Teachers had learned to use flash cards and objects while teaching beginners how to count, and students—who appeared to learn the numbers normally—were soon counting to twenty and to one hundred. Observation in the schools revealed, however, that children in their fifth year could not multiply and divide. Additional explanations and flash card drills did not help. Eventually, it was determined that none of the students could associate the correct quantity with a number name. We placed Cuisenaire rods in each school, thinking that the colored rods of different lengths would establish visual connections between quantities and number names, but to no avail.

Three years of observation elapsed before it was finally established beyond doubt that traditionally the Machiguenga used a biunique number system (one for you, one for me, one for him...). While they were able to memorize long sequences of number names and remember large numbers of individual transactions (e.g., I owe him salt; he owes me a woven bag), the only number name which for them carried invariant quantity was the number one. All the other number names merely represented "plural."

Having understood the problem, my husband and I returned to the beginning, asking the teachers to reteach the numbers slowly, using flash cards and a multitude of objects all arranged in set patterns—a triangle for three, a square for four, etc. A large workbook provided extra practice. The concept that each number name represented a different invariant quantity proved extremely difficult for the students at first. However, after half a school year, the majority could not only count and write the numbers to ten, but could select the appropriate quantity of objects for each number symbol. Thereafter, they progressed normally through the arithmetic textbooks. Interestingly, once the concept became established in the minds of one generation of students, it spread throughout the villages as children proudly practiced their counting at home. Succeeding generations of school children seem to have had less difficulty in learning their numbers. (See Wise and Riggle 1981, for "Mathematical terminology and instruction in basic mathematical concepts among ethnic groups of the Peruvian Amazon.")

Curriculum Development

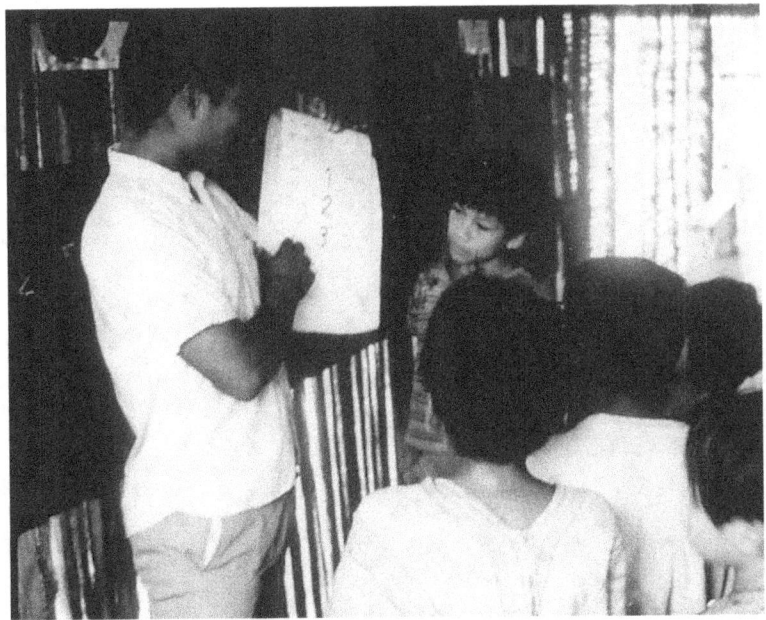

Above: The arithmetic workbook in use.

Below: Workbook pages were proudly displayed at home, providing practice for family members as well.
(P. Davis photos, Nueva Luz, c. 1968)

Above: Arithmetic practice is sometimes done on rocks beside the river.

Below: Teacher Andrés Vicente drills numbers with the aid of a snail shell abacus.
(P. Davis photos, c. 1969)

Reading

The Snells had never been satisfied with the Machiguenga reading series. Although the best teaching principles known at that time had been followed and some had learned how to read, the process appeared to be very difficult for Machiguenga students. Betty Snell attributed the difficulties to linguistic factors beyond the basic differences of differing worldviews and the Machiguengas' general lack of orientation to reading. In one way or another, all the methods we knew were oriented to languages in which nouns were predominant, or at least could be repeated frequently. They did not make adequate provision for the predominance of verbs in Machiguenga discourse. The problem was complicated by the fact that Machiguenga verbs are very long and the distribution of syllables within them is almost infinitely varied. It was very difficult, consequently, to find segments larger than the syllable which were similar enough to be usable for drill purposes. Furthermore, in idiomatic Machiguenga, exact repetition is infrequent except to mark continuation of an action.

Joining forces, Betty Snell and I faced the challenge of preparing readers to handle complex texts composed chiefly of long verbs without using too many practice drills (unnatural repetition). We also needed to make reading interesting and fun for a people who already were finding "paper too hard." The new primer series, built on a well-known folk story, contained a number of innovations and was introduced to the teachers for testing in the schools.

This reading program did not depend solely upon the use of the primers. Teachers were taught to practice words and syllables on the blackboard. They also were taught to use flash cards for each new word and syllable in Primers 1 and 2 and for the new syllables of Primer 3. (The cards were color coordinated with the cover of the primer to which they pertained and were organized in shoe-holder-type cloth pockets hung on the school wall.) The writing program was carefully planned to reinforce each day's reading lesson. New, coordinated writing books published in 1971 and 1972 provided additional help for the teachers and practice for the students. (See Davis 1981:265–271, for a further description of primer design.)

As the new series was tested in the schools, we found that students of average intelligence could complete Phase 1 and 2 of the program in three school years, sometimes less, and were able to read their language with comprehension.

Newly literate readers, however, needed additional practice to solidify and to maintain their skills. Over time, a number of advanced reading books were also produced (mostly by Betty Snell with the help of the Machiguenga)—traditional folklore, health books, trickster stories, the life of Simón Bolívar (the liberator of the Americas), and stories from the majority culture such as the race between the hare and the turtle.

School Supervision

Because Peruvian educational supervisors were seldom able to travel to the distant rivers of minority language groups, SIL members traveling in the area had been asked to provide counsel and to supply materials to bilingual school teachers. We added this task to our other duties and developed a format for school supervision which seemed to serve well. During January to March, we were present at the locale of the annual teacher training course, attending some classes, supplementing explanations, helping students with homework, and coaching teachers as they filled out year-end statistics and school reports. As the teachers finished and returned to their communities, we followed them, scheduling time with each one. While Harold attended to community development projects and upper levels, I visited the lower-level classrooms. My presence inevitably caused a stir—little ones unused to white faces were frightened; the teacher marshaled his best performance; and students were on their best behavior. But after approximately three days of sitting perfectly quiet in a corner, I found the classroom returning to normal. By that time, I had gained an idea of who the students were, where they were in their books, and who was having trouble with sight or hearing. I knew if books were lacking, if desks were the correct size, if the roof leaked, if the teacher had prepared well, if he/she was competent in lesson presentation, and if there were problems in class management.

Understanding that teachers labored under many difficulties, including a meager education and minimum pedagogical preparation, we sought always to be affirming—a number were working miracles with their students despite the handicaps. Usually, before much time had passed, teachers were asking questions—how to teach this lesson, or what to do about that learning problem. Occasionally, the consultants would demonstrate a lesson, but normally, in order to prevent embarrassment to students and to avoid undermining the teacher publicly, such matters were discussed in the afternoon. Afternoons, then, became in-service training sessions in which teachers reviewed lesson steps, received help in making lesson plans, thought through seat work assignments, discussed discipline problems, filled out forms, took inventory, and placed orders for material.

If a teacher was beset with many problems, the most serious one was addressed first. With help, the teacher prepared for the following day seeking to incorporate an improved technique into his new lesson plan. A debriefing session the next afternoon evaluated the lesson presentation and, again with help, the next lesson was prepared. Most teachers, when coached in this way over a period of two weeks to a month, showed permanent improvement. However, some appeared to comply only when the consultant was present, judging from the lack of progress evidenced by their students the following year.

At times, conversations with the teacher brought areas of need in school-community relations to our attention; community meetings were often suggested to help smooth difficulties and to enlist cooperation for the school. Normally, when they were consulted and needs were explained, Machiguenga parents were both interested and supportive. They came by the school to check on children's progress and behavior, gave time to maintain desks, roof and playing field, and later cleared bean fields which the children planted and harvested to earn money for school books and clothing.

A reading lesson shows syllable contrast. (P. Davis photo, c. 1972)

After school, homework goes forward on the front porch. (P. Davis photo, c. 1972)

Educational Reform

In 1968 a revolutionary coup ousted the democratically elected president of Peru and established a radical nationalist/leftist government, which described itself as socialist and humanist. Its goal was to bring in a new order. North American companies were ejected from the country, and a sweeping Agricultural Reform was instituted. In 1972 a new Educational Reform Bill was signed into law. It declared all the textbooks in the country obsolete, along with traditional education, substituting instead the consciousness-raising program of Paulo Freire, global teaching, units of experience, and modern math. The levels of elementary school (formerly called *years*) were reorganized into six grades. By 1974, SIL members were seen as disseminators of cultural imperialism and had to withdraw from all involvement in education. The educational system was decentralized, and the bilingual schools, which until that time had been directed from a central office in Pucallpa, were moved to the jurisdiction of some thirty-four districts, scattered over the vast jungle region.

Such sudden and profound changes disrupted the educational system of the nation, and much of the educational effort for the next years was directed towards sorting out administrative logistics and reorienting the teachers in seminars and workshops where, very often, ideology took precedence over pedagogy. The Machiguenga schools were supervised, first by educational offices in Atalaya, then in Quillabamba. Officials there had very little knowledge of bilingual education or the difficulties of an isolated minority-group teacher. The teachers did the best they could, but over all they felt disoriented, finding it hard to teach without textbooks or a schedule; as a result, the delivery of education suffered considerably. During this period, José Pereyra Kashiari, the most bilingual and highly educated of all the Machiguenga teachers, began to act as liaison between the teachers and the educational offices, helping educational authorities communicate new procedures to the teachers and acting as an advocate for the teachers to government officials. Recognizing his competence, the authorities eventually named him as an educational supervisor.

Unable to continue in education, SIL members nevertheless continued community development efforts—the establishment of a cooperative and a transportation system for agricultural produce; teaching the people how to organize, elect officers, keep financial records, and represent themselves according to new government guidelines; and putting them in touch with other agencies, such as the Ministry of Agriculture and World Neighbors-Peru, which could help them in areas of specific need. To maintain interest in reading, I produced an occasional bulletin, publishing the news that Machiguenga friends had written, often with the addition of a short article and illustrations authored by someone from Machiguenga-land who had an interesting experience to tell. These news sheets were well received.

A national bilingual education policy formulated under the revolutionary government included a new component—language maintenance and the revitalization of vernacular languages. Mother-tongue instruction was officially authorized. In approximately 1978, after the revolutionary government had been ousted and national policy had inched slowly back toward the center, SIL educators were again asked to help teach pedagogy in teacher training courses and to help rewrite all the textbooks which had been declared obsolete. This huge undertaking involved the development—under new guidelines—of the entire reading and writing series for twenty-eight jungle languages, as well as the math series, science series, health series, and Spanish as a second language textbooks used in all the bilingual schools (see table 5.1).

Table 5.1. Books recommended for the Bilingual Schools—1984

Reading	Writing	Spanish as L2	Mathematics	Natural Science	Social Science
Grade 1 Readiness *Readiness 1* *Readiness 2* Beginning reading *Primer 1*	Readiness *Readiness 1* *Readiness 2*—printing (in two lines) *Primer 1*	*Oral Spanish 1* (dialogues)	*Mathematics 1* (Teacher's guide)	*Our World 1* (Teacher's guide), *Mariquita, the dirty one* *Flies*	*We Live United 1* (Teacher's guide)
Grade 2 *Primer 2*	*Printing* (in one line) *Primer 2*	*Oral Spanish 1* continued	*Mathematics 2* (Teacher's guide)	*Our World 1* (Teacher's guide), *Mariquita, Flies*	*We Live United 1* (Teacher's guide)
Grade 3 Skill building *Primer 3* (Easy stories)	Cursive writing *Primer 3*	*Ana y Pepe, Pepe, el Travieso* —(reading and writing)	*Pedagogy Manual* pp. 48-66 (Teacher's guide), *Arithmetic 6-10*	*Our World 2 and Supplement* (Teacher's guide), *The Human Body*	*Nature and Social Life 2*, pp. 1–22

Reading	Writing	Spanish as L2	Mathematics	Natural Science	Social Science
Grade 4					
Stories with common words Readers 4–6, Mother Tongue Grammar Book, if there is one	Adventures in Spanish	Camino, Let's Write, Oral Spanish 2	Pedagogy Manual, pp. 48–66 (Teacher's guide), Arithmetic 6–10	Nature and Social Life 3, pp. 9–17, 23–44, Supplement 3, Care of teeth, Amoeba and hookworm, Tuberculosis	Nature and Social Life 3, pp. 3–9, 18–23, 45–62
Grades 5 & 6					
Advanced Readers 7–10		Reference books	Reference books	Progress, pp. 132–183	Progress, pp. 1–131

Fortunately, most of the Machiguenga textbooks had been modernized just prior to the educational reform law and met the guidelines of 1978; thus it was not necessary to revise them immediately. Betty Snell continued to prepare advanced reading material for the Machiguenga as her other duties allowed. By now I had been reassigned as SIL Peru Branch literacy editor and was—with a team—responsible for the development of the several scores of new textbooks urgently needed for the entire school system. Since the new government found itself in severe financial straits, SIL cooperated by seeking funding for the new bilingual school textbooks. The Canadian International Development Agency, as well as other entities, responded generously and publication was able to go forward—a strategic factor in rebuilding the morale of many teachers.

In approximately 1979, Machiguenga leaders presented a written petition (in the author's files) to the SIL administration requesting my continued services for bilingual school mentoring, but, given the political climate in the country, it was not possible for the administration to comply with the request. Subsequent reports from Professor Pereyra (personal conversation 1990) confirm our evaluation that things would have gone better in the opinion of at least certain of the Machiguenga leaders had mentoring in most areas been able to continue for another few years.

Author, Print Shop, and Translation Training

In the early 1980s an authors' workshop was held, during which Machiguengas were trained to write and publish their own materials on a silk screen press. This training has come into use at the Bible school and at the educational administrative offices, where materials and memos are constantly prepared, but only one manuscript of stories has been submitted for publication so far as I know. Lack of Machiguenga resources to fund spontaneously-authored materials is the greatest obstacle to the production of reading materials, coupled with the fact that the few people trained to produce materials now have too many demands on their time. In the educational and Bible school offices the silk screens have been replaced by mimeographs, which are used regularly but sparingly because of the difficulty of obtaining supplies. These facilities may also be used to publish bulletins for the church and for the cooperative.

During the 1980s, as well, Machiguengas apprenticed on the staff of the new bilingual print shop established at Yarinacocha to serve the bilingual schools. There they learned all of the steps involved in bookmaking, from the typing of stencils, and collating and binding the printed pages to servicing the mimeographs. The intent is that the Machiguenga will one day have a small print shop of their own to serve their growing school system.

In the early 1980s, the president of the church association and the director of the Bible Institute attended a brief course in translation principles. They received part of the information already possessed by the few who had spent concentrated time in on-the-job apprenticeship during the New Testament translation process. At least one of these students has made extensive use of the knowledge. All received a deeper understanding of the procedures required to achieve a good translation.

Textbook Revision

In the 1980s a new need arose. The new Machiguenga primer series had been a pioneer endeavor with a number of innovations designed to meet the needs of Machiguenga students. After observing its use in the schools for several years, we found that students appeared to be learning better than ever before and that teachers could follow the presentation without undue difficulty. Now the books needed to be regularized and reprinted in the format used by the newly-revised reading series of the other language groups. Irregular primers, though pedagogically adequate, could not be easily taught in teacher training sessions attended by representatives of many languages. Teaching steps had to be uniform for all.

From Canada, I (on extended furlough) mailed drafts to Betty Snell in Dallas. With the help of colleagues in Peru, the first two books were revised and published over a period of several years. Then in 1989 the two of us met in Peru. The goal was not only to write the last syllable book but to teach two Machiguenga educators—José Pereyra Kashiari and Edgar Barrientos Pereyra—the principles of textbook making. Capable and dedicated, these gentlemen assimilated primer making techniques as they helped coauthor the new reader (a combination of the two books previously known as Primers 3 and 4). The end result was two publications: the revised, enlarged Primer 3 and a thesis—a handbook for primer making—which earned the men baccalaureate degrees in bilingual education.

(4) Examples of the four-page lesson format used in the Machiguenga primer series.

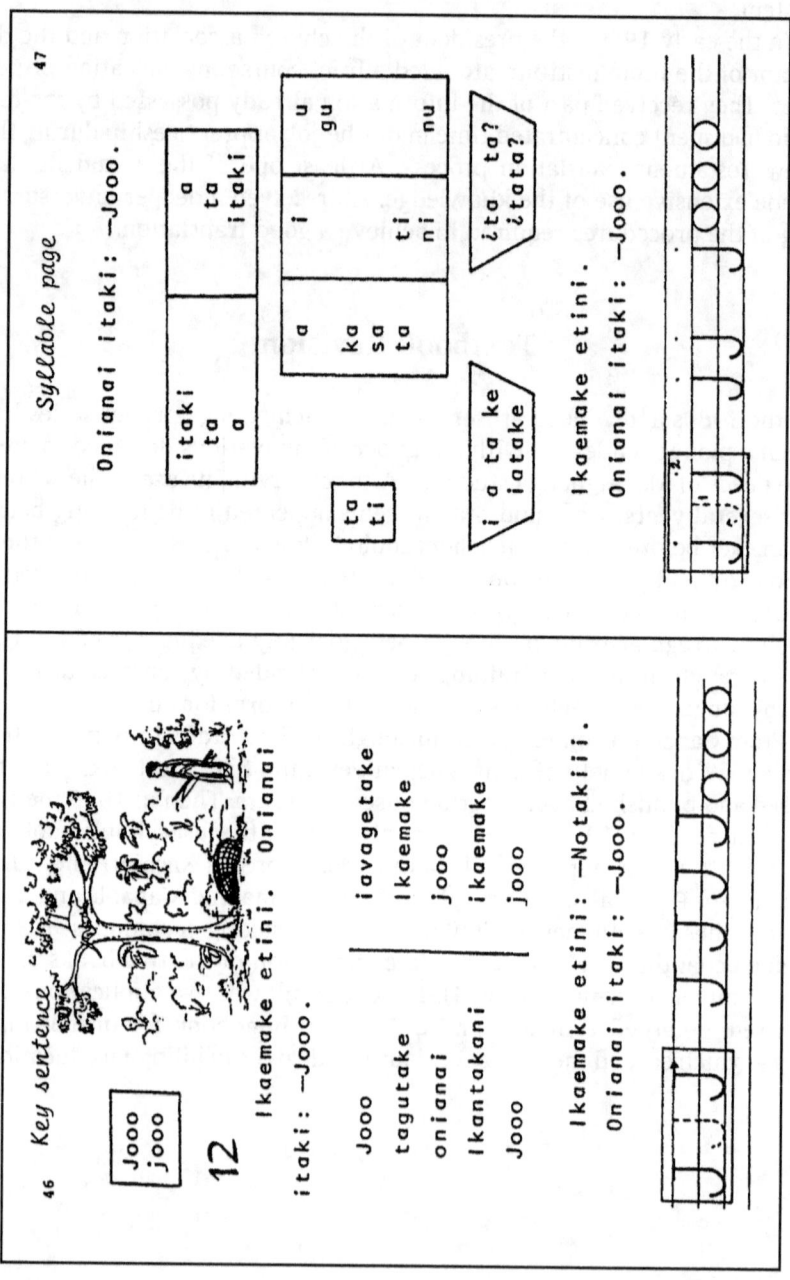

48 Grammar particle

Ikaemake etini. Onianai itaki: —Jooo.

| kaemake. | kaemake. |
| Ikaemake. | Ikaemake. |

Ikaemake
Ikemapaakeri
Itimi
Iavagetake
Ikantakani

Ikaemake
Onianai

Ikaemake etini: —Notakiii.
Onianai itaki: —Jooo.
Iavagetake samani matsigenka ikemapaakeri kaemake tagutake enoku.

Onianai: —Jooo.

Review 49

Itimi matsigenka inkenishiku ikantakani yanuivageti lavagetake samani.
Itimi etini inkenishiku ikaemake: —Notakiii. Ikemapaakeri matsigenka.
Onianai itaki: —Jooo.

itaki
ta
a

Ikaemake
Ikemapaakeri
Iavagetake
Itimi

ta gu ta ke
tagutake

no	ta	ni
ka	ni	o
ta	no	ka

tagutake enoku

Teacher Dedication

This chapter would not be complete without a word of tribute to the dedication and creativity of the Machiguenga teachers. With few resources, they pioneered new roles, built communities, took responsibility for problem solving, stemmed epidemics, traveled hazardous rivers, defended their people against injustice, spent their own money for school supplies for their pupils, and endured against many odds. The students they have taught, many of whom now surpass them educationally, have done so because they provided a solid foundation. Their years of faithful—often lonely—perseverance is now bearing fruit that can be seen by all.

The teachers' wives also deserve recognition. Assigned with their husbands, often far from their home community, they stood by their men, pioneering an unfamiliar role while creating a home for their children. It has been costly; at least one teacher and his wife lost a son because their assignment took them to a distant village where no medical help was available. Their willingness to suffer to help their people has made a huge difference in the outcomes visible today.

Chapter Summary

This chapter traces the development of the Machiguenga bilingual schools from 1953 when the Machiguengas of the Lower Urubamba were first offered the opportunity for education. Slowly, despite the considerable challenges—especially with regard to the teaching of reading and numeracy—teaching materials were developed which proved effective and primary teachers were trained. Assigned to remote communities, they pioneered in helping their people prepare to meet the outside world.

For the interest of educators, the chapter describes the methods developed for teacher training and supervision. The pedagogical methods used in the design of the Machiguenga primers are also presented briefly; they are described in more detail in Davis 1981b and c.

6
Developing New Research Methods

Long ago I lived in the headwaters and never had heard of a school. Now I have come here and my son attends. Ojojooo, that is good! It is wonderful. He is learning. I see what I missed...He can write, write, write. I see him handling books and doing it well. I WOULD REALLY LIKE TO LEARN, but I do not know how to write. Now I want my children to learn. I see the older one learns quickly. — Mother, House 16, Mayapo

Introduction

This chapter describes early preparation for the research project, the choosing of the sample, the setting of reading standards, and the content of the evaluation instruments which were developed.

Early Preparation

The research project was initiated nearly a year previous to my arrival on site by means of letters to SIL administrators in Peru and Professor José Pereyra K., the government Coordinator of Bilingual Education in the Machiguenga area, requesting permission to conduct a research project among the Machiguenga. Professor Pereyra's gracious letter of invitation (April 20,

1992, in my files) paved the way for my arrival in the village of Camisea by small plane in October of 1992, accompanied by Professor Edgar Barrientos K., the Supervisor of Primary Education for the Machiguenga bilingual schools. Professor Barrientos is a mother-tongue speaker of Machiguenga but is fully fluent in Spanish. His brilliant mind, *bachillerato* (baccalaureate degree) in bilingual education, and knowledge of the villages and of the people had prepared him to be an ideal research colleague.

Choosing the sample

The need to select a representative sampling precipitated several problems. First, exact figures for village populations were not available; in addition, not all homes included in village census records were accessible to the survey team because of distance. We did know, however, that Machiguenga bilingual school villages differed greatly and that no one community could be considered representative of the entire group. The villages could roughly be divided into those located on the Lower Urubamba River, which now have considerable contact with the outside world, and those located on tributaries of the Urubamba, most of which are still remote and difficult to access.

The reported population for the villages was as seen in table 6.1.

Table 6.1. Reported population of villages

Main river communities		Tributary communities	
Camisea	276	Camaná	318
Chokoriari	218	Mayapo	210
Nueva Luz	475	Montetoni	346
Nuevo Mundo	250	Pagoreni	25
		Puerto Huallana	353
		Segakiato	308
		Shivankoreni	346
Totals:	1,219, or 40.5% of the population		1,792, or 59.5% of the population

It was therefore decided to conduct the study in seven communities, covering one, Camisea, from the main river as thoroughly as possible and then sampling at random in six more villages: Camaná, Mayapo, Puerto Huallana, Segaiato, Shivankoreni, and Chokoriari. The reasoning for this approach follows.

Early Preparation

Among the four Machiguenga villages located on the Lower Urubamba, Nueva Luz had hosted the secondary school since 1982. Nuevo Mundo had been home of the Machiguenga Bible Institute since 1976 and is presently the headquarters of the Machiguenga *Central* (organizing body). Part of the population in both these villages is highly literate and is expected to maintain literacy skills. However, both villages also have a number of nonliterate and semiliterate adults and a mixed population of Piro speakers (in Nueva Luz) and Campa speakers (in Nuevo Mundo). Testing in those villages could be complicated by second language factors. Camisea, with its homogeneous Machiguenga population, had had a good primary school but no higher education until the creation of a secondary school in 1991. Its population was, therefore, deemed the most likely to place at a good, but not disproportionately high, level of literacy ability, without second-language complexities. On this basis, it was chosen for the entire-village sample.

The five villages located on tributaries were chosen for random sampling because schools had existed in them for many years (as contrasted with two very new communities where teachers had been assigned only a short time and the villagers were still largely nonliterate).

The sixth village, Chokoriari, was a newer community which, because of distance and location (upriver, where travel is more difficult), had always been isolated from the services provided to the other communities. Although accessible to travelers who pass by on the main river, educationally, it needed to be grouped with the more remote villages. Because of these factors and because no information was available on the state of literacy there, Chokoriari was selected for random sampling.

The random samplings aimed to cover ten percent of the village populations. The results, calculated as accurately as possible, are seen in table 6.2.

Table 6.2. Random sampling of remote villages

	Camisea	Camaná	Chokoriari	Mayapo	Pto. Huallana	Segakiato	Shivankoreni	Total
Reported population	276	318	218	210	353	308	232	1,915
Approximate accessible population	170	283	178	210	343	258	215	1,675
Number surveyed	119[*]	34	19	21	36	39	35	303

[*] Those of the accessible population not surveyed in Camisea included approximately ten adults who were absent at the time of our visit. The remainder were children under grade 2 level.

The total of 303 individuals represents 10 percent of the reported population (3,011) of all eleven Machiguenga bilingual school communities located in the Lower Urubamba region.

The ratio was 119 individuals in Camisea (39.3 percent of the sample) to 184 individuals (60.7 percent of the sample) from more isolated villages.

Community profiles

The communities chosen differed in location, historical antecedents, and length of school experience; thus a brief description is in order.

Camisea

Camisea, the oldest of the Machiguenga bilingual school communities, was founded in 1959 upon arrival of two groups of Machiguengas—one from upriver on the Urubamba and one from the Manú River. For twenty-seven years, until his retirement in 1988, the school was directed by expert teacher Professor Andrés Vicente. His teaching attracted upper-level students from other villages whose schools did not offer the upper grades of primary education. In 1991 the village was chosen as a central location for a regional secondary school, and since then the villagers have hosted both high school staff and secondary school boarding students.

Camisea adults have been characterized by their earnest desire to learn; a number have expended great effort to attend school along with their children. Adult classes have also been well attended. The good school, coupled with a location that provides opportunity for contact with the outside world, has enabled most villagers to acquire at least rudimentary concepts about literacy as well as a certain amount of Spanish. A large number of parents are literate (graduates from the early years of the bilingual school), and the younger generation expects to be.

In addition to those versed in traditional skills, the village boasts many technicians trained in agriculture, animal husbandry, saw mill operation, health care, store keeping, mechanics, and sewing. A number have attended Bible institute courses. Nearly all the young people have graduated from the bilingual primary school and are studying in secondary, tertiary, and technical institutions.

Camaná

Camaná is the most isolated of the villages in this study. It lies a full day of hard travel upstream by motorized canoe from Puerto Huallana, the point which most traders consider the end of navigable river. Sharply falling, dangerous rapids tax the boatmen's skill and strength, but the beauty of the foothills and of orchid-laden trees increases with every bend. The present-day location of the community is the fourth in the history of the village, which originally formed in 1967 in another, extremely isolated river valley but subsequently moved three times in search of land the people deemed more fertile, less flood prone, and more accessible to markets.

Originally, community members gathered upon the invitation of a relative. Dedicated teacher Venturo Cruz K., who had grown up away from his original homeland, returned to offer a school to his people. The community flourished under his leadership for some twenty years, and due to his superb teaching skill the primary students of this most isolated village, where the traditional way of life is still strong, became some of the best prepared, both in Machiguenga and in Spanish as a second language. Most of the young men attend high school in Mayapo. Several have trained in health care, animal husbandry, and at the Machiguenga Bible Institute. One has gone on to study business administration at a university on the coast.

In 1992, some years after Professor Cruz had been transferred to teach in the secondary school at Nueva Luz and later had retired, the village still retained the neatness and alertness which had characterized the people in the early years.

Chokoriari

The village of Chokoriari gathered on the Urubamba in 1973 just below the Pongo de Mainique, but has since moved downstream to a location only a few hours by motorized canoe from Camisea. Houses now extend perhaps two miles along the river. The dynamic teacher who founded the village has long since moved on, and the school has had a succession of other staff, but what caught my attention upon perusal of the school records was the large number of repeaters and then drop outs in the early years of the school. The villagers suggested that some of the children had been very young and that perhaps they had not taken their studies seriously. However, later there was opportunity to ask the original teacher about the matter.

"Ah, Señora," he replied. "I know exactly what happened. In the beginning I knew the steps for teaching the lessons, but I did not consider them important and I was not consistent in putting them into practice. It was only when I reached the Pedagogical Institute that I understood the importance of pedagogy and began to use the steps faithfully."

Nevertheless, by 1992, at least five of the village young people had graduated from secondary school. Two were contracted bilingual teachers, another was studying in Pedagogical Institute summer sessions, and a fourth was studying accounting in the city. In addition, fourteen young people were enrolled in secondary schools—six in Nueva Luz, four in Camisea, two in Cuzco, and two in Quillabamba.

The community also had specialists. In addition to those versed in traditional skills, an auxiliary health worker salaried by the Ministry of Health attended the medical needs; a trained cattleman cared for the forty-four head of cattle belonging to the villagers; an experienced barge commander/diesel mechanic served the Machiguenga cooperative; a lay pastor continued pastoral studies; and several community members had attended the Machiguenga Bible Institute.

Mayapo

Mayapo, the youngest and smallest of the Machiguenga bilingual school communities visited during this survey, was formed in 1975. At the request of the people, experienced teacher Professor Carlos Ríos Ríos moved from his teaching post on the Urubamba to open a school for his wife's relatives and others who lived scattered in the headwaters of the Picha River. They gathered at a point well above what was considered to be the navigable part of the Picha in order to reduce contact with the outside world. The village is still isolated and lacking in basic services and markets.

As is the case in new communities, the people were virtually all nonliterate, were unused to community living, and felt the pressure to build homes and fields as quickly as possible. In addition to his full-time teaching load, Professor Ríos spent long hours in orientation sessions, stemmed epidemics, recruited community development aid, and had—at the same time—to build his own home and maintain his own field.

Eighteen years later we found a neatly laid-out community—now in a new location. Professor Ríos had retired from teaching, but two of his daughters had replaced him in the school, and his son-in-law was now the school director. In 1991 the village had been chosen to host a regional secondary school; so in addition to their normal work, the men of the community carried the major responsibility for construction of the campus, and the women helped to feed the boarding students. Prior to the creation of the secondary school at least fourteen young people from the community had gone on to attend secondary schools in other places; one of these is now President of the community.

In addition to those versed in traditional skills, the list of specialists from the community now includes three bilingual teachers, one student in a Pedagogical Institute, one student in nurse's training, two health workers, three midwives, one storekeeper, one cattleman, two chain saw operators, one mechanic, and two seamstresses.

Early Preparation

This village, more than some, has experienced an exodus of young people. Nine young men left the area at about age fifteen (most after grade 5 or 6) to work for Peruvian landlords. They have now been away five to ten years, are probably married, and are presumed lost to their people. Rumor has it that some have been killed during logging operations or by terrorists, although this information has been disputed. The drain of manpower left the adult men, many of whom are now beginning to age, with a heavy work load as the community moved to a new location and, simultaneously, bore the major responsibility for the secondary school construction. The adults lament this lack of adult strength as well as the keen pain of family rupture, even though they partially understand their young people's desire for increased opportunities.

Puerto Huallana

The community now known as Puerto Huallana gathered on the Picha River in 1956. However, towards the end of that school year, or in early 1957, the original teacher died (of tuberculosis, it is said), about the same time a severe—although unrelated—epidemic ravaged the village. When the replacement teacher, Professor Mario Choronto Domingo, arrived to begin the 1957 school year, he found a sadly demoralized community in which some twenty school children had been orphaned. To their eternal credit, Professor Choronto and his wife took all of the orphans into their own home, bringing them up with their own six children. Professor Choronto continued as director of the school until 1982. As of 1992, ten individuals had graduated from secondary school; twenty-one were attending high school; one was attending a technical high school, one was attending nurse's training, two were attending carpentry training, and three were attending Bible school.

In addition to traditional specialists, graduates of the bilingual school were engaged in the following vocations and specialties:

7 bilingual teachers	1 mechanic
2 health workers	1 health worker's apprentice
5 seamstresses	1 cattleman
3 midwives	2 agricultural/community development workers
1 pastor	1 member of an editorial committee
3 evangelists	

Ten young men were away from the community working. Although some worked only during the vacation period in order to earn money for school, villagers feel that some of these young people may never return. One young father, who was murdered while working downriver in 1991, left a wife and four children. Villagers anguish over their absent family members and wish they could provide young people more income-generating work within the community, as used to be possible in years past. Because of the national financial crisis, however, they were left with few options until the national economy improves.

Segakiato

The community of Segakiato was founded in November 1971, with the arrival of a group of Machiguenga who had chosen to move from the Manú River to an isolated and sparsely settled area in the upper reaches of the Camisea River. The traditional way of life is still strong. From 1971 until 1986, faithful Professor Martín Vargas Cararoshi was the Director of the school and taught the beginners. The assistant teacher of many years, Victoriano Melchor Maruza, succeeded Professor Vargas as director upon his retirement. At different times adult literacy classes have been held, but no adults have reached independent reading level through these classes.

Although for some years the elementary school has taught all the grades, students have always had to leave the village to attend secondary school. Prior to 1992, approximately thirty young people had attended high schools outside the community, and at least four community members had attended the Machiguenga Bible Institute. In 1992, seventeen young people were attending secondary schools in other communities.

This was the only village in which we found the school building in disrepair. The floor sagged badly, and desks needed fixing. Due to a shortage of desks, students worked on the floor. The office was untidy; school records were missing. The school—which depends on the director and teachers to order supplies in advance—had experienced a severe shortage of books all school year and had been without notebooks the first trimester. Primary school children were two years behind the expected schedule in reading.

Two impressions have always been salient in Segakiato: (1) The earnestness with which an entire generation of young adults has struggled to learn, often repeating years several times so as to "learn it well," as they would tell us, and (2) the difficulty they have had in mastering the material, especially in the upper grades. Tragically, the upper-level teachers appear to have been unable to communicate the subject matter well. Perhaps their knowledge of Spanish was not adequate to allow them to comprehend and explain the lessons clearly. Perhaps—as one would suspect from the disrepair of the school campus—they have been negligent. In any case, teachers at the secondary school in Camisea complained that the Segakiato students as a group were poorly prepared. Our test scores bore this out: Seven out of eight secondary students from Segakiato failed to meet preset minimum standards on the Advanced reading test in Machiguenga. Five out of eight failed to meet preset minimum standards on the Spanish Test.

As a result of the lower educational achievement, fewer from Segakiato have qualified for specialist training than from other villages, although one health worker, one cattleman, and one pastor/diesel mechanic have received specialized training. At the time of our visit a number of young men—perhaps ten—were working outside the area for lumber workers and land owners. The villagers fear that some of these will never return, and one has been reported killed by a cable backlash during a logging accident.

Shivankoreni

The original Shivankoreni community gathered some distance upriver from the mouth of the Camisea in 1958 when the people of the area were contacted and invited to a school by pioneer bilingual teacher Silverio Perez Ganta. His informal class was recognized by a Ministry of Education Resolution No. 19967 in 1958, and since then the school has functioned as an official government entity with a number of different directors and teaching assistants of varying competence. Adult classes have been held and have been attended by most of the adults but have not brought anyone to independent reading.

For many years, the upper-level primary students commuted by river to attend classes under Andrés Vicente at the mouth of the Camisea, but more recently all the primary grades are offered in Shivankoreni. For about the last ten years, two teachers have been needed to handle the more than sixty primary students, and, more recently, a kindergarten teacher has also been assigned to the community. At the time of our visit, a new, large, adobe-brick school was being built by the villagers with the aid of engineers from CEDIA (a local community development organization).

In addition to those specialists versed in traditional lore, graduates of the Shivankoreni bilingual school have received the following specialist training. All but the two bilingual teachers are working in the village.

2 bilingual school teachers
1 health promotor/carpenter
1 sawmill operator/furniture maker
1 graduate of the agricultural secondary school who raises sheep.

1 health assistant
1 midwife
4 cattlemen
1 agriculturalist
1 pastor

1 mason (not educated in the bilingual school) who lives in the village and is called upon from time to time

Requesting authorization

A letter explaining the purpose of my coming to Camisea was presented to the village president, who, at the next General Assembly of the village, gave us opportunity to explain the nature of our visit. My explanation was necessarily detailed since the villagers had no acquaintance with research projects and would have reason to be suspicious.

I explained (in the Machiguenga language) that through their reading program they had realized unique accomplishments. Understanding how this came about could prove useful to others in far away places who wished to implement similar programs; however, in order to describe the program accurately I must have documentation. For that reason, I requested permission to visit every home and interview each family with reference to their thoughts about reading and the school. The opinions of the older people who could not read were as important as the opinions of younger literates. When the interview was over, we would ask those who felt able to read for us. Professor Barrientos, whom they knew, would conduct the interviews and reading tests which would need to be documented with tape recordings. Although we wished to visit everyone, participation was entirely voluntary. Participants would be given a coded identification so that they might remain anonymous.

We explained that this research was a university requirement, not a for-profit venture. I would write up the results and publish them. Many people would read the study and know what the Machiguenga have accomplished. A copy of the Spanish edition would be sent to their local Education Office. We assured them a second time that participation was voluntary, but requested that if they were in agreement they authorize their Executive Committee to sign a prepared form granting permission to interview and test in the homes. We would schedule visits with each family in advance, so as to avoid long waits and loss of work time for them.

This meeting with the community was culturally appropriate and, I felt, preferable to house-to-house requests. In the security of the group, individuals could feel more free to dissent or to question, and community leaders could sense the attitude of the majority towards the request. Professor Barrientos followed up my remarks with clarifying comments and answered questions. Discussion followed.

Early Preparation

Above: The purpose of the research project was explained in general assemblies in each village and permission was requested to carry out the study. (Rosemary Clayton photo, Mayapo, 1992)

Below: The Executive Committee of Camisea signed the authorization for research to be carried out in their community. (P. Davis photo, 1992)

The Machiguenga are a courteous people, and we were among old friends. Graciously, the community consented to our request. The Executive Committee signed the authorization form, and Professor Barrientos and I turned to the preparation of interview forms and test instruments.

In six other communities, the procedures followed were similar to those explained above: A letter of introduction was presented to each village Executive Committee, a community meeting was held during which we explained in detail the purpose of our visit, the methods we planned to use, and requested authorization to visit in the homes. In these six villages, however, we also explained that time did not allow us to test everyone. If the villagers were willing, we would select certain homes and visit them. Again, each village graciously assented.

With the help of village members, we had sketched a map of the village and had arbitrarily assigned a number to each house. Now the numbers were placed in a plastic bag and well mixed. While everyone looked on, the village president was asked to draw numbers representative of ten percent of the homes. This procedure generated hilarity and excitement akin to the interest on the eve of major drawings of the Texas lottery. As the names of home owners were called, each was asked if he were willing to have us come. After all had agreed and the Executive Committee had signed the consent form, we set up a visitation schedule.

Setting Standards for Machiguenga Readers

The research reviewed in chapter 3 indicates the range of standards which testing and quantification have established for the reading of English. I was not certain, however, whether expectations based on English could be transferred to reading in Machiguenga.

In the first place, Machiguenga literacy is new, having been introduced in the 1950s; thus, a literate environment is not as well established for the Machiguenga as for societies with a long history of public education. Second, the needs and expectations of a rainforest culture differ from those of the highly technological society which developed the English language reading standards. While in North America we demand business literacy and computer literacy, most Machiguenga adults still need only basic skills—i.e., fundamental reading, writing, and numeracy. So long as the message is eventually decoded, speed and fluency are not matters of great concern.[8]

Third, and most importantly, the Machiguenga language in no way equates to English. A non-Indo-European tongue, Machiguenga belongs to the Arawakan language family, which is characterized by agglutinative verbs. Rather than expressing meaning in isolated words, morphemes are added to the verb base forming very long sequences. Three examples:

According to field linguist Betty Snell (in Davis 1981c), Machiguenga verbs average twelve to eighteen letters. Example: *Yovirinitanakero* 'He made her sit down'.

It is not uncommon to find verbs of twenty-five to thirty-five letters. Example: *Impashiventaigavetanakempatyo* 'They will be ashamed, but they won't do anything about it'.

The longest sequence found thus far contains fifty-one letters and digraphs: *Irapusatinkaatsempokitasanoigavetapaakemparorokarityo*.

The analysis is seen in example (5).

(5) I-   r-   apusatink-   -aa   -tsempoki
     3rd pers.   future   head-over-heels   liquid   V-shaped (like
     masc.   or end-for-end   (action will   legs sticking out
                                                  happen in   of the water)
                                                  liquid)

     -t   -asano   -ig   -a   -ve   -t
     morpheme   emphasis   plural   morpheme   frustrative   morpheme
     separator   subject   separator   (the action   separator
                                                                    will be real-
                                                                    ized, then
                                                                    reversed)

     -apa   -ak   -empa   -rorokari   -tyo
     upon   nonrepetitive   reflexive   probability   exclamation
     arrival   action   action

Translation: 'They will probably really go head-over-heels into the water upon their arrival, but they won't stay that way!' [Said in the context of a group of parents watching children come pell-mell down the river in a canoe. The parents knew that the canoe would flip upon hitting the bank and that the children would go

---

[8]In contrast, Machiguenga leaders who deal with the outside world must develop higher-level skills, and young people who aspire to higher education must compete in the secondary and tertiary schools of a Western nation. Their needs will be similar to those of the majority society.

head-over-heels into the water, but since all could swim, there was no concern that anyone would drown.] (Davis 1981c:272)

Because of these long sequences, Machiguenga readers must learn to chunk units within words (*word* being defined as a fixed visual span bordered by space). Special techniques were employed to teach learners to chunk segments—to treat groups of syllables which commonly occur together as units—and thus to span long words in two to four eye fixations, rather than syllable by syllable.

Another point of difference is that Machiguenga syllables are, in the main, much shorter than English syllables, consisting only of vowel (V), vowel consonant (VC), consonant vowel (CV), or consonant vowel consonant (CVC). Remembering that the median oral reading rate of grade 1 children was sixty words per minute, according to Guszak (1985), I analyzed the first sixty words (212 letters) of a first primer story cited by Guszak (p. 122) and the story upon which the first Machiguenga primer is built (*Etini*, pp. 122–123, Ministry of Education of Peru 1987). Great effort had been expended during the preparation of the first Machiguenga primer to choose the simplest words possible while still preserving natural speech. The results from the analysis were as follows:

212 letters in English =	212 letters in Machiguenga =
60 words	31½ words
79 syllables	123 syllables

Adding to the complexity of Machiguenga reading is the fact that morphemes are frequently composed of only one letter. To miss one letter is to miss an important meaning, comparable to missing a word in English. Reading, therefore, must be very accurate or the meaning of the passage can be drastically skewed. However, since the core meaning is carried in the verb base, which occurs near the beginning of each verb, readers who can decode the first part of the verbs tend to ascertain the gist of the passage, even though they may miss crucial supporting information found in the verb suffixes, such as reversal of the action.

Positing minimal levels of skill as criteria for success

No guidelines could be found for reading evaluation in polysynthetic languages, but the available reading process research suggests that—despite language differences—certain characteristics are basic and common to all reading. For the purposes of this study, I therefore adopted Barr and Johnson's (1991) definition—that reading is a relationship between comprehension, prior knowledge, and skill with print. Skill with print must be developed for the process to function smoothly. Comprehension is the goal (pp. 16–17). Focusing on skill with print, I set the following minimum skill levels for Machiguenga readers which could be applied at any level of difficulty and which could be used as criteria for success:

Accuracy: 92%   Fluency: 2 (on a scale of 1–5)
Rate: 80 syllables per minute   Comprehension: 3- (on a scale of 1–5)

Accuracy

According to Ekwall and Shanker (1988:404), the reader of English will experience serious frustration below the 90 percent level of accuracy. While these authors, and the researcher, feel that students are able to cope with a certain amount of frustration for short periods, it seemed doubtful that Machiguenga readers could arrive at the meaning of a text if accuracy were to fall below the 92 percent level. This is especially true since many one-letter morphemes carry heavy information loads.

Fluency

For this study, fluency was defined in terms of prosody and Taylor, Harris, and Pearson's (1988) statement that fluency is "an index of the degree to which a reader's oral reading resembles everyday spoken language" (p. 123). It was rated on a scale of one to five:

1. Struggling, syllable-by-syllable
2. Reading word-by-word
3. Reading phrase-by-phrase
4. Observance of punctuation
5. Natural, communicative expression

This group of skills is commonly in focus in discussions of reading and informal reading inventories (e.g., Kennedy 1981:57; Ekwall and Shanker 1988:528–529; Bond et al. 1989:128–129). Although oral expression has received less emphasis in the most recent literature because of an increased emphasis on silent reading, prosody was preserved as a separate category in this study because beginning Machiguenga readers tend to call words in an unnatural sing-song fashion. As their intonation increasingly approximates everyday speech, the degree of naturalness serves as a measure of increased reading maturity.

The categories of the fluency scale are not mutually exclusive; in language, suprasegmental features occur simultaneously with segmental sounds. Some Machiguenga readers (the exception) can be heard blending syllables rather slowly, but their sense that print is meaningful is so strong that they still give the reading an overall sense of correct punctuation and communicative expression. Other readers, who race to finish, certainly are capable of reading phrase by phrase but overlook punctuation and natural expression entirely. The intent of the scale is not to dichotomize but rather to represent a continuum. All of the skills must be called upon simultaneously. The score reflects the success with which the components are blended to approximate natural speech.

Because most Machiguenga verbs are equivalent to an English sentence, it is possible for a word-by-word reader to approximate natural speech, if intonational patterns are correct. I hypothesized, however, that rarely will a Machiguenga who is truly reading perform at a level lower than two.

Comprehension

Comprehension, in this study, was rated on a scale of one to five and focused on literal reporting of facts, since this was the most easily demonstrable aspect of comprehension and the most reliable indicator available. The progression:

1. No demonstrated recall
2. Poor—fragments of the passage, but not the main topic
3. Fair—identified the topic and evidenced literal understanding of the most important facts
4. Good—identified the topic and elaborated on some facts, but did not cover all the supporting ideas contained in the passage
5. Excellent—identified the topic and also reported most of the supporting information given in the passage

I hypothesized that a Machiguenga reader who possesses basic skills would not perform at a level less than 3−, which would represent a sparse reporting of the main topic.

Rate

Although rate can be important to Machiguenga students, adults less frequently find themselves in situations in which speed is a prime requirement. Thus rate, for the purpose of this study, carried a lower priority than did the other reading measures. So long as a reader can decipher the meaning of a printed message, he is reading; the length of time required to do so is often irrelevant. However, I hypothesized that Machiguengas who are truly reading would cover at least eighty syllables per minute (spm). At slower rates, I expected to find decoding to require so much time that comprehension of the message as a whole would be impaired. Testing would reveal whether this rate was in fact an appropriate minimum standard for Machiguenga.

Levels of difficulty

Some information does exist giving guidance for the differentiation of levels of difficulty. Wendell (1982:25), a literacy specialist with many years of experience among preliterate peoples, identifies four stages of literature in easy-to-difficult progression.

Table 6.3. Easy-to-difficult reading material

Stage	Content in relation to:		Form of presentation
	Experience of reader	Experience of author	
1	Known	Direct, personal	Free
2	Unknown	Direct, personal	Free
3	Unknown	Vicarious	Free
4	Unknown	Vicarious	Translated

Author: Member of local culture; speaker of local language.
Readers: Members of local culture; speakers of local language.

Based on Wendell's progression, I chose the standards listed below to differentiate three reading levels. The intent was not to categorize readers solely on the basis of a particular passage but rather, by varying the material, to provide opportunity for more mature readers to demonstrate their skills. It is difficult to differentiate between beginning and mature readers if everyone reads the same low-level passage. However, to be useful the passages must be arranged in progressive order of difficulty. Wendell's categories inherently include increased sophistication of vocabulary and grammatical structure as well as sophistication of concepts.

Criteria for Basic (or functional) skill

The following criteria were set for Basic (or functional) skill:

Able to read text material familiar in daily experience and language genre which employs (potentially) all of the syllables of the language, while meeting at least the preset minimum standards of 92 percent accuracy, a score of 2 in fluency (on a scale of 1 to 5), a score of 3− in comprehension (on a scale of 1 to 5), and a rate of eighty syllables per minute.

Readers with basic skills are normally expected to function at the level of fundamental needs, thus the concepts and language genre should be those of daily experience. The beginning reading series in the Machiguenga language consists of two reading readiness books and three primers which teach the syllables of the language. Students who may read Primers 1 and 2 very well, are, nevertheless, unable to decode unrestricted material until they have finished (or nearly finished) Primer 3, the book that completes the teaching of the closed syllables. Neither parents nor teachers consider children full readers until they have finished this much instruction (normally, about the end of grade 3). Basic skills, consequently, are judged to include knowledge of all of the syllables of the language.

The oral readings of the Basic Tests were taken from Primer 3. In these readings vocabulary and syllables were controlled, but most of the syllables of the language were in use. The silent reading passage was a simple story about everyday activities in which the syllables and vocabulary were not controlled. Thus the stories of the Basic Tests met Wendell's criteria for Stage One difficulty.

Criteria for Intermediate level skill

The following criteria were set for Intermediate level skill:

Able to read with comprehension material unrestricted as to vocabulary and syllable patterning but moderately sophisticated in language genre and partially unknown in content, while meeting at least the preset minimum standards listed above.

Readers with intermediate skills have the decoding tools to decipher descriptions new to their experience and couched in more formal language. They also should be able to cope with some vicarious experiences. The folk stories chosen as test material for the intermediate level were all written by the same author and were similar in level of difficulty. They used the language genre of legends and were not entirely familiar to the audience, since story tellers from different regions tend to tell slightly different versions of the same tale. This placed the intermediate readings at Stages Two and Three of Wendell's levels of difficulty.

Criteria for Advanced (full) skill

The following criteria were set for Advanced (full) skill:
> Able to read unrestricted texts of formal genre which contain new information and abstract concepts, while meeting at least the preset minimum standards listed above.

Advanced Machiguenga readers need to be able to decode and understand conceptual writings which are formally (not colloquially) presented, such as those found in upper-level primary and secondary textbooks, instructions, editorials, reports of meetings, and explanations of the philosophy and functions of different organizations. To determine whether any readers had actually reached this level of skill, an advanced component needed to be included in the testing.

Advanced reading material which would meet a uniform standard was difficult to find, however. The few writings which exist are by different authors and employ different degrees of abstraction and formality. It was therefore decided to select conceptual passages from the Machiguenga New Testament—a high-quality, collaborative work of translation coedited by a committee of American linguists and native speakers of Machiguenga. This material met Wendell's criterion for Stage Four, the highest level of reading difficulty.

Content of the Evaluation Instruments

A series of interruptions—visitors, community celebrations, computer malfunction—delayed the preparation of evaluation instruments, but thanks to Professor Barrientos' superior skills and dedicated efforts we eventually completed the design of the following:

- An interview form
- 26 tests of basic reading skill in Machiguenga
- 25 tests of intermediate reading skill in Machiguenga
- 31 tests of advanced reading skill in Machiguenga
- 18 tests for Spanish reading

A selection of tests was needed because we would test by family groups (in which several people might be at the same level). We also expected a retinue of observers to follow us from house to house and, therefore, we needed a large number of tests in order to have new material for each participant.

The interview form

Designing the interview form caused us considerable difficulty. The Machiguenga language and worldview are markedly different from the English language and Western thinking. The great problem we faced was that of framing comprehensible, productive questions, for I knew from prior experience that most Western-type questions are difficult for the Machiguenga to understand and that, as a result, responses can be far from reliable. Worse yet, the types of questions usually asked in doctoral research are predominantly abstract and conceptual, and seem strangely irrelevant in the Machiguenga context. We were not alone in our dilemma. In 1978, researcher Orna Johnson wrote of her experience among the Machiguenga,

> It was only after many months in the field that we learned how to broach questions. We found that people would respond to specific examples related to known cases, but not to abstractions. Though loath to pass judgment...,when confronted with concrete cases they would offer explanations from which rules or values could be inferred. (p. 44)

Our questions, then, were necessarily as concrete as possible. They sought to assess personal use of reading and writing, self assessment of proficiency, attitudes towards literacy, and ability to count (in the context of buying, selling, and counting money). I had arrived with an idea of the information we needed to gather and had written a tentative interview form in Spanish. After a number of attempts, Professor Barrientos felt satisfied his reformulation of the questions in Machiguenga elicited correct responses and reached to the heart of our questions. (See appendix A for an example.) From the collective responses, I have sought to infer the answers to some of the more abstract questions of this study.

Reading tests

Because of the absence of standardized reading tests for Machiguenga, I turned to oral reading, choosing the Informal Reading Inventory method (devised by Betts in 1946 and used by teachers ever since) as the means of evaluation. The use of oral, rather than silent, reading tests is defended because oral reading provides the only observable measure of reading behavior. Also, reading aloud is common among the Machiguenga, even when individuals are reading to themselves. Oral reading tests were, therefore, a natural form of reading for research participants. The following set of reading tests was developed.

Content of the Evaluation Instruments

Basic skills assessment

A set of 26 tests. (See appendix B for an example.) Each test contained: a set of 10 syllables, one story to read aloud, and one story to read silently and retell.

The **syllables**—four open and six closed—were selected from charts containing the entire listing of the syllables of the language. The goal was to achieve a representation of each syllable type, particularly the closed syllables which are the hardest, are taught last, and which may double as morphemes to make important differences in meaning.

The **first story** of each test was selected from Primer 3, which completes the teaching of all of the syllables of the language. This book, recently off the press, had not yet been read by the majority of those sampled. Four additional stories were especially written to complete the 26-test set since Primer 3 included only twenty-two usable stories. The new stories matched those of Primer 3 as closely as possible in genre and difficulty.

Only very occasionally during the testing did we sense that the text was familiar to a reader who had studied the primer in school. Others, who actually had read the primer, did not appear to recognize the story when it was presented on a sheet of paper rather than in the book.

The type face and spacing was that of the primer page. Line length was slightly longer than in the primer. With one exception, none of the readings made use of hyphens, although students are taught to read hyphens, beginning in the middle of Primer 1. The stories were controlled for length as much as possible, but a syllable count was also done to provide a uniform basis for calculations. To assure accuracy, the syllables were counted twice and discrepancies in the counts were corrected.

The **second story** consisted of a procedural text, written by Professor Barrientos in simple, straightforward language, similar to that of the first story. These stories dealt with familiar occurrences: how to make a basket, arrows, a reed mat, a carrying bag, a canoe, etc. Both men's work and women's work were represented, but in every case the procedures involved were known to both sexes. Embedded in most of the texts was incorrect information of some type—for example, a sequence out of order or an incorrect listing of materials. The errors were intended to provide reasons for participants who understood to remark on the reading. That this purpose was accomplished—at least in certain of the texts—was attested to by the children and adolescents who wandered in to visit and who looked over our shoulders at the computer screen as manuscripts were prepared. Several objected strenuously to the errors in the text, much to the supervisor's suppressed amusement. We were not concerned, since individuals who could read as fast as I could type were advanced readers and would take a different test.

The second reading was reproduced in the same type face and format as Story 1, did not use hyphens, and was similar in length.

Titles written entirely in capital letters were used in all the Basic Level Tests. The goal was to ascertain if participants had learned to read capital letters, a task not all beginning readers have mastered.

Intermediate skills assessment

A set of 29 tests. (See appendix B for an example.) Each test contained: Reading 1—a portion of a traditional folk story to be read aloud, and Reading 2—a letter to be read silently and its contents recounted.

The intermediate readings dealt with common concepts but were somewhat more formal in style than the beginning level readings, and contained more new material and unpredictability.

Reading 1 was a Machiguenga folk story generally familiar to the public although variations in detail—regional or personal to the author—are inevitable in folk stories and provide an element of surprise. All of the stories were written by the same Machiguenga bilingual teacher as a draft for a book manuscript and so were comparable in genre and in sophistication. The type face was similar to that used in intermediate readers. Due to page limitations, the text was single spaced rather than reproduced at space and a half, as in the intermediate readers; however, students were familiar with single spacing in their other textbooks. Each text contained four words which were hyphenated at the ends of lines.

Length was controlled. Each story consisted of twenty-two typewritten lines, plus or minus not more than one line, when absolutely needed to complete the meaning of a section. Only a few of these stories were short; we used them if there was only one intermediate reader in the family. The longer stories were divided into segments, and if more than one person in the family was an intermediate reader, a portion of the story was given to each participant, and they were informed to that effect.

Reading 2 was a letter borrowed from school files or composed by Professor Barrientos. In contrast to the folk story, which was generally familiar to most participants, Reading 2 was a passage which the reader had never seen or heard. The concepts, however, dealt with common topics (such as an invitation to a game or a letter to a relative) and—although more sophisticated in style than the beginning level readings—were equivalent to each other in difficulty of concepts and of language. They averaged twelve typewritten lines each and contained four hyphenated words. The type face and spacing were the same as for Reading 1. Although twenty-nine Intermediate Tests were prepared, only seventeen were actually used, since few Intermediate Tests were administered. Titles written entirely in capital letters were used in all the Intermediate Tests.

Advanced skills assessment

At the advanced level, both Machiguenga and Spanish reading skill was tested. (See appendix B for an example.)

The only body of **advanced reading in Machiguenga** available beyond already-known school texts was the Machiguenga New Testament. It is written in a slightly more formal style than folk stories and letters; it is translated material (although the translation is very good), and it is set in another culture. All of these factors increase its difficulty. Advanced Machiguenga reading tests consisted of a set of thirty-one passages from the New Testament text, conceptual in nature. An effort was made to choose less familiar portions in order to reduce the unfair advantage churchgoers might have over nonattenders. Each passage was a unit containing a clear topic.

Participants read from the New Testament itself; consequently, there was no change in the type face or line length to which they were accustomed. Units of seventeen lines were chosen (plus or minus not more than one line when absolutely necessary to preserve the meaning of the section); these were marked off by covering the part of the page not included in the test with white paper. Use of hyphens was frequent in the text, as is normal in Machiguenga written material.

Spanish reading consisted of a set of eighteen passages excerpted from reports or business letters written by local authorities. The concepts were familiar to the participants and the style of expression normal and straightforward; thus the texts, although not simplified (and later considered demanding for second-language speakers by the interrater consultant), represented the easier end of the Spanish literary spectrum. They provided a reasonable sampling of the type of written language a Machiguenga speaker might frequently need to handle in Spanish.

The passages averaged twelve lines and were presented, in single spacing, in the type face used in the advanced readers. In the end, four of the tests which had been prepared were not used. (See appendix B for an example.)

Chapter Summary

This chapter outlines the steps taken during early preparation for the research project—the procedures followed when choosing the sample and requesting permission of the communities where we desired to conduct the study. The challenge of setting realistic standards for Machiguenga readers was complicated by a dearth of information concerning testing in minority languages and the vast cultural and linguistic divergence of the non-Indo-European Machiguenga language from English, upon which our knowledge of reading standards has chiefly been based. Minimal levels of skill were eventually posited as follows: To read with comprehension, a reader should demonstrate 92 percent accuracy, fluency of 2 (on a scale of 1–5), comprehension of 3 – (on a scale of 1–5), and a rate of 80 syllables per minute. To distinguish levels of reading skill, tests were written at three different levels of reading difficulty—basic (easy), intermediate, and advanced. The chapter then discusses the content of the interview forms and reading tests and the criteria used in their development.

7

Collecting Data the Cultural Way

I will keep on reading because I like to learn.
  - Father, House 38, Shivankoreni

Introduction

This chapter presents the methods employed for interviews and test administration, and goes on to describe the procedures used to assess and organize the raw data. Preparatory steps for analysis are also reported. They led to the preparation of a computerized data base which generated descriptive statistics, correlations, regression analyses, tables, and graphs. The chapter ends with a brief discussion of the strengths and limitations of these procedures.

Data Collection

Although informal data collection went on continuously, formal data collection took place during house-to-house interviews and by administering reading tests. The procedures adopted incorporated recommendations gleaned from the literature on cross-cultural testing as reviewed in chapter 3.

The passages chosen for the reading tests were carefully controlled for syllable content. To control for naturalness, the Basic readings were either authored by a Machiguenga speaker or thoroughly checked by Machiguenga speakers. The Intermediate readings were Machiguenga authored and edited. The translated advanced readings had been repeatedly checked by Machiguenga editors and readers for clarity and naturalness. These checks included syllable, word, phrase, paragraph, and discourse features.

The readings included sets of tests from three levels of difficulty—basic, intermediate, and advanced. A concerted effort was made to control each of the three sets of tests for uniform format and uniform level of difficulty. Accommodating to the group orientation of the culture, we planned to work with family groups; thus it was necessary to prepare a set of tests large enough that no one in the family need repeat a test previously read. We also wished to avoid the possibility of eaves-droppers (who might follow us from house to house) communicating to waiting test takers what the content of the test would be.

The interviews

Sessions began by setting up the tape recorder and recording the identity, age, and educational experience of each participant, as well as community responsibilities (public office), if applicable. An interview was next conducted in an informal, conversational mode, inquiring as to interviewees' opinions about and evaluations of reading. Professor Barrientos conducted the interview, covering as many of the questions on the form as time allowed, but also pursuing interesting topics as the situation suggested. As we had hoped, very often the "interview" turned into a spontaneous dialogue, both interviewer and interviewees carried away by the subject. Although we tried to involve everyone, often—in cultural fashion—the father or mother spoke for all. In a minority of cases the home owners seemed nervous and aloof, but usually by the end of the conversation, the participants appeared relaxed.

I felt considerable concern that: (1) interview questions might not be clear to Machiguenga respondents and (2) that the questions might inadvertently cue respondents to tell us what they thought we wanted to hear rather than reflecting honest opinions. Attempting to avoid these problems, I spent time with Professor Barrientos, orienting him to the interview goals and to techniques and pitfalls. After initial attempts in which he tested his questions and refined them, both he and I felt they were communicating accurately. An honest attempt was also made not to influence responses. However, a researcher must always be aware that respondents' lack of familiarity with research-type questions and their desire to please the research team may affect answers to some degree. I felt comfortable with the data compiled, however, because it matched information both

Data Collection

observed and communicated to me by the people on various occasions over previous years.

Questions on the interview form were revised several times to clarify their intent. However, the information collected from the beginning was valuable; so it was not discarded. The last revision of the forms was made in November of 1992. Five and one-half villages of the seven villages visited were sampled after this revision.

The reading tests

After the interview, readings were given out, based on the level of education of the participants and their self-assessed competence. The procedures for the reading assessment were as follows:

1. To keep the atmosphere as relaxed as possible, the mother tongue was used for all conversation and instructions.
2. Participants were given opportunity to read the passage before testing began.
3. Parents (who were usually less nervous) were asked to read first, and thus set a model for the children.
4. The testing was carried out by Professor Barrientos, who was known to everyone.

Basic and Intermediate reading tests

To begin, our instruction was, "Read the first passage to yourself. When you are ready, please read it aloud for us all to hear." Time was allowed for practice, then each group member read out loud, usually beginning with the parents and taking turns around the circle. Reading in turn is a familiar practice in school so was not a novel procedure for participants. The tape recorder was turned on for each reading, and the time required for the reading was noted. Finally, participants were instructed to read the second passage to themselves, and, when they had finished, to tell what it said. This recount was recorded.

Advanced reading tests

To begin, our instruction was, "Read the passage to yourself. When you are ready, please read it aloud for us all to hear. After that, please give back the book and tell us what it said." Our next instruction was, "Read the Spanish passage to yourself. When you are ready, please read it aloud for us all to hear. After that, please give back the paper and tell us what it said."

Both passages were timed, and both reading and recount were tape recorded.

Writing

Our last instruction to advanced readers was, "Please take this piece of paper and the pencil and write the following dictation." The Supervisor dictated a sentence or two (in Machiguenga) from an Intermediate reading test. The writing samples then were clipped together with the reading tests and filed by family group. Although the Machiguenga seem to expect that individuals—after the first years of school—can write whatever they can read, time constraints prevented our testing all participants. Only advanced readers were asked to write a short dictation. Writing has been beyond the scope of this paper, but I noted that very few participants used cursive handwriting. (See appendix C for samples.)

Changes made as the result of early testing

The procedures described were followed from the beginning of the testing, but with experience we made refinements.

1. Prior to the reading, we added an explanation that participants would be expected to retell the story. In the beginning, that point, if overlooked, may have put readers at an unfair disadvantage by not alerting them to the fact that they needed to read for recall.

2. If participants seemed hesitant (or unable) to retell the story, we found that prompt questions helped substantially to enable them to give evidence of comprehension. Thus, after the preliminary testing, cue questions were used as standard procedure except when readers retold the story on their own initiative, without hesitation. An effort was made to ask questions which did not give away information but required that understanding of the passage be demonstrated (e.g., What is this story about? or, Can you think of something else?). However, since the texts described common activities, participants inevitably drew upon their general knowledge to some extent.

3. After we began to suspect that the stop watch might be giving participants the impression that speed was the main goal, we tried to indicate that time was not a concern to us. We also tried to make the use of the stop watch less conspicuous.

4. We had expected a retinue of observers to follow us from house to house and therefore to need a large number of tests. As it turned out, we had few observers. Upon realizing this, we limited the number of tests used and repeated the same ones as often as possible. This reduced somewhat the variability attributable to differences in test instruments.
5. The Reading Score Chart was revised several times to fit with the data and with the aspects of reading we desired to focus upon. (See appendix C for the final version.)

The Population Surveyed

In all, ninety-four households were visited:

Camisea	33
Camaná	9
Chokoriari	8
Mayapo	9
Puerto Huallana	12
Segakiato	11
Shivankoreni	12
Total	94

The ratio was thirty-three households in Camisea (35 percent of the sample) to sixty-one households (64.9 percent of the sample) from more distant villages.

In-depth interviews were conducted in eighty-nine households as well as with one individual from the community of Nueva Luz—ninety interviews in total. Altogether, the survey included a population of 303 individuals. Reading tests were given in each household where there were readers. All of the participants in the reading test were either adults or students at or above grade 3 level. Children of grade 2 level and below were not included, since none were encountered who could read the Basic Test.

The testing intentionally focussed on adults. However, as many primary and secondary school students as possible were surveyed in Camisea and, in other villages, students who were home at the time of our visit were also included. (When school was in session, school age children were not present during our visits.) The hope was to provide an indication of the present effectiveness of the community schools. Many of the secondary school students, however, were not children but were old enough to classify as adults in the society; indeed, some were fathers with families. Three Pedagogical Institute students were bilingual teachers. The number of students (people in school whether children or adults) who took our tests turned out to be 32.3 percent of the total population surveyed (table 7.1).

Table 7.1. The number of students who took the tests

Grade	Camisea	Camaná	Choko-riari	Mayapo	Pto. Huallana	Segakiato	Shivankoreni	Total
Gr. 3	8	3	0	1	1	0	0	13
Gr. 4	6	0	0	1	4	1	2	14
Gr. 5	10	0	0	2	1	1	4	18
Gr. 6	4	5	0	0	2	2	3	16
1st Secondary	5	0	1	0	1	5	0	12
2nd Secondary	12	1	0	2	1	3	1	20
3rd Secondary	0	0	0	0	1	0	0	1
4th Secondary	1	0	0	0	0	0	0	1
Pedagogical Institute	3	0	0	0	0	0	0	3
Total	49	9	1	6	11	12	10	98

Altogether, a total of 340 reading tests were administered to participants in our study; 226 tests assessed literacy skills in the Machiguenga language, and 114 tests evaluated ability to read in Spanish. (The number of tests exceeded the number of people because most advanced readers took two tests, one in Machiguenga and another in Spanish.) The breakdown is seen in table 7.2.

Table 7.2. Summary of the Reading Survey

Tests	Camisea	Camaná	Choko-riari	Mayapo	Pto. Huallana	Segakiato	Shivankoreni	Total
Basic								
Adults	12	0	0	2	2	8	11	35
Primary	13	3	0	1	6	1	6	30
Secondary	0	0	0	0	0	0	0	0
Intermediate								
Adults	4	0	0	0	0	0	0	4
Primary	11	0	0	1	0	0	2	14
Secondary	0	0	0	0	0	0	0	0
Advanced								
Adults	37	17	11	6	19	3	5	98
Primary	2	5	0	1	2	1	1	12
Secondary	18	1	1	2	3	7	1	33
Spanish								
Adults	32	15	9	4	13	1	5	79
Primary	4	0	0	1	1	1	2	9
Secondary	12	1	1	2	3	6	1	26
Total	145	42	22	20	49	28	34	340

The ratio was 145 tests (41.9 percent) completed in Camisea; 195 tests (58.03 percent) completed in more isolated villages.

Preparation for Analysis

Several steps were required before analysis of the raw data could go forward. This section describes the preparatory procedures.

Transcription of the interviews

As soon as possible after the home visit, all the tape-recorded interviews were transcribed. Because the amount of material recorded was very large (forty 90-minute tapes roughly divided between interviews and reading tests), transcription time ran into hundreds of hours. Machiguenga high school graduates were hired for this task, and their willingness to help was much appreciated. That schools have been successful is evidenced by the fact that in every community bilingual school graduates capable of performing this demanding task could be hired, even though their handwriting, spelling, and punctuation was a source of consternation to one retired bilingual school teacher who later helped me with the translation of difficult passages.

Syllable counts

Because it was necessary to calculate an accuracy score based on the total number of syllables in the passage, the syllables of the first reading of each test were counted, first on one set of tests, and then—as a check for accuracy—on a second set.

Score charts

Interview Forms were designed to summarize the answers given to the interview questions. Individual Reading Score Charts were designed to record the passage read and the accuracy, fluency, comprehension, and rate scores for both Machiguenga and Spanish (appendix C). Both forms allowed space for the participant's identity code, community, sex, age, studies completed, and last year of study.

Interlinear translations

A free interlinear translation was prepared for certain of the second readings of the Basic Test set and for selected second readings of the Intermediate Test set. Translations of the Advanced Test set already exist in both Spanish and English, but some additional interlinear translations were also prepared. I had thought that these translations would aid in checking comprehension, but when the advantages proved few (because test participants used vocabulary very different from the readings during their recounts) and the time expenditure large, translations were prepared only in cases of special difficulty.

Coding the Raw Data

The interviews

Following the written transcription, I recorded the information for each person on an Interview Form, translating directly into English from Machiguenga. The data were organized by topic—self evaluation of literacy skill and use, attitudes, and numeracy skills.

The Machiguenga reading tests

Scoring the reading tests required months of time. The following was the procedure.

Scoring for accuracy

Professor Barrientos listened to each Machiguenga reading test on a Sony tape recorder coding the errors. An error was defined as any observed response which deviated from the expected response to the printed text.

The coding system used was the following;

Circle	= omission	Overline + A	= attempted correction
Caret	= insertion	Overline + C	= successful correction
Overwrite	= substitution	Parenthesis	= aid received
Overline	= repetition		

I listened to each test at least five times, using both a variable speed control transcriber and a high-quality Maranz tape recorder. Although the Supervisor's work was highly accurate, the superior equipment available to me enabled me to hear and code errors he had not been able to perceive.

An error count was established, using the following criteria:

1. Each error counted as one point.

2. A missed segment (word, phrase, line, or lines) counted as one point.

3. Within a word, each incorrect syllable was counted as an error, if the errors were separated from each other by intervening syllables. This decision was influenced by the great length of many Machinguenga words and the fact that they are composed of many morphemes, a large number of which equate with syllables. Very often, to miss a syllable (i.e., a morpheme) is to miss a meaning equivalent to a word in English.

4. Within a word, a sequence of incorrect syllables was counted as one error.

5. Each insertion was counted as one error, no matter how many syllables it contained.

6. Each substitution was counted as one error, no matter how many syllables were involved.

7. Dropped endings were counted as an error, even though certain dropped endings are common in natural speech and these omissions are especially noticeable in readings of superior readers whose production approximates normal speech.

8. Regressions such as false starts, stutters, and repeating for no apparent reason were considered to be simple repetitions. They were not included in the error count.

9. Correction strategies. Successful corrections were mistakes which were self corrected and thus were not included in the error count. Each attempted (but unsuccessful) error correction was counted as one error.

Here it would have been desirable to have analyzed miscues; however, distinguishing miscues from errors requires psycholinguistic intuitions beyond my ability as a nonnative speaker of Machiguenga and the time limitations of this project. It was, therefore, deemed wiser to mark all deviations from the text as errors, even though many attempted corrections were undoubtedly miscues. A subsequent study, undertaken in collaboration with mother-tongue speakers of Machiguenga, could profitably focus upon the analysis of miscues.

10. Multiple tries at the same word were counted only once. It was judged that the rate would reflect the time lost in repetition.

The accuracy score was determined by totaling deviations, less the number of successful self corrections. The scores were recorded on the Reading Score Chart. (See appendix C for an example.)

Scoring for fluency

The fluency characteristics evident during the reading were ranked on a scale of one to five as follows:

1. Syllable-by-syllable
2. Word-by-word
3. Phrase-by-phrase
4. Observance of punctuation
5. Natural, communicative expression

Scoring for comprehension

Upon completion of the reading, readers retold the passage in their own words. Professor Barrientos listened to the recount, highlighting—where this was possible—the segments which corresponded to the text. Often the recounts did not match the text exactly although they contained the same ideas in other words. Other recounts contained some of the ideas of the text but added or deleted information. A few imaginative readers, who evidently had not understood the passage, invented a different story! The Supervisor then noted his impression on a scale of five—nothing, poor, fair, good, or—occasionally—perfect. (See appendix D for a sample of the comprehension scale.)

I listened to the recount, making note of the amount of material covered. Taking my assessment and the Supervisor's rating into consideration, I assigned a score between one and five, according to the following scale:

1. No demonstrated recall. Could not, or did not, convey any part of the message read. Often these readers said they did not understand the passage; others appeared too nervous or too shy to respond.
2. Poor—scattered points only. Fragments of the passage might be retold, but these were few, unconnected, and failed to convey the main idea.
3. Fair—reported the main idea of the passage without elaboration.
4. Good—gave the main thrust and more, but did not cover all the ideas presented in the text.
5. Excellent—thorough coverage of the main idea and also the additional ideas contained in the text.

Some recounts diverged significantly from the original text using vocabulary unfamiliar to the researcher. In these cases, I:

1. Listened carefully, comparing with translations of the reading. The goal was to ascertain whether the recount bore relation to the text. Here it was necessary, as much as possible, to differentiate between statements generated not from the text but from general knowledge, and to recognize the occasional cases in which readers talked energetically but failed to give information based on the reading.
2. Listed the number of items mentioned. In most cases, when the recount bore relation to the text, the number of items mentioned was in proportion to the fullness of recall.
3. In the few cases where it was difficult for the researcher to form a judgment even after following the above procedures, the Supervisor's evaluation was given most weight.

Scoring for rate

The time required for each reading was noted. A syllables per minute (spm) rate was found by means of the formula in (6).

(6) $\dfrac{\text{Number of syllables read} \times 60}{\text{Time in seconds}} = \text{spm}$

The syllable (rather than the word) is considered the unit of reading. In the Machiguenga language, the syllable is the unit most accurately measured and is more uniform in length than either words or morphemes.

The Spanish reading tests

The procedures explained above were also applied in the evaluation of the Spanish readings, with the following exceptions:

1. Field time was too short for the Supervisor to listen to the Spanish readings. They were checked by the researcher (level of Spanish: four on the Inter-Language Roundtable—formerly Foreign Service Institute—Scale), then validated with a rater who was a native speaker of Spanish.
2. Words mispronounced because of first language interference in the second language (not because of reading problems) were coded with a wavy underline. Points were not taken off for second language pronunciation problems as long as the words were recognizable.
3. Many of the Spanish Tests contained numbered paragraphs. So few readers read the numbers that it was decided not to count these omissions, especially since a tradition had already been established of omitting verse numbers when reading Scripture passages aloud.

Recording the reading scores

The reading scores were entered on individual Reading Score Forms (appendix C). They were then transferred to summary charts and entered into the computer data base.

Interrater Reliability

To test the accuracy of the researcher's evaluation of the readings, interrater checks were carried out by means of the following procedures.

Machiguenga readings

On Machiguenga readings which were clearly recorded, a high degree of interrater agreement occurred between the Machiguenga Supervisor and me. In the rare cases of serious disagreement, the Supervisor's (mother-tongue speaker's) evaluation was the final authority. With a transcriber, however, I was able to hear errors too brief to respond to with a normal tape recorder. The total of errors that I marked is thus considerably higher than the number marked by the Supervisor. I also had more time to listen for repetitions of all types than did the Supervisor; perhaps this also contributed to my totals being higher than his.

To test the accuracy of our combined evaluations of the Machiguenga readings, a consultant was requested to check a selection of twenty tests—six from the Basic skills set, four from the Intermediate skills set, and ten from the Advanced skills set. Betty Snell, the consultant, is one of the field linguists who analyzed the Machiguenga language and who speaks it at Level 4+ proficiency (Inter-Language Roundtable/Foreign Service Institute Scale). I am grateful to her for leaving other important tasks to provide this help to me.

I explained the evaluation process, providing written examples of the procedures to be followed. The consultant then listened to the readings independently, coding deviations from the printed text on a clean copy of the test. Subsequently, a joint session resolved problem cases. The results were then transferred to a clean evaluation sheet, and the consultant's sheet was compared with the combined evaluation sheet of the Machiguenga supervisor and me. The percentage of agreement between evaluators was 100 percent for fluency ratings and 94.44 percent for comprehension ratings.

Spanish readings

To test the accuracy of my evaluation of the Spanish readings, a mother-tongue Spanish speaker was requested to serve as consultant. Elisa Goodson holds two M.A.s in education and works as a professional evaluator of oral Spanish tests. I owe her a deep debt of thanks for taking time to help me.

I explained the evaluation process, providing written examples of the procedures to be followed. The consultant then listened to a sampling of twenty readings independently, coding her findings on a clean copy of the test. Subsequently, a joint session resolved problem cases.

The results were then transferred to a clean evaluation sheet, and the consultant's sheet was compared with my evaluation sheet. The percentage of agreement between evaluators for fluency ratings was 95 percent.

Ms. Goodson could not check comprehension on the Spanish Tests, since the majority of the recounts were in Machiguenga. It was necessary for me to score this portion of the test.

Data Analysis

The data was divided into two parts—the interview data and the reading scores.

Upon completion of the scoring, the personal information for each participant (identity code, gender, age, years in school, last year of school, extra education) was compiled in a large table along with the interview data and the reading test sores. This table was then imported into Systat, a program designed for statistical analysis on Macintosh computers, forming a data base which generated the descriptive statistics, tables, graphs, correlations, and regression analyses presented in chapters 8 through 12. In some cases, one-way analysis of variance and chi-square goodness of fit tests were also applied to ascertain whether variance among the different communities was significant.

Strengths and Limitations of the Methods

The research methods and data analysis procedures followed in this study have both strengths and limitations.

Strengths

The Informal Reading Inventory proved very helpful in the Machiguenga situation. In the absence of standardized tests, it provided a method for a relatively uniform treatment of material and of arriving at scores. It is a method which any teacher or local language supervisor can use, and it can be applied in nonstandard situations, in any language, with different genres of material.

Strengths and Limitations of the Methods 149

Tape recording the readings proved an important aid to scoring. It is not possible to code all the mistakes during a reading; in addition, tape recordings relieve readers of the pressure of seeing themselves being graded. The help of a mother-tongue speaker of the language, who coded the reading errors, also proved important, especially in cases which were difficult to hear. The aid of a good but inconspicuous microphone for recording and a good quality player for transcription also were crucial to scoring.

Scoring of rate (done with a stop watch) and of accuracy proved to be the most reliable parts of the testing. As long as the tape recording is clear, even a second language speaker can hear deviations from the text clearly and mark them correctly. Since accuracy is important to comprehension, especially in the long sequences of Machiguenga, I was grateful to be able to assess accuracy levels with precision.

My overall impression after working with the tests was that they were satisfactory for the purpose for which they were designed—namely to provide material which would make possible a gross sort of reading ability. It was recognized that without standardized tests, miscue analysis, and multiple test opportunities for each participant, individual scores could not be definitive; nevertheless, the aggregate scores of 303 individuals are sufficient statistically to produce an overall picture which, insofar as we can judge, matches reality in the general population.

Our efforts to make the evaluation as low key and casual as possible by interviewing and testing in family groups in home settings seemed to be successful in reducing tension. One helpful element was the use of a relatively inconspicuous tape recording system, which was set out by the Supervisor at the beginning of the visit and then ignored. Most Machiguengas had seen tape recorders but would have been very uncomfortable with a microphone placed close to their face. The Realistic PZM microphone picked up normal conversation at a distance, looked merely like a piece of metal, and within a few minutes of its being placed in the center of the circle, tended to be forgotten. The use of the mother tongue was another key factor in this facet of the research. Most Machiguenga are not at home in Spanish, although some members of the family may be able to speak it. As one woman told us, "I go into my house when I see Spanish speakers coming. I shut my door and don't come out until they are gone" (Mother, House 28, Segakiato). With the use of the mother tongue, however, we had a much greater sense of normalcy and of freedom of expression.

Placing the interview before the testing provided several positive results. Adults, even though illiterate, were given a sense of importance; participants were familiarized with the research team, and confidence was built. Very frequently, the interview, although begun formally because the research team was not well known to the participants, lost its formal character and became a conversation, both interviewer and interviewee carried away by the subject. This not only permitted us to collect more reliable data but also the testing could take place afterwards in a more relaxed atmosphere.

The intent of the testing was to obtain information concerning the numbers of readers produced through the Machiguenga reading program and the levels of skill these readers have achieved. Although it is recognized that many readers may have demonstrated less ability in the testing situation than they might have under non-test conditions or during silent reading, the study nevertheless accomplished its purpose by providing approximations never before available. In addition, the rather large number of tests administered helps to compensate for individual variation and collectively to provide a higher degree of reliability than would otherwise have been the case.

Limitations

Reading teachers understand that Informal Reading Inventories suffer from the subjective criteria necessarily used in determining "increasing difficulty" and "frustration level." They also understand that one Informal Reading Inventory is insufficient to permit a firm diagnosis of a reader's ability. For precision, a battery of tests is needed. The goal of this study was not so much exactitude as a general picture of reading ability, which—it was reasoned—could be achieved through the gross sort (approximate scores) of many tests. Thus, while any one individual's score must be recognized as tentative, the compilation of test results permits a global view of reading ability which, I believe, matches reality fairly closely.

Because group testing required sets of tests rather than a single test which could be administered to each person, tests necessarily varied, even though care was taken to make them as similar as possible. It is recognized that this variation diminished the rigor of control.

Although effort had been expended to select readings which were equivalent in genre and in difficulty, my colleague and interrater checker for the Machiguenga reading tests pointed out that in fact the difficulty of the Advanced reading tests did vary. In her judgment, certain passages seemed either harder to read because of lack of prefixation or harder to recall because of the variety of themes they included. These factors may well have affected recall and lowered some comprehension scores. However, since it was the Advanced Tests which were mainly in question, the gross sort of literate versus illiterate was not affected.

We found that tests became too long if more than two (Machiguenga and Spanish) were administered to each person in the family group. During the early testing, we began with Basic Tests and moved to Intermediate and Advanced Tests if readers proved able to do so. However, the time required for retesting seriously inconvenienced the family, interrupting their schedules for hours. We adjusted by first inquiring about the participant's reading ability and then selecting one mother-tongue reading test at whatever was judged to be the appropriate level. This shortened the test time but prevented us from retesting participants whose test proved too easy or too hard. Even so, tests became too long in large family groups; participants grew tired and sometimes left the circle. The readers most affected by our inability to retest were those who were given Intermediate and Advanced Tests but who needed easier material. Their test scores would have been higher had they been reading at a lesser level of difficulty; nevertheless their ability to struggle through gave evidence that they possessed basic literacy skills; so the gross sort of literate versus nonliterate was not affected.

The field situation allowed virtually no time for analysis. More analysis time would have been desirable and would have alerted us to the danger of overplacing grade 5 and 6 students.

We were not as successful as we had hoped in taking attention off testing and getting people to listen to and enjoy each other's stories. Under the stress of the situation, participants felt compelled to practice until it was their turn to read.

In a few cases (e.g., a daughter in House 29, Camaná), we suspected that the presence of parents embarrassed school children, particularly if the parents were good readers and the child was not. Normally, however, this presented no observable problems.

Comprehension was the least precise of the reading test measurements. Some participants, who inadvertently had been given tests too difficult, were working at frustration level. They would easily have understood a less difficult passage. Another group of participants understood the passage but did not retell it because of nervousness under the test situation. This was particularly true of children and certain women. Other participants, who appeared not to understand, would certainly have done so had there been more time to go over the passage. Given all of these realities, the comprehension scores should be considered very tentative.

No mother-tongue speaker of Machiguenga was available for consultation after Professor Barrientos' first coding of the tests. Although further consultation was not indispensable, it would have been preferable.

Test results for a few readers were so poor that accuracy could not be scored fairly. For example, a participant in Mayapo, House 32, was given an Advanced reading test. When we discovered that because the test was too difficult he was attempting only to read the first part of each word and mumbling a guess for the rest of the word, no time remained to try an easier test. Some readers stumbled badly, then gave up in the middle of the test. Two individuals invented readings rather than admit that the text was too difficult for them. Tests of this type had to be disqualified because it was not possible to score them accurately. I have assumed, however, that any reader who could sound out an Intermediate or an Advanced Test, possessed at least basic-level skills.

In spite of these limitations, I consider the accuracy, fluency, and rate scores to be fair representations of the ability demonstrated at the time of each test. The comprehension scores, however, must be considered tentative.

Chapter Summary

This chapter describes the culturally-adapted data collection procedures used in this study, which included testing by families rather than individually. It explains the protocols developed for conducting the interviews and reading tests and describes the population surveyed. Before the raw data could be processed, several steps were required: preparation of syllable counts, score charts, interlinear translations, and transcription of the interviews. I then describe the coding systems used for the interviews and reading tests as well as the procedure adopted for interrater reliability checks. The results of the interview data and the reading scores yielded a data base from which descriptive statistics, correlations, regression analyses, and chi-square goodness of fit could be calculated. A final section discusses the strengths and limitations of these research procedures.

Chapter Summary 153

The Machiguenga people graciously gathered their families together for the interviews and reading tests conducted by the research team.
(Rosemary Clayton photos, Mayapo, 1992)

8
Literacy in Machiguenga Society

I want to continue learning. As long as I live I hope to keep on. And I would like to take more courses. If I do not die, and as long as there is money, I will keep on buying books and learning.
                              - Father, House 18, Puerto Huallana

Introduction

What has made literacy a pleasure to the Machiguenga, whereas in some other societies it has not been valued? Since educational factors alone cannot account for people's response to literacy, this chapter reports on societal factors which appear to have furthered literacy acceptance and use. Proceeding in chronological order, background theory, and events presented in chapters 2 through 5 are discussed with reference to Machiguenga literacy and the Machiguenga people's concept of literateness.

Factors Influencing Literacy Acquisition

A complex of factors, many of them beyond the control of the Machiguenga themselves, appear to have influenced literacy acquisition from the beginning. These include congruence with national policies, congruence with literacy predictors, a favorable sociological situation, constructive patterns of accommodation, and productive coping strategies.

Congruence with national policies

The Machiguenga are fortunate to live in a democratic nation in which mother-tongue education has been permitted. The bilingual program was government initiated and supported, and teachers from their language group were both trained and then assigned to schools in their own language area. These factors have been crucial to the success of the program (Goodman, Goodman, and Flores 1978:9–10). A staff of well-trained roving consultants, who worked in cooperation with the Ministry of Education—volunteers whose livelihood did not depend upon income generated by the Machiguenga and who were occasionally able to obtain some seed money for key projects—also enabled education and community development to progress faster than it might have otherwise. However, it is the Machiguenga themselves who have borne the brunt of the work and who have made good use of the opportunities offered them under national policies.

Congruence with literacy predictors

Motivation has long been considered a key factor in the acceptance of literacy (Gray 1961:23). In Machiguenga-land, ever since people understood the function of the school, motivation has not been lacking. In our survey, when asked, "Who needs to read?," 89.4 percent (101 respondents out of 113) replied, "Everyone." Nine replied, "Everyone who wishes to." One replied, "Men." One replied, "Children," and only one was unsure.

In answer to the question, "Why do you say it is good to read?," we received the following replies:

To know (things)	To learn	To read/send letters and documents	To help husband	To teach one's children
43	57	15	2	3

In Machiguenga the words translated into English as 'to know' and 'to learn' derive from one verb *yogotake*. Thus one hundred responses focused on the importance of knowing and obtaining information. Examples follow: " I like knowing" (Mother, House 16, Camaná). "I was able to learn, then study to be a health worker. Now I hold an office. We can become whatever we want" (Father, House 17, Camaná). "We used to live separately, scattered. We were not many. It is good the way we live now.

Children are learning" (Father, House 4, Shivankoreni). "I will keep on reading because I like to learn" (Father, House 38, Shivankoreni).

Because the Machiguenga have experienced exploitation, ability to defend oneself against it was cited at least seventy-two times during our interviews as motivation for education. The thought was expressed in a variety of ways: To defend one's self (twelve times), to avoid being cheated (fourteen times), to be able to speak Spanish (twenty-five times), to be able to buy and sell (twenty-one times).

In the early years of the first school in Camisea, the names of several adults appeared in the school register; in 1972, a beginning class was composed entirely of adults. At least three of these adults continued to enroll with the children until they could read well—a telling demonstration of their earnest desire to learn. One illiterate father expressed the sentiments we heard from many: "I have sent all my sons and daughters to school. They should know how to read and write and to defend me. I say to them, 'Learn to read. Don't be like me. If you don't know how, how will you manage later?'" (House 12, Puerto Huallana).

The Machiguenga, then, fulfill all of Spolsky, Engelbrecht, and Ortiz's (1983) conditions for the introduction of vernacular literacy to be successful in a traditional society, and, subsequently, for it to be maintained:

1. The group sees value in literacy.
2. Local uses for literacy have been developed.
3. The language is widely spoken.
4. Those who introduced literacy supported mother-tongue literacy.
5. Literacy is supported by a school system over which the people themselves have some control.

In regard to autonomous control, while normally it may be true that successful pilot projects tend not to be as successful when implemented on a large scale, in the case of Machiguenga teacher training, we have seen Machiguenga bilingual supervisors perform at a high level of competence, quite apart from outside presence or help.

Furthermore, the linguistic choices made by those who reduced the language to writing, the writing system chosen, the dialect used as the basis for the alphabet, and the teaching materials prepared for reading, did strongly affect the "taking hold" of literacy, as Ferguson (1987:2) predicted. The Machiguenga alphabet, which was simple and facilitated transfer to Spanish, met with the approval of the people. Literature was prepared in a major, well-accepted dialect, and the teaching materials were revised until they proved effective. All of these facilitated successful literacy introduction.

In order for literacy to be maintained, training should not be discontinued before students become proficient in literacy skills (Gray 1961; Cairns in Watters 1990:53; and others). Among the Machiguenga, the median length of school attendance for Basic readers was 4.6 years, for Intermediate readers 5.4 years, and for Advanced adult readers 6.57 years. The fact that the Machiguenga have been willing to move into communities so as to be proximate to schools has made it possible—at least in recent years—for most children not only to attend but also to complete all the years of schooling available in the village. This has allowed time for literacy skill to be made permanent.

In addition, eleven of the predictors tentatively postulated by Heath (1987) have been fulfilled among the Machiguenga.

1. *The Machiguenga people think and talk about language.* They comment on dialect differences, pun, use double talk, and place high value on oratorical skills.

2. *Literacy is not in competition with any other symbolic system legitimizing power* (as is true among the Australian Aborigines).

3. *Opportunities exist to talk about information from written materials in institutions other than the family and the school.* The Machiguenga local and central General Assemblies, church meetings, parents' associations, clubs, health posts, sawmills, rice hullers, and stores all provide opportunities to speak about written information.

4. *Collective sociopolitical discussions take place as an established practice.* In the monthly General Assemblies the villagers take part in decision making, rather than only a select group of elders.

5. *It is acceptable to borrow vocabulary from other languages, and mechanisms exist for doing so.* Machiguenga has incorporated not only Spanish nouns, but roots of verbs to which Machiguenga prefixes and suffixes are added, as in *nojuegatake* ' I play [soccer]' from the Spanish *juego* 'I play'.

6. *The society has a broad range of oral narrative types.* The Machiguenga have origin stories, oral history, folklore stories, instructional stories, and they also preserve many of their beliefs in song. A special speech form is reserved for oration on formal occasions such as arrivals, departures, and exchange of information between people who may or may not know each other well.

7. *Speakers do not hold unusually strong valuations of their language as being either bad or good,* i.e., they do not hold their language so sacred that they are unwilling for anyone else to learn it; neither do they reject it or feel that the time spent learning to read it is worthless.

8. *Speakers have opportunity to explicate the scope and sequence of tasks.* Machiguenga parents can be seen instructing their children on procedural tasks, although not as frequently as in Western societies. For example, I have observed a mother explaining the steps involved to her daughter as she set up a loom.

9. *There is opportunity for interactive (not merely one-sided) exposure to the outside world.* Although these opportunities have been limited, Machiguengas have traveled to cities, and officials, tourists, and oil workers have visited Machiguenga villages.

10. *A diversity of skills has been promoted and rewarded* through the community development program, the agricultural cooperative, and the church. Thereby, more uses for literacy and more opportunities for employment have been provided than would otherwise have been the case, even though the national economic crisis of recent years has drastically—and it is hoped, temporarily—curtailed jobs and economic opportunities in the Machiguenga homeland.

11. There is *opportunity for membership in a modern religious group* which holds frequent meetings to discuss religious texts involving both men and women of all ages. They also attribute significance to membership rites, and encourage members to share their faith.

Many of Trudell's (1993) positive indicators for literacy acquisition in Amazonia have also been true of the Machiguenga. They include: control over their own economic development, a sense of control over life and the future, ethnic and economic self-sufficiency (under normal circumstances), sentimental attachment to the mother tongue, viability of traditional customs, strong domains for vernacular literacy, high regard for learning, willingness to live in communities for the sake of bilingual schooling, a strong bilingual education program, perceived purpose for learning and education, availability of vernacular literacy instruction, family "habit" of vernacular literacy, and indigenous control in the schools.

A favorable sociological situation

Wallace (1956) warned that catastrophic demoralization and extinction can result from massive social change. The Machiguenga, although candid about the magnitude of the changes and problems they face—cultural loss, privation resulting from the national economic crisis, oil company concessions for exploitation of the natural deposits in their area, the difficulty of defending their land titles and of receiving equal treatment in a majority society which historically discriminates against indigenous minorities, despite favorable laws—are nevertheless increasing in number and, in 1992, were reasonably optimistic. I suggest that key factors contributing to their stability include the following.

1. Isolation. Because of their remote location the Machiguenga have not experienced the extreme subjugation suffered by some other indigenous groups and consequently were less demoralized when prolonged contact with outsiders began. Although they are very isolated, widely-scattered, and live in difficult terrain, the group is small enough to be manageable administratively yet large enough to maintain ethnic identity and some collective strength. The fact that they do not have clans or moieties may also make their language a more important unifying factor than might otherwise be the case.

2. A written language which a majority of the population can read has engendered a sense of linguistic equality with the dominant society.

3. Positive reinforcement of the Machiguenga culture and language from the beginning of prolonged contact with outsiders on the Lower Urubamba has helped enhance self esteem.

4. A community development policy directed towards Machiguenga autonomy has fostered independence rather than dependence.

5. A comparatively lengthy period (some twenty years) of preparation before heavy impingement began allowed time for new knowledge to be diffused and internalized with minimal pressure to perform.

6. The community development program generated jobs for the first literates (and since then for many others) and thereby provided immediate uses for literacy.

7. Knowledge of math, Spanish, Peruvian history and geography, and of majority society civic and judicial systems alleviate helplessness and afford the group some options for problem resolution (Gram Vikas and Pradan 1990; Varese 1985).

8. The emergence of educated leaders who have learned how to approach government offices has allowed for some self representation.

9. The experience of managing a large and successful cooperative has resulted in expertise which the Machiguenga know they can draw upon in the future, even though agricultural cooperatives have not proved economically viable in many places and are now looked upon as more

valuable as a means of giving people official representation (Perez-Crespo 1986:262–263).

10. Shared leadership may also be a factor in the maintenance of equilibrium. Since school teachers depended upon community leaders and parents for the support of the school program, leadership has been, and continues to be, shared between young people and elders to a larger degree than in some societies which have experienced wrenching generational gaps as young people became educated. A parent in the community of Mayapo put it this way, "I say that the bilingual school is good because it respects the adults" (Father, House 2).

Constructive patterns of accommodation

When adjusting to changing circumstances, some societies, like the individuals within them, appear to employ adaptive measures which produce more satisfaction than do others. Among the Machiguenga, individuals can be found who exhibit each of the patterns identified by Spindler and Spindler (1971)—traditionalist (resisting change), syncretistic (seeking to reconcile the two cultures), transitional (exhibiting identity problems because of alienation from both the native and the majority cultures), and elite acculturated (having become psychologically mestizo rather than Machiguenga). The more extreme cases are easy to identify. Traditionalists escape to remote locations and avoid contact with village life; syncretistic individuals blend church practices with shamanism; transitional individuals demonstrate considerable ambivalence as they try to be accepted in cities but also seek to maintain family ties; a few better-educated individuals are respected on the outside as well as on the inside and are truly bilingual and bicultural.

In 1992, however, the majority of villagers in the bilingual school communities gave evidence of maintaining equilibrium: "Sometimes I get upset with the gossip around here and say, 'I am going to move out of the community,' but I'll never really do it" (Father, House 42, Camaná). "We want to live together because there is more help. When we live in a community, there is more stealing, illicit love affairs, and gossip. That makes me sad, but we will still continue living here" (Mother, House 41, Camaná). A national code for rural communities legalizes disciplinary action both for villagers and for visiting mestizos who overstep the bounds of propriety (school supervisor, November 1992, personal communication). Knowing that they are not defenseless in the face of blatant injustice has significantly enhanced Machiguenga self assurance. I was told of several instances in which village police and justices of the peace had meted out fair punishment both to Machiguengas and to mestizos.

Although the Machiguenga respect their environment and in many ways preserve it well, large villages tax natural resources over time, especially if the population increases. The SIL team has sought to meet the problem by introducing additional crops—beans, rice, peanuts, citrus, and other fruit trees—and alternative protein sources. Increasing shortages of materials for house construction, firewood, and land for gardens are on-going concerns, although these were ameliorated in 1991 through enlarged land grants procured with the help of CEDIA, a local community development organization. Cash crops permit the purchase of construction materials and food supplements, but if the economy continues to be so depressed that sale of agricultural produce cannot meet basic needs, some villagers may opt to scatter. Fortunately, the Machiguenga still produce the items that were necessary to maintain themselves prior to the availability of Western items (Baksh 1984:447).

In Wayne Snell's opinion, the greatest secular achievement in the program was the procurement of birth certificates for the Machiguenga. This legitimization of individual personhood allowed them to become a people and created a sense of worth and belonging difficult to describe. Prior to that time they did not exist insofar as the law was concerned and were called animals and dogs to their faces.

Betty Snell emphasizes that the community development program would not have progressed had the Machiguenga not been given a hope for the future. For many years the most common farewell we heard was, "I won't be here when you come back; I'll be dead." Since they truly expected to be overtaken by death, there was little incentive to plant fields, build a school, or plan for a future for their children. Scripture provided spiritual hope; community development has supplied medical aid and tools with which they can help themselves. Both factors worked together to free the Machiguenga from debilitating fear, which in turn has enabled them to achieve a commendable degree of self-sufficiency.

All of these factors represent adaptive measures which appear to have promoted satisfaction for villagers. Betty Snell also points out that it was important to provide help and to lay foundational knowledge as early as possible in the program. In our experience, once Paulston's (1980) politicalization phase begins, the presence of outsiders may not be acceptable.

Productive coping strategies and sense of control

The tendency noted by Foster (1973) and Paulston (1980) for a post-contact generation to desire majority society acceptance so strongly that the indigenous language and culture is rejected has been observed among the Machiguenga only to a moderate degree. "Sometimes students (young women as well as young men) drop out and leave the community. They become proud and don't care about helping their people" (Father, House 17, Chokoriari). As a result, some individuals—perhaps as many as a score—appear to have been lost to their people. The pressure has been more evident in the adoption of Western clothing, the loss of some native lore and skills among the young people, and the wish to conduct themselves in ways Peruvians consider appropriate (which, for example, has motivated the acceptance of majority society dances). Fortunately, teachers, parents, and church and civic leaders have recognized the danger of cultural extinction and are joining to combat these tendencies by teaching crafts in school, encouraging the composition of new hymns with traditional music, incorporating traditional music and dance in civic programs, and counseling young people to learn the traditional stories and skills from their elders.

While not all young people cooperate, several indicated to us their intent to remain in their home communities (where mastery of most survival skills such as house building and hunting is obligatory) and to use their education on behalf of their people. As in Fiji (Clammer 1976), the "literate revolution" which has taken place among the Machiguenga appears to have "allowed the individual...to embark on a personal voyage of self-education" (p. 201). Thus the Machiguenga exhibit characteristics similar to those of the students (described by Mehan, Hubbard, and Villanueva 1994), who accommodate to new and stretching realities in ways comfortable for them without feeling they have to assimilate entirely, since they have learned some coping mechanisms and expect—through effort—to achieve some successes.

From the above, it can be seen that the Machiguenga have enjoyed unusually favorable conditions for literacy acquisition. They have taken advantage of the opportunity.

Special challenges

Our experience has demonstrated, however, that local-level development and education endeavors which might appear to function independently because they are geographically remote, nevertheless depend upon and are deeply affected by central government decisions and policies. In the case of the Machiguenga, government decisions, such as those which created bilingual schools, required cooperatives to be organized, and declared obsolete all of the textbooks of the school system, have radically changed circumstances and required a whole new set of responses. Frequently, rapid change, which even urban dwellers find difficult, entails yet more disruption, bewilderment, and expense for isolated minority groups.

In addition, the Machiguenga have been strongly influenced by many other factors in their immediate milieu over which neither they nor the SIL team has had control. Included among these factors have been: the national society's attitudes towards indigenous peoples; contacts with traders, lumber men, tourists, oil company laborers, anthropologists, government officials, and educators; the ridicule and long-term opposition of institutions and private citizens in the area who did not wish the Machiguenga to be autonomous; the ideologies of opinion makers and politicians; the teachings of religious organizations; experiences the individuals have had when visiting towns and cities outside of their area; the modeling of members of the majority society; and cross-cultural communication with other native groups. The Machiguenga have had to devise their own responses to each of these. The fact that thus far they have been able to do so without massive demoralization speaks well for the patterns of accommodation which they have adopted.

How the Machiguenga Define a Literate Person

The Machiguenga had no literate tradition, and in the early days of contact experienced considerable difficulty in understanding the concepts underlying reading and writing. Not surprisingly, then, respondents struggled to put their ideas about literacy into words. In answer to our query, "What do you think reading/writing is?" several replied, "I don't know, I have never thought about this before." Nevertheless, sixty individuals from five communities offered thoughtful answers to our query which indicated four areas of understanding.

To read and write is to comprehend print

Two verbs occurred interchangeably in the definitions relating to comprehension: *okoneatakena* 'it is clear to me' and *nokemakero* 'I understand it'. In addition, a few individuals included ability to say (speak) what is written as part of the definition, for example,

"I look at it and it is clear" (Father, House 16, Segakiato).

"I can look and understand what is written" (Father, House 33, Segakiato).

"I look and don't know what it says. Then someone else looks and says, 'It says this.' I see that it is clear to her" (Mother, House 13, Shivankoreni).

"I look at what is written and I can speak it" (Mother, House 31, Camisea).

To read and write is to master a skill

A number of answers indicated that this skill must be demonstrated to prove its existence, but other participants considered that the skill would exist—even apart from demonstration—if it had been taught/learned.

"When I say, 'What is this? this? this?' and she can tell me [correctly], then I know she knows how to read" (Father, House 18, Camisea).

"Those who can't, don't read; those who can do" (Father, House 6, Shivankoreni).

"I see he writes *tsirin, tsirin,* and then it is clear to him and he can speak what it says" (Father, House 40, Puerto. Huallana).

"If they have gone to school, they will have learned because the teacher will have taught them" (Father, House 8, Camisea).

To read and write is to undergo a learning process

Respondents made clear that some readers knew only a little; they had not yet finished learning to read and write. A verb often used in this connection was *yogotanake* 'he is in the process of learning'.

"When I had not yet seen paper or letters, they were not clear to me. I looked at written things but could not say them. Later, when the teacher taught me the syllables, I found the letters becoming more clear" (Father, House 11, Camisea).

"My son knows a little (i.e., first primers), but is still learning; he does not yet know everything" (Mother, House 31, Camisea).

"I never finished learning to read" (Father and Mother, House 36, Camisea).

To read and write relates to the self

Certain responses focused on individuals' awareness of their ability: "I hear them say they don't know how" (Father, House 40, Shivankoreni). One respondent related writing to self expression: "It is for saying whatever we want in writing" (Father, House 38, Shivankoreni).

The breakdown of responses are summarized in table 8.1.

Table 8.1. Concepts of literateness

	Comprehending print		Mastering a skill		A process	Self related	
Question:	Clear/un-derstood	Able to say it	Demon-strate it	Teach/Learn it		Evaluation	Expression
What is reading?	25	13	2	7	10	3	0
How is it distinguished?	0	0	23	1	0	0	0
What is writing?	6	1	4	4	1	2	1
How is it distinguished?	0	0	6	0	0	0	0
Total	31	14	35	12	11	5	1

A perceptive father in Camisea (House 31) gave perhaps the most graphic description: "I look [at the paper]. Depending on what is written, I understand it in my head. I know I am not mistaken about what I have understood in my head. I think about what I am reading. The person who does not know how to read does not understand what he is looking at, and so he babbles. He cannot read alone [without being told what the words are], and he does not know how to write."

Our observations indicated that in the villages the literate person is expected to be able to interpret at least simple writings in the Machiguenga language and to help others do so. In this culture, which places high value on sharing, the sharing of literacy skills appears to be as much expected as the sharing of food. Literates can write their official signature. Usually, they can also write friendly letters in Machiguenga and can do simple computations on paper both for themselves and for others. In church services, when a hymn or a Scripture passage is announced, everything stops until the literates have helped all the nonreaders around them find the correct page. The fully literate person is expected to be able to read all writings in Machiguenga and may be able to write business letters; however, it is possible to be literate in Machiguenga without being literate in Spanish, and vice versa. Literates, especially those who have learned Spanish, bear the responsibility of representing their people to the outside world—of receiving visitors, negotiating with traders, dealing with officials, and answering official letters—and receive respect commensurate with their knowledge and ability.

Reflecting...

The Machiguenga, as a group, have never appeared to be ashamed of their mother tongue. Some theorists suggest that their psychological health can, in part, be attributed to this fact (Guiora 1984:10). Learning has also been made easier for the Machiguenga in that new concepts, taught first in their own language, were more easily understood and then could be transferred to Spanish (as recommended by UNESCO 1953a; Modiano 1973; Freire and Macedo 1987; and many others). Although the acquisition of literacy is not a guarantee of development (Cairns 1985; Gough 1968; Freire and Macedo 1987), literacy has made possible almost all of the specialized training received by the Machiguenga and has formed the basis for their schools, churches, health posts, stores, sawmills, internal government, and appointment as government officials to positions such as education coordinator, school supervisor, justice of the peace, civil registrar, and state senator.

Never having had a literate tradition, the Machiguenga have developed concepts of literacy representative of their experience in the bilingual schools.

Although many struggled to vocalize their understandings, their composite definition of literacy showed a high level of comprehension, analysis, and expression for a people unused to dealing with Western abstractions.

Institutionalization of Literacy and Group Custom

Seeking to find institutions and domains which support Machiguenga literacy, I observed carefully as we visited. The following is a report.

The institutionalization of literacy

Upon my first visit to Machiguenga-land in 1963, fledgling school and church groups provided the only institutionalized support for reading. In 1992, I was surprised to find the following entities in each Machiguenga bilingual school community (unless an exception is noted). The impetus for most of the newer organizations has come from the people themselves without direct pressure from outsiders of which I am aware, although a general sense of need for coping strategies and a desire to identify with the majority society frequently are indirect factors. The pride, which was obvious as people told me of the ways they had organized, led me to interpret the new structures as indication that the Machiguenga people are quick to take note of ideas which they deem useful and to adapt the models for their purposes.

The following institutions now exist in each community.

1. A school, which is part of the government school system.
2. A church, affiliated with the incorporated Machiguenga Evangelical Church which holds regular services, Sunday school, and Bible studies.
3. A health post where records are kept, signs posted, and medications with directions are dispensed. These health posts operate under an agreement with the Ministry of Health.
4. A General Assembly (organized in about 1990 in accordance with the Law of Native Communities with the help of CEDIA, a regional community development organization). Since all villagers are expected to take an active part in the administration of their community, attendance at General Assembly meetings is required for adolescents and adults, and roll is called.
5. A Parents' Association for the primary school. If a secondary school also is located in the community, a separate Parents' Association is convened to handle secondary school affairs.
6. A men's Sports Club. If a secondary school is located in the community, the secondary school also organizes men's and women's teams for soccer and volley ball as a part of the physical education program. Intercommunity tournaments, with the appropriate written invitations and ceremonies, are convened. Adult women play on teams but tend not to be formally organized.
7. A Mothers' Club (with the exception of Camaná). This organization supports the men on their community work days by preparing a noon meal and has taken responsibility for the building and maintenance of village streets. Projects in support of the school—like breakfast for the children—may also be undertaken.
8. A church General Assembly.
9. A church Women's League.

Institutionalization of Literacy and Group Custom 169

The community health post in Mayapo displays health posters; inside, the few medicines available are neatly arranged and labeled. (Rosemary Clayton photos, 1992)

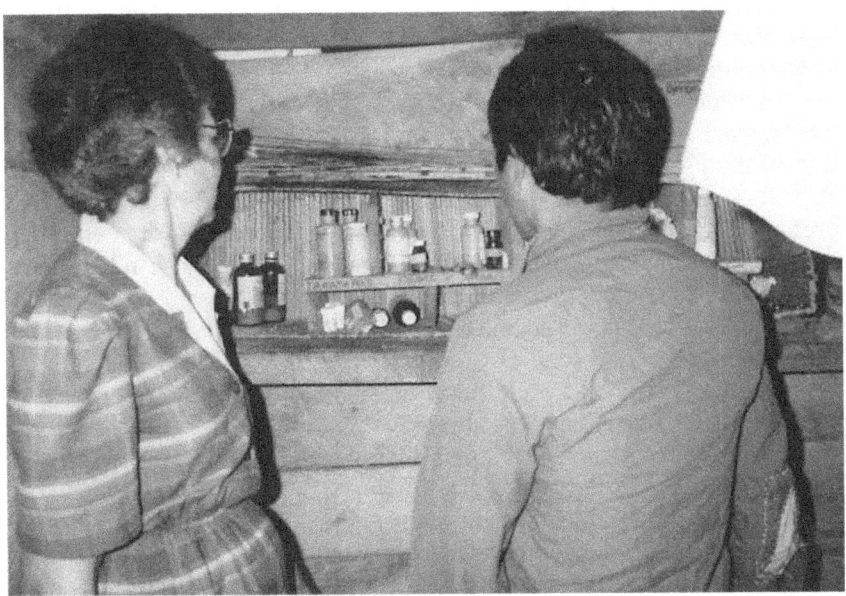

Each of these organizations meets monthly in official session. A panel of elected officers—composed of a President, Vice-President, Secretary, Treasurer, and one or two Delegates from the community—presides over the meetings. A written agenda is prepared on a chalkboard at the front of the assembly room, and items are erased as they are handled. The Secretary keeps and reads official minutes. The Treasurer keeps written financial records and may put the monthly report on the chalkboard. Because of the number of organizations now functioning, most of the villagers —at one time or another—have a turn serving as an elected officer with closer exposure to written records.

Although the organizations and the meetings themselves are based on Western innovations, a participant observer senses that they have been adapted to Machiguenga cultural needs—where group consensus is a high value—and form a unique and satisfying part of village life. Seating patterns (men in front, women and children at the back and around the sides, or families together) reflect traditional visiting patterns. As information is given from the podium, a dialogue often develops between the speaker and an elder (or elders), who acts as spokesperson for the assembled public—a traditional feature of Machiguenga formal speech. Women, who normally remain silent, nevertheless wax eloquent on matters about which they feel strongly, often in the high-pitched whining style used when problems are being aired in the home.

Monthly meetings accommodate to the patterns of this face-to-face, event-oriented society by carefully including all matters relating to village life so that all may be informed. As a result, meetings are very long—frequently six to eight hours. The social value of these meetings is high: news is shared, marriages are approved, field space is allotted, and tensions are aired. As well, the community must come to agreement on budgets and school needs; coordination between community, school, and church schedules; work projects; discipline cases (when these arise); preparation for special events (such as hosting a soccer tournament or an anniversary celebration); and how to respond to notices and requests from government and other outside entities. At the end of the meetings—at least in the well-managed communities where I observed—one can sense relief (everyone is tired of sitting), satisfaction (at knowing about and having dealt with current issues), a strong consciousness of again being in control of community affairs, and sometimes apprehension (if difficult interpersonal problems still linger, or a matter such as a threat to their retention of land titles is still unresolved).

Increasingly noticeable in recent years, perhaps as a result of their increasing self-government, has been the Machiguengas' increasing self-esteem and sense of their right to make their own decisions. On a 1990 visit, I remember asking three young adults how the Machiguenga people feel about single-family homes, which have now to a large extent replaced traditional multi-family communal houses. I was asking, I explained, because SIL members had come under criticism for imposing this change in cultural patterns, although I had no knowledge of team members ever suggesting it. The indignation of my respondents was startling, "Why don't people *ask us* before they write this stuff? We *like* to live in single-family dwellings; with fewer people there is less interpersonal tension."

Each community has had a store, although with the economic crisis, the stores fell upon hard times and in 1992 were temporarily closed. Two communities, however, still oversee the operation of sawmills and rice hullers donated for the use of all Machiguenga villagers. These and the community health posts continue to involve the people in measuring, weighing, counting, computing, and ongoing record keeping.

In addition to the above, at least four communities have also formed pro-CONCODE committees, whose mission is to apply for government grants offered for specific purposes, such as the building of schools and clinics, and to oversee the use of the money.

Most communities now have civil registrars, who record births and deaths and provide birth certificates. In 1992 for the first time, teams of military registrars were sent to key villages to provide military inscription services for the Machiguenga. Also for the first time in 1992, polling booths were set up in one central location, thus enabling many to vote who could not travel to the cities.

In 1975 the Machiguenga bilingual school communities of the Lower Urubamba formed an agricultural cooperative which has changed with the times to become the Machiguenga *Central,* a central organizing body. Each of the bilingual school communities in the area belongs to the *Central,* and sends a delegate to its yearly General Assembly. A *Central* Executive Committee—composed of a President, Vice-President, Secretary, Treasurer, and a Delegate from each community—is elected each year at the General Assembly meetings. This Executive Committee is active in handling formal business with government entities and all affairs which affect the Machiguenga bilingual school communities of the Lower Urubamba as a group. After the General Assembly meetings of the *Central* a report of the proceedings is sent to member communities, and this report is then presented in the village meetings. The *Central* Executive also visits communities to disseminate information and sends written communications as the need arises.

Certain key individuals who have been involved in cotranslating and coediting the Machiguenga New Testament and Old Testament portions have had extended experience in editorial processing. Their families and communities have helped read preliminary versions of the translation, checking for comprehensibility. This process furthered public awareness of the written word.

Group use of literacy

Letter writing is now a common practice among the Machiguenga, as well as the writing of formal invitations to special events. People draw designs on T-shirts and other articles of clothing and also label their clothing by writing their name on an inside seam. One young father who left the community to work and was tragically murdered under dubious circumstances is reported to have been identified by the name written on the inside of his shirt cuff, even though his documents had been stolen. Private citizens keep records of bills owed, and churchgoers write notes on occasion, either in preparation for a service or to remember verses and important points of a lesson. Preachers illustrate their sermons with annotations on the chalk board. Bible reading is carried on privately in many homes.

Public signs—both in Machiguenga and Spanish—are in use everywhere, particularly around the health posts, churches, and town halls. At times letters are written on walls or are carved on plants and gourd pots. (Some of the writing appears to have originated with young children who were practicing their letters while at play, but one wall boasted elegant Old English calligraphy as part of a chalk-drawn mural.)

Mothers frequently mentioned that they help their children with school work, and students can be seen doing their homework. People also pore over new writings that come to their hands, both individually and in groups. Villagers store birth certificates with care—often in lengths of hollowed-out bamboo—and take pains to understand the written instructions on their medicine bottles.

Although nonliterates can still function quite comfortably in the society, it is interesting to note that in bilingual school communities virtually every nonliterate person has a literacy mediator—someone to whom he or she goes when there is a need to understand print, write a letter, or buy and sell with cash.

Literate Machiguengas also express their sense of having become part of their nation and the world. "If there had not been a school, I would not know now. Now I can write, add, study, read what the newspapers say, and understand a little Spanish. It was not like this long ago" (Father, House 18, Puerto Huallana).

Reflecting...

The Machiguenga are now moving from primary oracy (Ong 1982) to secondary oracy (speech supported with written materials). More than that, they are developing what Heath (1991) calls "the sense of being literate" as well as "literate behaviors," which include comparing, sequencing, arguing with, interpreting, and creating extended chunks of spoken and written language in response to a written text (p. 3). Examples include the school-related tasks required of both teachers and students; reports issued by the Machiguenga *Central;* the monthly meetings of community organizations; health posters which elicit questions and comments, instructions for medications, bills for the health post, saw mill, and stores; and correspondence, both business and personal.

These uses of literacy serve a dual function: they provide instrumental reasons for learning to read and for maintaining the skill. They also give practice in analyzing, categorizing, interpreting intent, following written instructions, doing numerical calculations, and managing records. These skills contribute to success in school.

Chapter Summary

This chapter lists factors which have contributed to the acceptance of literacy among the Machiguenga. Among them we find favorable national policies, geographic isolation, a strong sense of cultural and linguistic identity, a written language with a well-accepted orthography, positive reinforcement of the language and culture from the beginning of prolonged contact with outsiders, a community development policy directed towards Machiguenga autonomy, a comparatively lengthy period of time in which to adapt to changes, constructive patterns of accommodation, and coping strategies which have fostered a sense of being in control and which have enhanced self esteem.

Questioning revealed that the Machiguenga consider that a literate person has the skill to understand and speak correctly the word symbols on a page, that learning to read is a process, and that writing is a means of self expression.

Institutional uses for literacy are found not only in the school and church but also in community meetings, parents' associations, sports clubs, women's clubs, and the Machiguenga *Central* (organizing body). Each of these has regular meetings where correspondence is handled, minutes are recorded and read aloud, and agendas are written on the chalkboard. Health posts, stores, saw mills, rice hullers, civil registers, and community income-generating projects all provide continual uses for reading and writing.

Letter writing, labeling of clothing, public signs, note taking, Bible reading, private record keeping, and printing on cactus leaves, gourds, walls, and T-shirts are further evidence that literacy has become part of group custom. All of these provide strong support for literacy.

Chapter Summary

A sign placed by the door of a temporarily vacant home in Puerto Huallana says, "Now all of you who live here in Puerto Huallana, I want you not to enter my house, and not to take what is in it. Also, when you go by, stay on the trail." (P. Davis photos, 1992)

9

Personal Perspectives
Attitudes and Usage

Our daughters need to enter school in order to be able to help us. Other girls need to study so they can help their husbands. Sometimes when I am treating patients I need my wife to help me. She works [with patients] too. - Father, House 23, Puerto Huallana

Introduction

This chapter focuses upon attitudes towards literacy reported by the Machiguenga and literacy activities which we observed. In ways expected and unexpected reading and writing are permeating village life and contributing to literacy retention.

Attitudes Towards Literacy

Wishing to understand whether the Machiguenga valued literacy enough to retain it, we asked a series of interview questions. The queries produced a virtually unanimous consensus that reading and writing are good. Even nonliterates and those who did not wish to study themselves considered literacy to be worthwhile and wanted their children to learn. Seeking to probe a little further, we asked a series of questions of different participants in different communities. These questions and their answers are given in the following tables. The categories listed are those expressed by the Machiguenga themselves, not categories predetermined by the researcher.

Table 9.1. Do you read well?

Community	Unable to read	Fair	Only a little	Not well	No–bad eyes	Yes	Yes–but bad eyes	Total
Camisea	2	14	3	28	0	14	1	62
Camaná	1	2	0	3	0	0	0	6
Chokoriari	0	0	0	9	0	3	0	12
Mayapo	1	0	0	9	0	1	0	11
Nueva Luz	0	0	0	0	0	1	0	1
Pto. Huallana	0	0	0	6	0	1	0	7
Segakiato	1	0	0	20	0	0	0	21
Shivankoreni	3	2	1	13	1	1	0	21
Total	8	18	4	88	1	21	1	141

Of 141 participants who answered this question, eight were unable to read, eighty-nine felt they did not read well, four read only a little, and eighteen rated themselves as fair readers. Only twenty-two (15.6 percent of these respondents) considered themselves to be good readers. All of the responses were undoubtedly conditioned by the Machiguenga sense of modesty, which does not permit a claim in the affirmative unless skills are superior.

Table 9.2. Do you read much?

Community	None	Every day	A little	A little (bad eyes)	No	No (bad eyes)	Often	Some	Very little	Total
Camisea	2	52	8	1	12	2	11	27	2	117
Camaná	3	11	1	0	4	0	3	7	0	29
Chokoriari	1	2	0	0	5	0	1	9	1	19
Mayapo	1	6	2	0	6	0	1	5	0	21
Nueva Luz	0	1	0	0	0	0	0	0	0	1
Pto. Huallana	0	12	0	0	3	0	6	9	1	31
Segakiato	2	13	5	0	10	0	1	3	2	36
Shivankoreni	3	10	5	0	5	0	0	9	2	34
Total	12	107	21	1	45	2	23	69	8	288

Of 288 participants, fifty-nine responded that they did not read; 229 (79.5 percent) read at least a little. Among the latter, 107 individuals,

Attitudes Towards Literacy 179

mostly students, read every day during the school year. The others who read every day tended to be school and church leaders.

Table 9.3. Do you write much?

Community	None	Every day	A little	No	No (bad eyes)	Often	Some	Very little	Total
Camisea	2	51	9	16	1	6	29	3	117
Camaná	3	10	4	4	0	2	6	0	29
Chokoriari	1	1	1	6	0	1	6	1	17
Mayapo	1	6	0	10	0	0	4	0	21
Nueva Luz	0	1	0	0	0	0	0	0	1
Pto. Huallana	0	12	0	5	0	5	8	1	31
Segakiato	2	13	6	13	0	1	1	0	36
Shivankoreni	3	10	5	11	0	0	5	0	34
Total	12	104	25	65	1	15	59	5	286

Of 286 respondents, seventy-eight replied that they did not write; 208 (72.7 percent) indicated that they write at least occasionally. Again, students write every day during the school year, school teachers and administrators write constantly, and church leaders write often. Secretaries of the village organizations write at least once a month.

Table 9.4. Will you continue reading?

Community	None	Only a little	Some	Very little	Yes	Yes, qualified	Total
Camisea	0	4	1	1	43	1	50
Camaná	0	0	0	0	6	0	6
Mayapo	0	0	0	0	1	0	1
Nueva Luz	0	0	0	0	1	0	1
Pto. Huallana	0	0	0	0	13	0	13
Segakiato	0	0	0	0	8	0	8
Shivankoreni	4	2	0	0	10	1	17
Total	4	6	1	1	82	2	96

Of ninety-six respondents, eighty-two (85.4 percent) gave strong affirmative answers, and a total of ninety-two expected to read at least a little. "If I leave off, I'll regress. I want to keep on reading" (Father, House 6, Camaná). "I want to learn more and more" (Father, House 17, Camaná). "Yes, I will read a lot. I would like to become a doctor" (Father, House 10, Camisea).

Women had strong opinions too about the need for reading and the need for children to persevere until they become good at it. This question evoked the following response from one mother:

> Long ago when I went to school, I did not think about what kind of work I might want to do later. I said, "I'm not going to go back to school; I'm just sitting there for nothing." In vain Mother said to me, "My daughter, go to school." I didn't want to; I was tired of it.
> Now it is the same with my daughter. She goes to school and gets tired of it. I say to her, "Go to school. Look at me. Long ago I had a good chance [to learn]. Mother said to me, 'Go to school and learn. Learn to write and read and talk Spanish. Learn to add so you can sell and learn to sew.' I said, 'I don't want to; I'll just listen to the radio.'" I said that, but now it is hard for me. (Mother, House 18, Puerto Huallana)

Table 9.5. In which language will you read?

Community	None	Both	Spanish	Spanish, qualified (I know my own language)	Machiguenga	Total
Camisea	0	75	1	0	25	101
Camaná	2	13	0	0	5	20
Chokoriari	1	7	1	0	3	12
Mayapo	0	9	0	0	4	13
Nueva Luz	0	1	0	0	0	1
Pto. Huallana	0	20	0	0	9	29
Segakiato	0	16	0	0	9	25
Shivankoreni	2	17	1	1	8	29
Total	5	158	3	1	63	230

Of 230 respondents, five did not expect to read in any language; four preferred Spanish, sixty-three expected to read only in Machiguenga, and 158 (68.7 percent) anticipated reading in both languages. Participants frequently indicated that Spanish was more difficult for them, but for that very reason they wished to practice it and learn it better. "I want to learn more Spanish to talk to visitors" (Father, House 7, Camisea). The thrust of all but two or three conversations was that Spanish was in addition to, not a substitute for, Machiguenga. Those who read mostly in Spanish did so because they had exhausted all material in Machiguenga and because the new material to which they had access was written in Spanish.

Attitudes Towards Literacy

Table 9.6. Who needs to read?

Community	Children	Everyone	Everyone who wishes	Men	Unsure	Total
Camisea	0	47	5	0	0	52
Camaná	0	13	0	0	0	13
Mayapo	0	4	1	0	0	5
Nueva Luz	0	1	0	0	0	1
Pto. Huallana	0	8	0	0	1	9
Segakiato	0	17	0	0	0	17
Shivankoreni	1	11	3	1	0	16
Total	1	101	9	1	1	113

When asked, "Who needs to read?," one respondent out of 113 replied "Children." One respondent replied, "Men"; 101 (89.3%) replied, "Everyone." Nine others qualified the concept of *everyone* to mean, "everyone who wishes to," and one respondent was unsure. The majority opinion was expressed in many ways: "I don't want anyone to be left out" (Father, House 7, Mayapo). "...Boys, girls, men, women. Children should go to high school so they will know how to defend us" (Father, House 16, Mayapo). "I want everyone to know things, like book knowledge and the Bible. All children need to learn" (Father, House 41, Camaná). "There is now no one who doesn't need to know" (Father, House 23, Shivankoreni). "[They need to know] so that they can read without being ashamed wherever they are" (Son, House 3, Camisea).

Table 9.7. Do women need to read?

Community	No	Unsure	Yes	Yes, if they wish	Total
Camisea	0	0	25	1	26
Camaná	0	1	5	1	7
Mayapo	0	0	3	0	3
Nueva Luz	0	0	1	0	1
Pto. Huallana	0	0	5	2	7
Segakiato	1	0	6	0	7
Shivankoreni	0	0	2	2	4
Total	1	1	47	6	55

Of fifty-five participants asked this question specifically, forty-seven (85.4 percent) answered "yes." Six more qualified the statement by adding, "if they wish to." This favorable attitude towards women's learning is worked out in practice. I heard of only one, perhaps two, children (both girls) of primary school age who were not enrolled in school, and the fact was represented to me as an unhappy exception to custom.

"Women also need to learn" (Father, House 34, Segakiato). "Our daughters need to enter school in order to be able to help us. Other girls need to study so they can help their husbands. Sometimes when I am treating patients I need my wife to help me. She works [with patients] too" (Father, House 23, Puerto Huallana). "Girls also need to go to school; then they can hold positions in the community" (Father, House 8, Camisea). "Women should have the same opportunity as men—learn to read, write, attend high school....The only problem is money" (Father, House 17, Camisea). I heard of no primary school children who had been held out of school, however, solely for lack of money.

Table 9.8. Do officials need to read?

Community	No	No, but will need help	Unsure	Yes	Yes, unless there is help	Total
Camisea	2	1	0	35	1	39
Camaná	0	2	1	6	0	9
Mayapo	0	1	0	4	1	6
Nueva Luz	0	0	0	1	0	1
Pto. Huallana	0	3	0	7	0	10
Segakiato	0	1	0	13	0	14
Shivankoreni	0	3	0	12	0	15
Total	2	11	1	78	2	94

Because head men in the past have been very effective without being literate, special effort was made to converse with representatives from all age groups and levels of responsibility to determine whether the Machiguenga now feel that village officials need to be literate. Of ninety-four respondents, seventy-eight (83 percent) participants responded unequivocally in the affirmative, one answered in the negative, and one was unsure. "Things are different now," we heard over and over. "Long ago it was possible to be a chief and not read. Now it would be hard to know how to do everything" (Father, House 6, Camaná). "They need to know how to read letters that come and tell the information to the people" (Father, House 4, Camisea). "They need to be literate to do their work; otherwise, they can't sign documents" (Daughter, House 4, Shivankoreni), and "They will be cheated when they sell" (Father, House 6, Shivankoreni). Thirteen conceded that "If illiterates are capable [people] they can organize the community without being able to read" (Father, House 13, Camisea), and can be elected to public office. However, they pointed out, "They can call people and tell them how to do the work, but they will not know how to read or be able to talk Spanish to visitors" (Father, House 12, Puerto Huallana). "He could become an official and function here, but if he needed to go downstream on business, or if a visitor were to come here, he would need to speak Spanish" (Father, House 40, Camaná).

To cope with these demands, illiterate leaders would at least need the services of someone who could read and write. "He can find a helper—the Secretary—then he will be able to deal with our people, but not with Whites" (Father, House 14, Puerto Huallana). "[Leaders] need to know Spanish. Things have changed since long ago" (Father, House 4, Shivankoreni). "They may have to attend seminars and courses" (Father, House 14, Shivankoreni).

The respondents made it clear that a further dimension is also needed—"Now [leaders] need to know in order to be able to think about and direct how we live here and how to really help everyone. They should not just parcel out work but think about many things. That's where it is different from long ago" (Father, House 23, Puerto Huallana). "They need to read documents and explain to us what they say" (Father, House 28, Segakiato). "They have to defend us—prevent our land from being taken away, for example. If someone is illiterate, he can direct work crews, but...leaders need knowledge to help with our economic problems so we can pay our debts" (Father, House 10, Camisea). "[The job] requires those who have studied and know about organization" (Father, House 38, Shivankoreni).

Evidences of Literacy

When literacy is both valued and used, evidence of it tends to appear around homes and community buildings. We asked ourselves, "What visible evidence of literacy is found around homes?" Types of evidences were categorized as follows:

- books (Bibles figured significantly in this category)
- clothing with print (either purchased logos or hand written by the owner)
- crafts (such as sewing or carpentry) which imply use of print or numbers
- writing practice on walls and plants
- printed matter (pamphlets, magazines, etc.)
- school textbooks
- school work (drawings, papers, etc.)

- household utensils (such as letters carved on water gourds or containers with printed labels) which imply some use of print
- wall decorations (such as posters, calendars, signs, drawings, pictures, slogans, announcements)
- writing materials (such as notebooks, pencils, ballpoint pens)

An informal survey was then taken in fifty-eight homes. The number of different types of literacy evidence visible around the home or in the visiting area at the time of our arrival was recorded with the following results.

Table 9.9. Number of types of literacy in evidence

Community	1.0	2.0	3.0	4.0	5.0	6.0	7.0	Total
Camisea	13	9	7	3	3	6	3	44
Camaná	7	5	1	2	0	0	0	15
Chokoriari	2	0	12	2	2	0	0	18
Mayapo	3	2	2	2	0	0	0	9
Pto. Huallana	10	2	6	0	0	0	0	18
Segakiato	10	3	0	0	0	0	0	13
Shivankoreni	9	2	0	2	2	0	0	15
Total	54	23	28	11	7	6	3	132

In fifty-four homes one evidence of literacy was noted; two types of evidence were found in twenty-three homes; three types of evidence were noted in twenty-eight homes; and four to seven types of evidence were seen in twenty-seven homes. We knew printed material existed in most of the other households we visited, but it was carefully put away in inside rooms, away from small children and blowing rain. Also, if we arrived during school hours, most of the school texts and notebooks which normally might have been visible were not at home but at school with the children.

In our sampling, the frequency of occurrence of visible literacy evidences was as follows.

Frequency	Type
34 homes	books
24 homes	wall decorations
22 homes	writing materials
16 homes	printed materials
14 homes	household utensils
12 homes	school texts
9 homes	writing practice on walls, plants

8 homes	school work
5 homes	clothing with print
2 homes	crafts which imply use of instructions (knitting, carpentry)

Numeracy

Because knowledge of numbers is a highly-desired aspect of literacy among the Machiguenga and because ability to buy, sell, and count money is another measure of literateness, we also asked the questions displayed in the following tables.

Table 9.10. Can you buy and sell?

Community	Only a little	No	Yes	Yes, but unsure on big numbers	Only barter	Total
Camisea	5	19	48	1	1	74
Camaná	1	11	9	0	0	21
Chokoriari	0	7	11	0	0	18
Mayapo	0	6	7	0	2	15
Nueva Luz	0	0	1	0	0	1
Pto. Huallana	2	4	14	0	2	22
Segakiato	1	16	6	0	0	23
Shivankoreni	6	13	5	0	0	24
Total	15	76	101	1	5	198

According to their responses, seventy-six respondents did not consider that they could buy and sell without someone more knowledgeable to help them; sixteen could handle only simple purchases, not the making of change or calculating with big numbers; five reported being able only to barter (although we know that many more actually do barter both with traders and within the community); 101 participants of the 198 who responded to this question, felt able to buy and sell using money.

Table 9.11. Can you count money?

Community	A little	No	Yes	Yes, but not perfectly	Total
Camisea	8	19	51	1	79
Camaná	1	10	12	0	23
Chokoriari	0	7	10	0	17
Mayapo	1	7	7	0	15
Nueva Luz	0	0	1	0	1
Pto. Huallana	0	6	19	0	25
Segakiato	4	14	13	0	31
Shivankoreni	9	9	8	0	26
Total	23	72	121	1	217

Of the 217 who responded to this question, seventy-two responded in the negative; twenty-four felt able to count only a little; 121 answered "yes."

The Personal Face of Literacy

If we think of literacy only as an abstract object, we fail to appreciate its impact in people's lives. The following account illustrates the significant change reading skill brought into the life of one young boy.

In December of 1992, retired bilingual teacher Andrés Vicente P. sat down at his desk in the Camisea Civil Registrar's Office, took up his pen, and proceeded to create a word picture. Professor Vicente had been born in the remote headwaters of a small stream where no one had ever heard of paper or pencils. Now he wrote:

> When I was a child, I used to go to the jungle with my father for a week at a time to extract the milk of the rubber tree. Everyone worked [for a *patrón*]....Mr. Torres was good; he did not give us much heavy work. The men could work in groups, taking their time until they had large quantities of resin. Then they would be asked to take it to the mouth of the stream. That was when they suffered intensely because in summer the stream was very low. The loaded canoe could not pass and would have to be pushed. They would strain and push until they arrived and could deliver the cargo to the *patrón*. I remember I was still little; I must not have been more than seven years old.

Shortly after this time, Professor Vicente was able to attend the first bilingual school. Eventually, he learned enough to train as a teacher. Now, after completing high school and twenty-seven years of service to the Ministry of Education, his world is greatly expanded. When asked what he read and wrote, he compiled the following list in writing.

What I read:

- New Testament
- Pamphlets
- Stories and legends
- Information about herbal cures
- Spanish texts, primary and high school
- Natural science texts
- Books about family life
- Material about the Christian life
- Newspapers, when available
- Statutes of the community
- Constitution of Peru
- Many other things

What I write:

- Letters in Spanish
- Business letters re:
  sports
  district council affairs
  community bylaws
- Civil birth register
- Civil death register
- Letters in Machiguenga
  friendly letters
  business letters
- Copies of laws, Bible verses, community affairs excerpts from books; other things I want to learn or remember.

What I wrote when I was Director of a bilingual school:

- Business letters:
  letters of coordination
  letters requesting leave
  letters to Shell Oil Company
  letters to/for the Machigenga *Central*
  letters to CEDIA setting up meetings
  letters to other communities
  invitations to sports events
- Decrees
- Petitions
- School attendance records, evaluation records, reports
  Lessons and lesson plans

Professor Vicente's account is representative of the experience of many others. They also speak with earnest intensity about the value of literacy.

Attitudes Towards Change

How do the Machiguenga feel about the changes in their society? The man who in 1993 was treasurer of the *Central* of Machiguenga Native Communities and coordinator of the Machiguenga Evangelical Church presented me with the following written list which captured in essence most of the commentary gleaned in our house-to-house interviews.

Positive consequences of education
- community organizations
- an ecclesiastical organization
- judicial organization (which includes a lieutenant governor, police chief, and police constable)
- Machiguenga students enrolled in higher education
- Machiguenga men who have served their country in the military

Negative consequences of education
- new ideologies, including communism
- strife between organizations
- pride in knowledge
- abandonment of traditional culture
- rejection of the language and ethnic identity
- materialism—desire for luxuries, things, money
- substitution of Western music for traditional music
- an exodus of young men to work for mestizo *patrones*

(Díaz, January 1993)

The concerns expressed by Díaz were echoed by villagers during our interviews. "Sometimes a student leaves school, goes to work far away, and he stays away. In vain they say to him, 'Live here; think about your studies.' Sometimes this is what happens; they become proud" (Father, House 16 Camaná). "Some of those who come back from secondary school sometimes are resentful of their homeland. They say, 'It's not good here. Huallana doesn't give me any money. I'll go to Lima (or some other town) and become like a White person. I don't want to be like a Machiguenga....' I don't know where they go. But I see that our homeland is good. There is fish, game, and wood for building and for fires. Here things don't cost and we can go to town when we want" (Father, House 18, Puerto Huallana).

Interestingly, despite their recognition of and concern about the negative side effects of education, villagers did not blame the school for them. "Sometimes a young person will go off, but in the case of my son it was his decision, not because of the school" (Father, House 41, Camaná). "Some don't finish—they go off to work lumber....Some get tired of it and start having boy-girl affairs. They don't think straight—they need to settle down and finish. But it is not the school's fault. The school is good" (Brother, House 38, Puerto Huallana). "Some teachers are not training their students as well as the old teachers did. There is a lack of discipline and good counsel. [But] it is the students' fault. They are the ones who do not listen and cooperate even when they are taught and counseled" (Father, House 27, Chokoriari).

Villagers recognize that young people have legitimate needs, even as they complain that some are too greedy: "Young people no longer want to dress in the traditional clothing. They want to wear pants. That's why they go downstream to work. They want blankets, shoes, plates, pots...." (Father, House 40, Puerto Huallana). Community members distinguish between those who leave to work temporarily in order to earn money for basic necessities and for schooling and those who have abandoned their people. A retired teacher summarized the prevailing attitudes thus: "The school is an institution. An institution is neutral. It is people—teachers and students—who do good and bad, and they do it by their choice" (Father, Nueva Luz).

I found it encouraging that many people were aware of difficulties that they faced as a result of increased contact with the majority society, and that rather than taking a fatalistic view they were proactive—within the limitations of their situation—in seeking to ameliorate problems. A conference convened with regional authorities in 1991, for example, resulted in increased economic help and the provision of military inscription services and electoral polls for the first time.

Reflecting...

Interestingly, although survey participants listed many uses of reading, no one mentioned reading the hymnbook (the most popular book after the New Testament and one which is in constant use in the church), reading signs (which are posted on health posts and community buildings in every village), or reading agendas (which are written on the black board for every public meeting). This gave me to understand that much unconscious as well as conscious reading is taking place. It also may mean that the respondents think of reading only in the context of sitting down with a book and perusing it with serious intent, rather than also including incidental reading tasks.

Fewer than five gave the impression that they wished Spanish to replace Machiguenga; for most the desire to know Spanish was additive and pragmatic—more reading material is available in Spanish. Literacy evidences around both homes and public buildings contrasted significantly with a previous nonliterate era observed by the author in the 1960s. I noticed too that—in contrast to the early years of the bilingual schools—literacy is now expected of anyone who has grown up in a school community, rather than being the exception to the rule. These favorable attitudes towards literacy and its uses indicate that literacy skills will continue to be maintained.

Factors Influencing Literacy Retention[9]

What factors have influenced the retention of literacy skills? To answer this question, adults were again separated from students, since only those who have finished formal study are apt subjects for a study of literacy retention. The four scores (five scores in the case of the Basic Test) corresponding to each adult's test were first standardized and then averaged into one composite score. General linear regression formulae were then applied to find correlations between variables. The levels of correlation were showed with Pearson r, and probability values were noted. Regression analysis could not be conducted on the Intermediate Test for lack of data—only one adult met standards on the Intermediate Test.

Interestingly, no significant correlations were found between success on the Basic Test and age, gender, evidences of literacy in the home, or number of years since those tested had left school. These findings suggest that all students learned the same basic skills at beginning level. Only for the Spanish Test was the correlation with number of years of school attendance barely significant ($N = 77; r = 0.226; p = 0.048$). Continuing to read, however, yielded a highly significant correlation ($N = 30; r = 0.545; p = 0.002$). Obviously, those who had continued to use their reading skills placed well when suddenly called upon to do so.

For the Advanced Test, no significant correlations were found between participants' ability to meet preset standards and their age, gender, or evidences of literacy in their homes. A mild, though nonsignificant, positive trend was noted for years of schooling ($N = 95; r = 0.169; p = 0.101$). Again, continuance of reading correlated with success at a highly significant level ($N = 88; r = 0.35; p = 0.001$). One infers that Advanced readers who continued reading had had more practice than Basic readers, thus the difference in the probability score: ($p = 0.002$ for Basic readers; $p = 0.001$ for Advanced readers).

The results showed a significant correlation between success on the Advanced Test and the number of years since participants had left

---

[9]Refinements and corrections in the statistical analysis have resulted in a somewhat different presentation of the data in this section than in earlier versions of this study.

school ($N = 93$; $r = -0.228$[10]; $p = 0.028$). These data appear to indicate that, in the Machiguenga case, literacy skills have not deteriorated after participants left formal study but rather have improved over time, just as they reported to me.

Possibly—as some villagers suggested—the early teachers taught better than newer teachers; thus children learned better under the old school system which allowed more time for the early grades. This could explain why those who had been out of school longer demonstrated stronger skills than those who finished more recently. The suggestion was disputed by other villagers, who felt that the new teachers were better trained and therefore children were learning better than previously.

I interpreted both comments to be true, but in different situations. In general, the reduction of teaching time in the early grades under the new school system has created stresses for both students and teachers but has been partially ameliorated in most villages by the creation of preschool programs. Education in individual communities, however, has been—and continues to be—greatly affected by the varying skill of the teachers assigned over the years.

For the Spanish Test, the analyses showed no correlation between success in meeting preset standards and age, gender, or evidences of literacy around the home. The number of years of school attendance showed a mildly significant correlation ($N = 77$; $r = 0.226$; $p = 0.048$), indicating that knowledge of Spanish tends to be dependent on the length of time students study it. A mildly significant correlation was also found for continuance of reading ($N = 108$; $r = 0.193$; $p = 0.045$).

Compared with the Basic Test ($p = 0.002$) and the Advanced Test ($p = 0.001$), the correlation between continuance of reading and proficiency on the Spanish Test showed considerably lesser significance ($p = 0.045$). Doubtless because of the second language factor, continuance of reading in Machiguenga does not assure comprehension in Spanish.

The number of years participants had been out of school tended to correspond negatively to their success on the Spanish Test ($N = 76$; $r = -0.121$[11]; $p = 0.296$), indicating that for many, their Spanish reading skills had improved over time. This phenomenon may be explained by the fact that the more Spanish villagers know, the more they are called upon to use it. Due to increased contact with the outside world, Spanish is

---

[10] The negative r is an artifact of the fact that the values on the x axis were given in years (1950–2000), with the result that the smallest year is equivalent to the largest number of years out of school.

[11] The negative r is an artifact of the fact that the values on the x axis were given in years (1950–2000), with the result that the smallest year is equivalent to the largest number of years out of school.

heard in the communities more frequently now, and more Spanish communications are received and written. With this continued practice, Spanish reading skills have improved rather than deteriorated.

Gender

The fact that gender showed no significant correlation to success on any of the reading tests is an unusual finding which merits elaboration. In many developing countries, marked discrepancies are found between males and females. In the Machiguenga situation, however, education has been accessible to all since the very beginning of the bilingual schools. Most have taken advantage of the opportunities, as evidenced by the fact that the majority of children complete all the grades available in their village. A few fathers have attended school along with their children; mothers have been known to bring their babies and toddlers to class. Although wives and mothers are somewhat less free to attend, adult classes have been held at appropriate hours, and those who really want to enroll can usually find a way to do so. In my sampling, the following profile was found.

	Total Survey Population			Literates		
	M	F	Total	M	F	Total
Non literate	6	7	13			
Semiliterate	39	55	94			
Functional	43	58	101	43	58	101
Fully literate	49	46	95	49	46	95
Total	137	166	303	92	104	196

Calculating a chi-square independence test on the full set of data for the variables of gender and literacy, we found a nonsignificant result ($x^2 = 2.908$; $df = 3$; $p = 0.406$), indicating no significant difference of distribution between literate males and literate females.

The slightly larger number of literate women reflects what appears to be a slightly larger number of females in the population at large. Also, at the time of our visit, the female population may have been artificially high since a number of young adults (mostly male) were away from the communities studying and working. The analysis indicates, however, that gender is not a significant factor in the acquisition of literacy among the Machiguenga. Numerically, the genders were most unevenly distributed in the semiliterate category. Older wives and mothers who had little opportunity to attend school, and school drop-outs who have let their literacy skills grow rusty may possibly account for some of the discrepancy between men and women in the semiliterate category.

Chapter Summary

This chapter reports individuals' attitudes towards reading and writing. (Eighty-nine percent of respondents believed everyone needs to learn to read, even though they recognize the tensions it can cause.) The Machiguenga concept of literacy is explored, and a retired school teacher lists the uses he makes of reading and writing. Finally, the discussion turns to factors which appear to have influenced literacy retention. For this set of data the only item of statistical significance which could be identified was whether the individual had continued to read much. In the main, age, gender, the number of years readers had attended school, the time elapsed since they had left school, and literacy evidences around their homes showed little or no correlation to meeting preset standards on the Basic, Advance, and Spanish Tests.

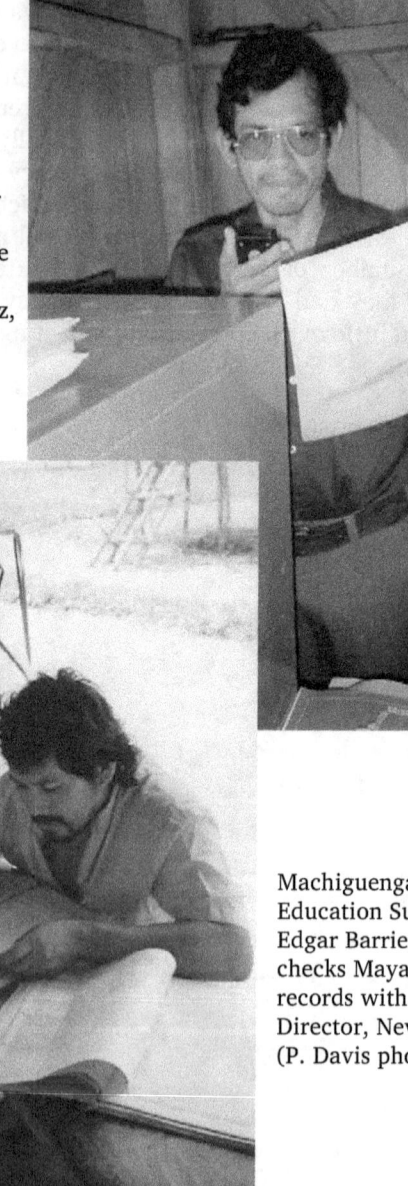

José Pereyra K., Regional Coordinator of Bilingual Education, communicates by ham radio from his isolated jungle office to the district headquarters in the city of Quillabamba.
(P. Davis photo, Nueva Luz, 1992)

Machiguenga Bilingual Education Supervisor Edgar Barrientos K. checks Mayapo school records with school Director, Never Allui.
(P. Davis photo, 1992)

10

Literacy Levels

[They need to know] so that they can read without being ashamed wherever they are.   - Son, House 3, Camisea

Introduction

This chapter focuses upon the educational achievements observed among the Machiguenga at the time of this study. Culturally-adapted evaluation instruments measured the levels of literacy; test results are reported for the sample population as a whole and also by community.

Reading Levels Attained

In order to ascertain what percentage of the population had attained basic (i.e., functional), intermediate, or advanced (full) levels of reading skill, surveys were carried out in seven communities. Four sets of tests were prepared, with the goal of giving readers opportunity to demonstrate their level of reading skill. I hypothesized that, no matter what the level, a truly independent reader would attain minimum scores of:

- 92% (out of 100%) in accuracy.
- 2 (on a scale of 1 to 5) in fluency, i.e., word-by-word reading.

- 3 – (on a scale of 1 to 5) in comprehension, i.e., a scanty recount of the main idea.
- 80 syllables per minute.

The Basic Test contained short readings about everyday matters, potentially drawing on most of the syllable patterns of the language. The Basic Test also contained a list of ten syllables, since ability to read words (or syllables) in isolation was considered to be a possible predictor of reading skill.

Two levels of more difficult text material—the Intermediate and Advanced Tests—were used to test Machiguenga reading. Advanced readers were also tested on Spanish reading ability. These upper-level tests were provided to give more accomplished readers an opportunity to demonstrate their superior skills. A *Met preset standards?* column in the statistical data base indicated whether the participant had

		Codes
a.	declined to take the test, feeling it was too hard	−1
b.	failed to meet all four preset standards	0
c.	taken the test but scored so poorly that the test was disqualified	1
d.	met all four preset standards	2

The Basic Test

Seven individuals were unable to take the Basic Test because of bad eyesight, a disability, or illness; however, all of these were known to be functional readers. Of 118 potential test takers, 53 adults (17.5 percent of the total number of individuals surveyed) declined to take the Basic Test believing it was beyond their skill. One participant could not read Machiguenga, only Spanish; the remainder classified themselves as illiterate or semiliterate. Since peers confirmed their statements, I had no reason to believe these respondents were misrepresenting their abilities.

Sixty-six Basic Tests were administered, but twelve were disqualified. The results of the remaining tests are discussed below.

Accuracy

The following graph in figure 10.1 displays the accuracy scores for the Basic Test.

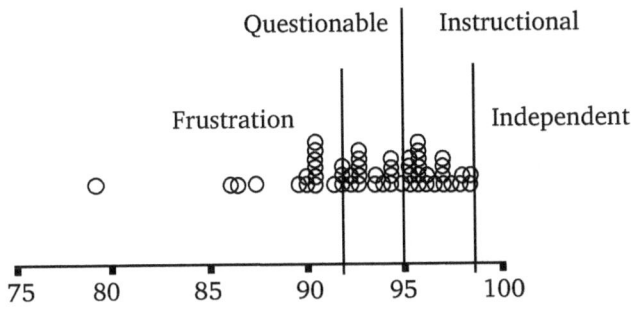

Figure 10.1. Basic Accuracy.

Fifty-four participants took the accuracy portion of the Basic Test. The scores were grouped according to the Betts Informal Reading Inventory scale (which was slightly modified to accommodate my preset minimum standard of 92 percent accuracy).

Modified Betts scale:		Distribution of Basic Test accuracy scores:
99–100%	- Independent level	0
95–99%	- Instructional level	21
92–94%	- Questionable level	16
Below 92%	- Frustration level	17

Fluency

Fluency was measured on a scale of one to five by means of the following categories:

1. Struggling, syllable-by-syllable
2. Reading word-by-word
3. Reading phrase-by-phrase
4. Observance of punctuation
5. Natural, communicative expression

With pluses and minuses to identify the borderline cases, a 14-point scale evolved. For purposes of statistical computation, however, the entire scale had to be converted to numeric values as follows:

Scale		Numeric values	Scale		Numeric values
1	=	0	3+	=	7
1+	=	1	4−	=	8
2−	=	2	4	=	9
2	=	3	4+	=	10
2+	=	4	5−	=	11
3−	=	5	5	=	12
3	=	6	5+	=	12.5

Conversion to numeric values elongated the scale; so when the computer generated frequency polygons to show the distribution of the fluency scores, some unnatural dips resulted. To compensate, both scales will be shown.

The frequency polygon in figure 10.2 displays the fluency scores for the Basic Test.

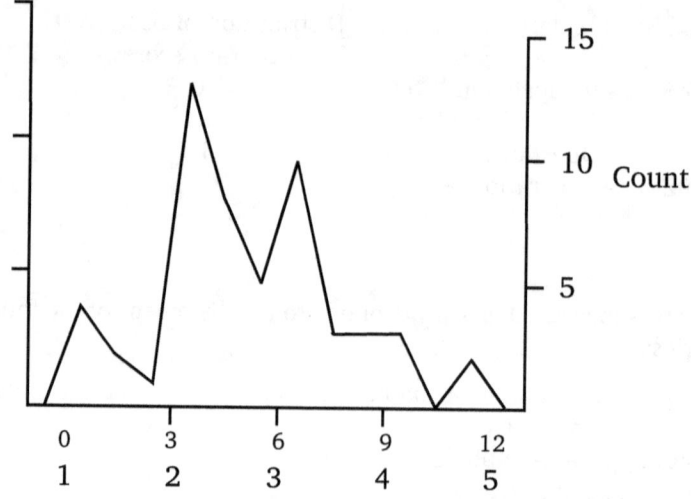

Figure 10.2. Basic fluency.

The spread of scores by community can be seen in table 10.1.

The Basic Test

Table 10.1. Basic Test: Fluency

Fluency scale:	1	1+	2−	2	2+	3−
No. participants per community:	0.0	1.0	2.0	3.0	4.0	5.0
Camisea	1	1	0	4	5	2
Camaná	0	0	0	1	0	0
Mayapo	0	0	0	0	1	1
Pto. Huallana	0	0	0	2	0	0
Segakiato	1	0	1	2	1	2
Shivankoreni	2	1	0	4	1	0
Total participants	4	2	1	13	8	5

Fluency scale:	3	3+	4−	4	5−	
No. participants per community:	6.0	7.0	8.0	9.0	11.0	Total part.
Camisea	5	1	2	2	1	24
Camaná	1	0	0	0	0	2
Mayapo	0	0	0	0	0	2
Pto. Huallana	1	0	1	0	0	4
Segakiato	1	1	0	0	0	9
Shivankoreni	2	1	0	1	1	13
Total participants	10	3	3	3	2	54

On the fluency measure, only seven participants fell below 2, the preset standard representing word-by-word reading. Thirteen participants scored 2 exactly. The remaining thirty-four fell between 2+ and 5− on the scale, with ten of these scoring at a level of 3 (reading phrase-by-phrase).

ANOVA[12] calculations for in-group variation on the fluency scores yielded no significant results ($F = 0.424$; $df = 5, 48$; $p = 0.8297$). Thus, on the Basic Test, levels of fluency appeared to be comparable across communities.

Comprehension

As with the fluency scoring, comprehension was evaluated on a scale of 1 to 5:

1. No demonstrated recall.
2. Poor—fragments of the passage only.

---

[12]In this section and following, refinements and corrections in the statistical analysis have resulted in a somewhat different presentation of the ANOVA and regression analyses than in previous versions of the manuscript.

3. Fair—identified the topic and showed literal understanding of the most important facts.
4. Good—identified the topic, with some elaboration.
5. Excellent—identified the topic and most of the information given in the passage.

In order to include pluses and minuses in the statistical analysis, this 1 to 5 scale was converted to the same numeric scale of 0 to 12.5 as shown above for fluency; both scales are included in the graph. Again, the frequency polygon is expanded by the additional numbers, which accounts for the unnatural dips.

The frequency polygon in figure 10.3 displays the Basic Test comprehension scores.

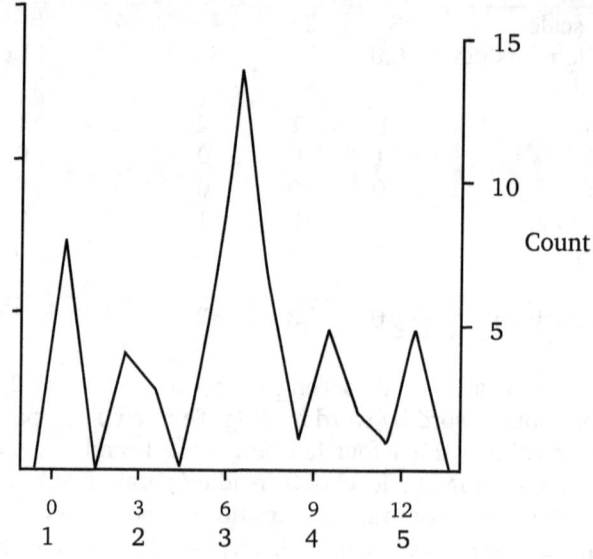

Figure 10.3. Basic comprehension.

The spread of scores by community can be seen in table 10.2:

Table 10.2. Basic Test: Comprehension

Compreh. scale:	1	1+	2	3−	3	3+
No. participants per community:	0.0	2.0	3.0	5.0	6.0	7.0
Camisea	1	3	3	4	6	4
Camaná	0	1	0	0	0	0
Mayapo	0	0	0	0	0	0
Pto. Huallana	0	0	0	1	3	0
Segakiato	5	0	0	0	1	1
Shivankoreni	2	0	0	0	4	1
Total participants	8	4	3	5	14	6

	4−	4	4+	5−	5	
	8.0	9.0	10.0	11.0	12.0	Total
Camisea	0	1	0	1	1	24
Camaná	1	0	0	0	0	2
Mayapo	0	0	1	0	1	2
Pto. Huallana	0	0	0	0	0	4
Segakiato	0	1	1	0	0	9
Shivankoreni	0	3	0	0	3	13
Total participants	1	5	2	1	5	54

Of the fifty-four individuals who were scored on the Basic Test comprehension measure, seven said they could not read the comprehension passage on their own, and although they did answer questions when the passage was read to them, they were assigned a score of 1. Additionally, eight participants scored below the preset minimum of 3− (scanty recall of the main idea). The mode on this test was 3 (solid recall of the main idea), a score attained by fourteen participants. Twenty more individuals scored between 3 and 5.

In order to determine whether there was significant variation among the communities, a one-way ANOVA was calculated, with the following results: ($F = 2.299$; $df = 5, 48$; $p = 0.595$). Here the results did not quite meet the level of significance. We infer from this that comprehension was comparable across communities.

Rate

The Basic Test scores for rate are displayed in the frequency polygon in figure 10.4.

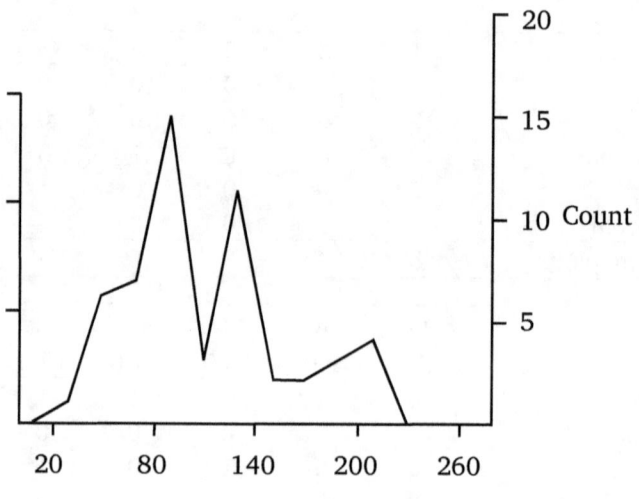

Figure 10.4. Basic rate.

Of the fifty-four Basic Test takers:

- 14 read less than 80 syllables per minute (spm)
- 15 read between 80 and 100 spm
- 15 read between 100 and 150 spm
- 6 read between 150 and 200 spm
- 4 read slightly over 200 spm (up to 204.3 spm)

Number of syllables correct

The following frequency polygon and table display the spread of scores for the list of ten syllables included in the Basic Test.

The Basic Test

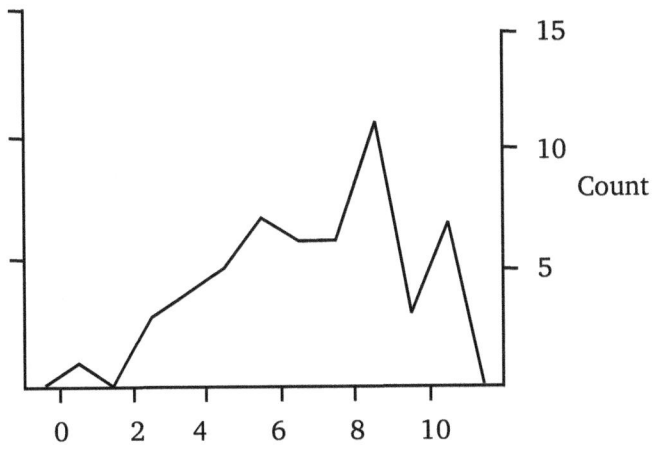

Figure 10.5. Basic syllables.

Table 10.3. Basic Test: Number of syllables correct (out of 10)

Syllables correct:	0.0	2.0	3.0	4.0	5.0	6.0	7.0	8.0	9.0	10.0	
Participants per community:											Total part.
Camisea	0	2	1	2	3	4	1	5	1	3	22
Camaná	0	0	0	0	1	0	1	0	0	0	2
Mayapo	0	0	0	0	0	0	1	1	0	0	2
Pto. Huallana	0	1	0	0	0	0	1	0	0	2	4
Segakiato	0	0	0	0	3	1	1	1	2	1	9
Shivankoreni	0	0	3	3	0	1	1	4	0	1	13
Total participants	0	3	4	5	7	6	6	11	3	7	52

Of fifty-two participants (two more omitted reading the list of ten syllables), nineteen read five or fewer correctly, twelve read six to seven correctly, and twenty-one read eight to ten correctly. I felt that the scores would have been higher had all the participants studied the last syllable book and learned all the syllables of the language. Other participants, perhaps, had forgotten syllables they had once known.

To determine if within-group differences existed between communities, a one-way ANOVA was calculated for the scores on the syllable portion of the Basic Test with nonsignificant results ($F = 0.469$; $df = 5, 46$; $p = 0.797$). These calculations may be conditioned by the fact that in two communities only two people took the Basic Test. Although remote communities have had the most difficulty procuring school books, the analysis did not reflect significant difference overall on the syllable portion of the test.

Met preset standards?

Table 10.4 summarizes the results.

Table 10.4. Basic Test: Met preset standards?

Participants per community:	Declined to take test (too hard)	Test disqualified (too poor to score)	Did not meet standards	Met standards	Subtotal	Disabled
Camisea	11	1	14	10	36	5
Camaná	4	1	1	1	7	0
Chokoriari	6	0	0	0	6	0
Mayapo	6	1	0	2	9	1
Pto. Huallana	4	4	1	3	12	0
Segakiato	16	1	7	2	26	0
Shivankoreni	5	4	6	7	22	1
Total participants	52	12	29	25	118	7

Seven individuals could not take the test because of illness, eye problems, or disability; however, all of these were known to be functional readers. Fifty-three declined to take the test feeling it was too hard for them; thus to a potential group of 118 people, sixty-six Basic Tests were administered. Of these, twelve had to be disqualified because they were too poor to score, and twenty-nine more met from one to three of the preset standards. Of the twenty-nine who failed to meet all four requirements, seventeen were adults—eight men and nine women—most of whom had been out of school for many years. The remaining twelve were students—seven in grade 3, one in grade 4, three in grade 5, and one in grade 6. Grade 3 children were included in the testing because at the end of grade 3, students are expected to be able to read, but, according to information we received, books had been lacking and school schedules had lagged behind, with the result that many grade 3, 4, and 5 students had not yet completed the study of the last syllable primer.

Basic Test participants, students and adults, who were unable to meet all of the preset standards totaled twenty-nine, or 43.93 percent of the sixty-six who took the Basic Test. Reasons for failure to meet the preset standards fell into the following categories:

Accuracy	Fluency	Comprehension	Rate
16	6	15	15

Those who met all four of the preset criteria numbered twenty-five. This is 37.8 percent of the sixty-six who took the Basic Test or 8.25 percent of the entire population surveyed. Of these, fifteen were adults—five men and ten women. The remaining ten were students—four in grade 3, and six in grade 4.

The Intermediate Test

Comparatively few Intermediate Tests were administered—eighteen in three communities. (Two more individuals who potentially should have taken the test were unable to do so, one because of illness, one because of a disability.) Three of the eighteen tests were later disqualified because their score was too poor. The small number was not by design; it was a reflection of my on-the-spot estimation of what participants might be able to do. Although those who failed to meet the preset standards (especially six grade 5 children in Camisea) might better have been given a Basic Test, and those who failed to meet the standards for the Advanced Test might better have been given an Intermediate Test, we had no way of knowing this until after the fact. Unfortunately, time limitations and participant fatigue precluded retests.

Neither analysis of variance (because of the small number) nor chi-square (because it was impossible to know what expected results might be) were appropriate tests for this set of data; thus these tests were not performed.

The results of the testing were as follows.

Accuracy

This graph displays the accuracy scores for the Intermediate Test.

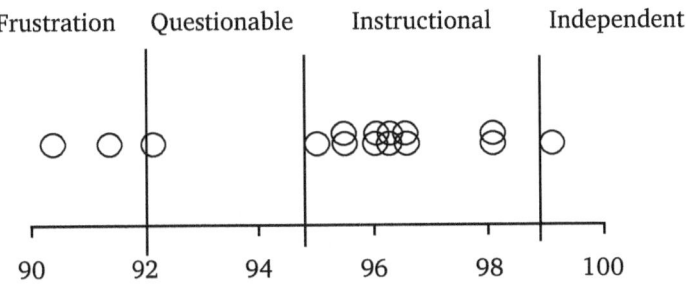

Figure 10.6. Intermediate accuracy.

The spread of scores by community is seen in table 10.5.

Table 10.5. Intermediate Test: Accuracy (percent of syllables correct)

Accuracy level:	90.3	91.5	92.1	95.0	95.4	95.5	95.9	96.2
Participants per community:								
Camisea	1	1	1	1	1	0	2	0
Mayapo	0	0	0	0	0	0	0	1
Shivankoreni	0	0	0	0	0	1	0	0
Total participants	1	1	1	1	1	1	2	1

Accuracy level:	96.3	96.5	96.6	98.0	98.1	99.0	
Participants per community:							Total part.
Camisea	1	1	1	0	1	1	12
Mayapo	0	0	0	0	0	0	1
Shivankoreni	0	0	0	1	0	0	2
Total participants	1	1	1	1	1	1	15

The scores of the fifteen participants who took the Intermediate Test were distributed as follows when compared to the Betts Informal Reading Inventory scale, as modified to accommodate my preset minimum standard.

Modified Betts scale		Distribution - Intermed. Test accuracy scores
99–100%	- Independent level	1
95–99%	- Instructional level	11
92–94%	- Questionable level	1
Below 92%	- Frustration level	2

Fluency

The following frequency polygon displays the fluency scores for the Intermediate Test.

The Intermediate Test

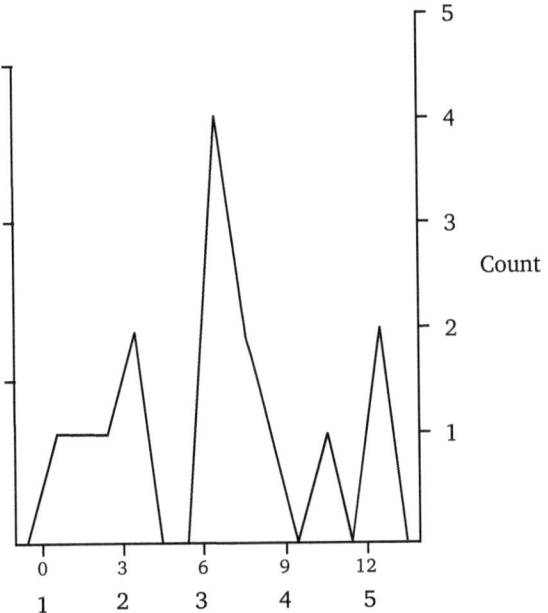

Figure 10.7. Intermediate fluency.

The spread of scores by community is seen in table 10.6.

Table 10.6. Intermediate Test: Fluency

Fluency scale:	1	1+	2−	2	3	3+	4−	4+	5	
Participants per comunity:	0.0	1.0	2.0	3.0	6.0	7.0	8.0	10.0	12.0	Total part.
Camisea	1	1	1	1	2	2	1	1	2	12
Mayapo	0	0	0	0	1	0	0	0	0	1
Shivankoreni	0	0	0	1	1	0	0	0	0	2
Total participants	1	1	1	2	4	2	1	1	2	15

Three participants scored below the preset standard of 2. Two met the minimum standard exactly. Four (the mode) scored 3, and six scored between 3+ and 5.

Comprehension

The frequency polygon in figure 10.8 displays the Intermediate comprehension scores.

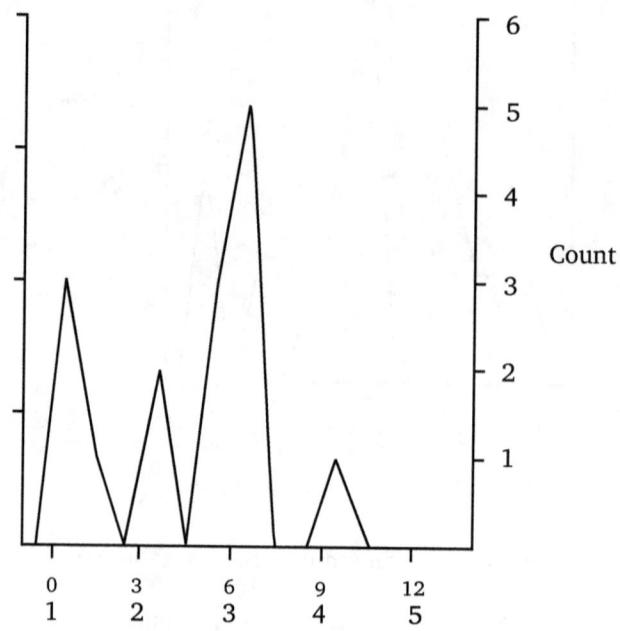

Figure 10.8. Intermediate comprehension.

The spread of scores by community is seen in table 10.7.

Table 10.7. Intermediate Test: Comprehension

Compreh. scale:	1	1+	2	3−	3	4	
Participants per community:	0.0	1.0	3.0	5.0	6.0	9.0	Total part.
Camisea	3	0	1	3	4	1	12
Mayapo	0	1	0	0	0	0	1
Shivankoreni	0	0	1	0	1	0	2
Total participants	3	1	2	3	5	1	15

On comprehension, six participants scored below the preset minimum of 3−; three scored 3− exactly; six scored between 3 and 4.

Rate

The Intermediate Test scores for rate are displayed in the frequency polygon in figure 10.9.

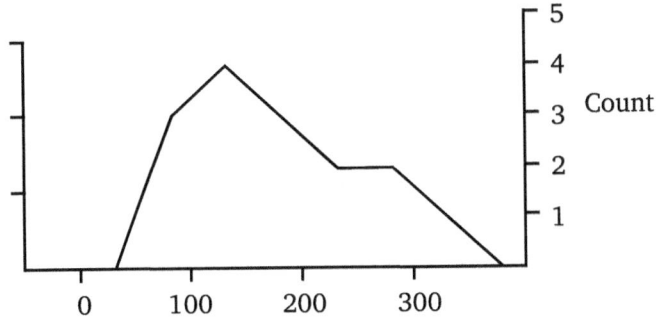

Figure 10.9. Intermediate rate.

The breakdown of the scores by community is seen in table 10.8.

Table 10.8. Intermediate Test: Rate (in syllables per minute)

Rate scale: Participants per community:	64.7	79.1	97.1	129.7	140.4	140.8	143.2	151.2
Camisea	1	1	1	0	1	1	0	1
Mayapo	0	0	0	0	0	0	1	0
Shivankoreni	0	0	0	1	0	0	0	0
Total participants	1	1	1	1	1	1	1	1

	190.0	196.8	201.8	231.8	256.2	259.8	316.5	Total
Camisea	1	1	0	1	1	1	1	12
Mayapo	0	0	0	0	0	0	0	1
Shivankoreni	0	0	1	0	0	0	0	2
Total participants	1	1	1	1	1	1	1	15

Of the fifteen participants who took the Intermediate Test:
    2 scored below the preset minimum of 80 syllables per minute,
    1 scored between 80 and 100 spm
    4 scored between 100 and 150 spm
    3 scored between 150 and 200 spm

3 scored between 200 and 250 spm
2 scored over 250 spm (up to 316.5 spm).

Met preset standards?

Table 10.9 summarizes the results.

Table 10.9. Intermediate Test: Met preset standards?

Participants per community	Test disqualified	Did not meet standards	Met standards	Subtotal	Disabled
Camisea	3	6	6	15	2
Mayapo	0	1	0	1	0
Shivankoreni	0	1	1	2	0
Total participants	3	8	7	18	2

Two individuals were unable to take the test, one because of illness and one because of a disability, but they were known to be functional readers. Eleven of the eighteen who took the Intermediate Test did not meet all four of the preset minimum standards. Of these eleven, three were adult women; seven (three disqualified tests plus four who did not meet standards) were grade 5 students, and one was a grade 6 student. Two participants failed two sections of the test. Failing scores were distributed as follows:

Accuracy	Fluency	Comprehension	Rate
2	3	6	2

The seven participants who did meet standards included one adult woman, and six students—one in grade 4, one in grade 5, and four in grade 6.

The Advanced Test

There were 143 participants who took the Advanced Test: 139 tests were scored; three were too poor to score and were disqualified; one test, although accurate, was read so rapidly it could not be heard well enough to score.

Accuracy

This frequency polygon displays the scores for the Advanced Test.

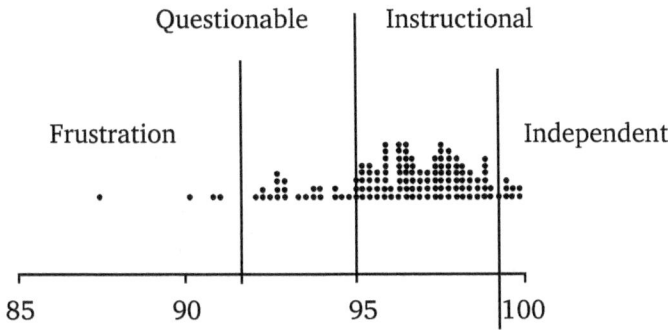

Figure 10.10. Advanced accuracy.

The test results for accuracy for the 139 participants whose Advanced Tests were scored were distributed as follows when compared to the Betts Informal Reading Inventory scale, as modified to accommodate my preset minimum standard of 92 percent accuracy.

Modified Betts scale		Distribution of Advanced Test scores
99–100%	- Independent level	12
95–99%	- Instructional level	102
92–94%	- Questionable level	21
Below 92%	- Frustration level	4

Fluency

This frequency polygon displays fluency scores for the Advanced Test.

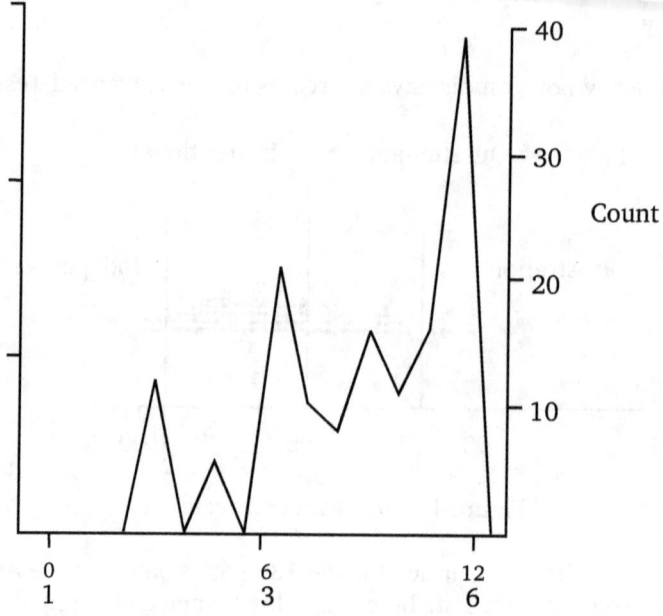

Figure 10.11. Advanced fluency.

The spread of scores by community can be seen in table 10.10.

Table 10.10. Advanced Test: Fluency (Scale of 0 to 12.5)

Fluency scale: Participants per community:	2 3.0	3− 5.0	3 6.0	3+ 7.0	4− 8.0	4 9.0	4+ 10.0	5− 11.0	5 12.0	5+ 12.5	Total part.
Camisea	2	0	8	3	4	7	5	5	19	2	55
Camaná	1	3	2	0	2	3	1	4	7	0	23
Chokoriari	0	1	2	0	1	0	1	3	4	0	12
Mayapo	2	0	0	1	0	1	2	1	2	0	9
Pto. Huallana	4	1	4	4	0	3	2	1	4	0	23
Segakiato	2	1	3	1	1	1	0	1	0	0	10
Shivankoreni	1	0	2	1	0	1	0	1	1	0	7
Total participants	12	6	21	10	8	16	11	16	37	2	139

Of the 139 participants whose Advanced Tests were scored for fluency, none fell below the preset minimum standard of 2. Twelve scored 2 exactly. The mode—a score of 5, representing a close approximation to natural speech—was attained by thirty-seven participants; two very skilled individuals scored a perfect 5+.

The Advanced Test

Wishing to determine if communities differed significantly, an analyses of variance was computed with significant results ($F = 3.079$; $df = 6, 132$; $p = 0.00747$). This result indicated that fluency did vary between communities.

Comprehension

The Advanced Test scores for comprehension are displayed in the following frequency polygon.

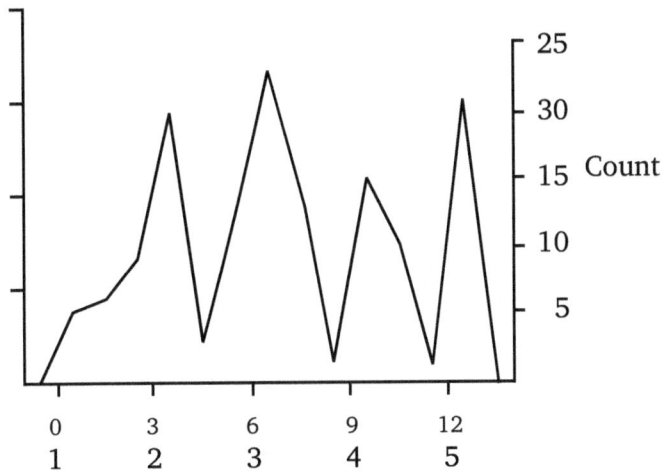

Figure 10.12. Advanced comprehension.

The spread of scores by community can be seen in table 10.11.

Table 10.11 Advanced Test: Comprehension

Compreh. scale:	1	1+	2−	2	2+	3−	3	3+	4−	4	4+	5−	5	
Participants per community:	0	1	2	3	4	5	6	7	8	9	10	11	12	Total part.
Camisea	2	4	2	6	1	6	8	6	0	8	3	1	9	56
Camaná	0	1	2	3	2	3	5	1	0	3	0	0	3	23
Chokoriari	0	0	0	0	0	1	1	4	0	0	3	0	3	12
Mayapo	0	0	1	1	0	0	3	0	1	1	1	0	1	9
Pto. Huallana	0	1	1	4	0	2	5	1	0	2	2	0	5	23
Segakiato	2	0	2	4	0	0	0	1	0	0	0	0	0	9
Shivankoreni	0	0	1	2	0	0	1	1	0	1	1	0	0	7
Total participants	4	6	9	20	3	12	23	14	1	15	10	1	21	139

Of the 139 participants whose Advanced Tests were scored, forty-two failed to meet the minimum standard for comprehension (a score of 3−, which represents a scanty retelling of the main idea). Twelve scored 3− exactly. The mode fell on 3 (a solid recount of the main idea) with twenty-three participants achieving this level. Another sixty-two scored between 7 and 12.

A one-way within-group ANOVA was calculated for the Advanced Test comprehension scores, with significant results ($F = 3.389$; $df = 6, 132$; $p = 0.00377$). This result indicates large variation on the comprehension measure among the seven communities; our observations supported these findings.

Rate

The Advanced Test scores for rate are showed in this frequency polygon.

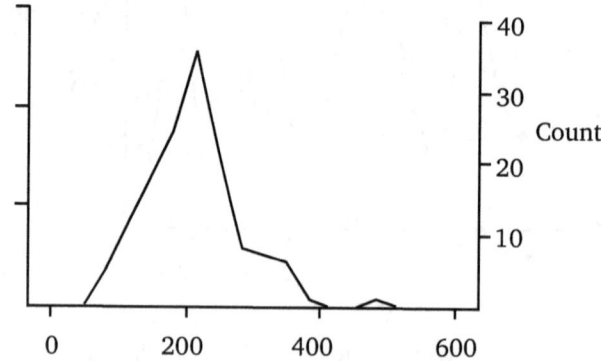

Figure 10.13. Advanced rate.

Of the 139 participants whose Advanced Tests could be scored,

  2 fell below the preset minimum of 80 syllables per minute,
  3 scored between 80 and 100 spm,
 23 scored between 100 and 150 spm,
 31 scored between 150 and 200 spm,
 41 scored between 200 and 250 spm,
 17 scored between 250 and 300 spm,
 10 scored between 300 and 350 spm,
  4 scored between 350 and 400 spm, and
  1 incredible individual read at 492.2 spm. (Although as far as the checkers could tell, this reading was correct, it could not be heard clearly enough to score.)

Met preset standards?

Table 10.12 summarizes the results.

Table 10.12. Advanced Test: Met preset standards?

Participants per community:	Test disqualified	Did not meet standards	Met standards	Subtotal	Misc.
Camisea	1	17	39	57	1
Camaná	0	8	15	23	(Dis-
Chokoriari	0	0	12	12	abled)
Mayapo	0	2	7	9	
Nueva Luz	0	0	1	0	
Pto. Huallana	1	6	17	24	
Segakiato	1	9	1	11	
Shivankoreni	0	4	3	7	
Total participants	3	46	95	144	145

One individual could not take the Advanced Test because of poor eyesight; however, he was known to be a functional reader. One official, who was interviewed but not tested, was counted as having met preset minimum standards because he was known to be one of the best readers in the language group. One hundred forty-three participants actually took the Advanced Test; however, forty-nine readers (forty-six, plus three disqualified) were unable to meet all four of the preset minimum standards. Of the forty-six tests which did not meet standards, twenty-four belonged to adults—six men and eighteen women. Another twenty-two belonged to students—three in grade 6, eight in First Year of secondary, and eleven in Second Year of secondary. Failing scores were distributed as follows:

Accuracy	Fluency	Comprehension	Rate
4	0	43	2

The comprehension scores on all the tests—not only the Advanced reading—were noticeably conditioned by participants' nervousness (too anxious to remember), their shyness (too timid to respond to the questions), and, in a number of cases, by their concentration on speed rather than on meaning. Unfamiliarity with the format (being asked to retell a passage) may also have had some effect on the test scores. However, since almost all of these participants were skilled in the mechanics of reading, under normal, non-test conditions I would expect their "actual" comprehension to be high.

Another ninety-five participants met all four criteria. The group included forty men, one of whom had never attended school (he had taught himself to read with occasional help from family and friends). There were also thirty-three women and twenty-one students—one in grade 5, six in grade 6, two in First Year of secondary, ten in Second Year of secondary, one in Third Year of secondary, and one in Fourth Year of secondary. Additionally, one official (a skilled reader) was included in this grouping, making a total of ninety-five. These accomplished readers formed 31.4 percent of the total population surveyed in this study.

The Spanish Test

One hundred thirty-one of the 143 participants able to read the Advanced Test in Machiguenga were also asked to take a Spanish reading test. (Twelve were not asked to do the Spanish reading, either for lack of time or because they took part in pilot testing of Machiguenga reading tests, when Spanish reading was not yet in focus.) Of the 131, seventeen readers declined to take the Spanish Test; 114 individuals consented to do so. Since, to my knowledge, no standards for Spanish reading have been established, the Spanish reading tests were tape recorded, coded, and scored in the same way as the Machiguenga reading tests, using the same criteria for accuracy, fluency, comprehension, and rate.

Accuracy

The following graph charts the accuracy scores for the Spanish Test.

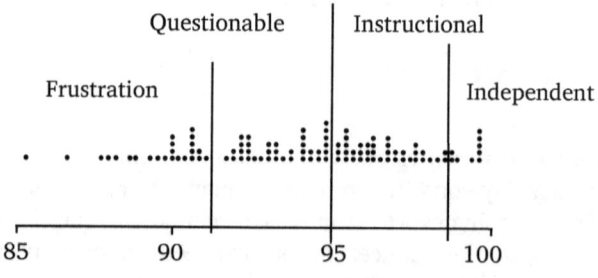

Figure 10.14. Spanish accuracy.

The accuracy scores of the 114 participants who took the Spanish Test were distributed as follows when compared to the Betts Informal Reading

The Spanish Test

Inventory scale, as modified to accommodate my preset minimum standard of 92 percent accuracy.

Modified Betts scale		Distribution–Spanish Test accuracy scores
99–100%	- Independent level	9
95–99%	- Instructional level	41
92–94%	- Questionable level	36
Below 92%	- Frustration level	28

Fluency

This frequency polygon displays the fluency scores for the Spanish Test.

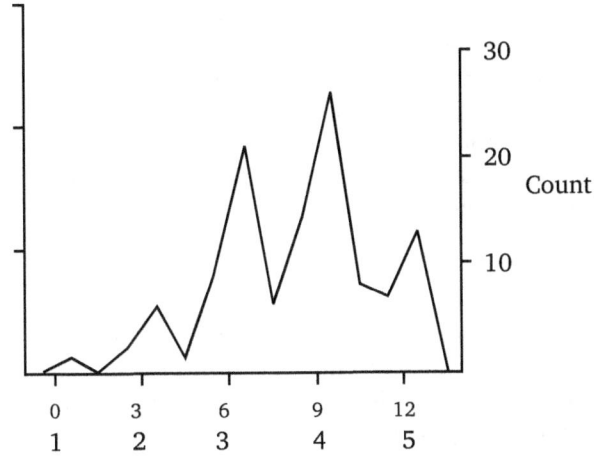

Figure 10.15. Spanish fluency.

The spread of scores by community can be seen in table 10.13.

Table 10.13. Spanish Test: Fluency

Fluency scale:	1	2−	2	2+	3−	3	3+	4−	4	4+	5−	5	
Participants per community:	0	2	3	4	5	6	7	8	9	10	11	12	Total part.
Camisea	0	0	0	0	3	6	0	5	11	6	7	8	46
Camaná	0	0	4	0	0	5	3	3	3	0	0	2	20
Chokoriari	0	0	0	1	1	0	0	0	5	1	0	2	10
Mayapo	0	0	1	0	0	0	0	0	5	0	0	0	6
Pto. Huallana	1	1	0	0	1	5	2	4	1	1	0	1	17
Segakiato	0	1	0	0	1	3	1	2	0	0	0	0	8
Shivankoreni	0	0	1	0	3	2	0	0	1	0	0	0	7
Total participants	1	2	6	1	9	21	6	14	26	8	7	13	114

Only three of the 114 who took the Spanish Test scored below 2, the preset standard representing word-by-word reading; six others scored 2. Twenty-one scored at level 3 and fourteen more at 4−. The mode for fluency—level 4—was attained by twenty-six participants. Twenty-eight test takers scored between levels 10 and 12.

A one-way ANOVA for homogeneity of the seven communities was calculated. It yielded highly significant results ($F = 5.8$; $df = 5, 107$; $p = 0.0000$), indicating that variation does exist between communities on the fluency dimension of the Spanish reading test. Our field observations suggested that Spanish reading fluency in Camisea and Camaná was on a par. This was surprising since Camaná is the most remote of the villages visited; however, it has had a very good teacher. Others of the remote communities scored considerably lower. In Camisea, the higher scores may be attributable to increased contact with the outside world, for it has long been a hub for travel and now has a secondary school.

Comprehension

The following frequency polygon displays the Spanish Test comprehension scores.

The Spanish Test

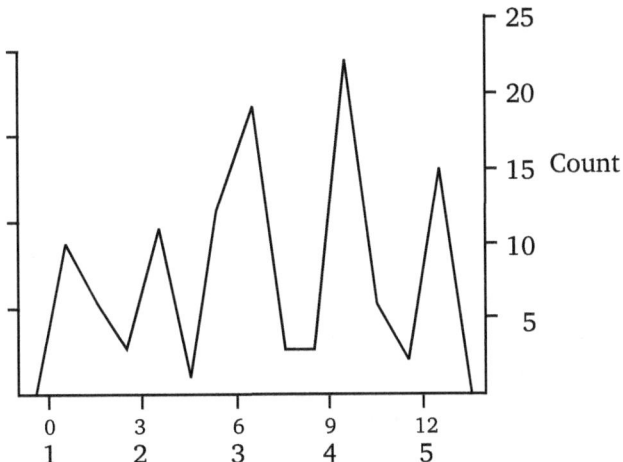

Figure 10.16. Spanish comprehension.

The spread of scores by community can be seen in table 10.14.

Table 10.14. Spanish Test: Comprehension

Compreh. scale Participants per community	1 0	1+ 1	2− 2	2 3	2+ 4	3− 5	3 6	3+ 7	4− 8	4 9	4+ 10	5− 11	5 12	Total part.
Camisea	2	2	1	2	0	3	9	0	3	12	3	2	7	46
Camaná	3	2	0	4	0	2	2	0	0	2	2	0	3	20
Chokoriari	1	0	0	1	0	1	0	1	0	4	0	0	2	10
Mayapo	0	0	0	1	0	2	0	0	0	2	1	0	0	6
Pto. Huallana	2	1	2	1	0	1	3	2	0	2	0	0	3	17
Segakiato	2	0	0	2	1	0	3	0	0	0	0	0	0	8
Shivankoreni	0	1	0	0	0	4	2	0	0	0	0	0	0	7
Total participants	10	6	3	11	1	13	19	3	3	22	6	2	15	114

On the Spanish Test comprehension measure, thirty-one individuals did not meet the preset minimum standard of 3− (representing a scanty recount of the main idea); thirteen scored 3− exactly, and nineteen scored 3 (solid recount of the main idea). The mode fell at level 4, a score attained by twenty-two participants; twenty-three more test takers scored between 4+ and 5.

When a one-way ANOVA was calculated for community variation, the results were significant ($F = 2.374$; $df = 6, 107$; $p = 0.0342$), confirming our field observation that considerable difference existed between communities as regards their ability to comprehend the Spanish Test passage.

Rate

The Spanish Test scores for rate are displayed in this frequency polygon.

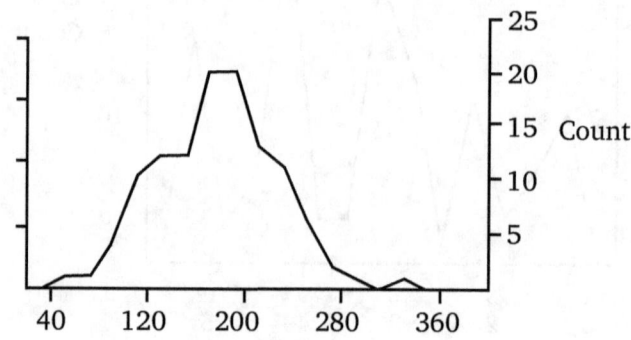

Figure 10.17. Spanish rate.

Of the 114 Spanish Test takers,

> 2 scored below 80 syllables per minute,
> 4 scored between 80 and 100 spm,
> 30 scored between 100 and 150 spm,
> 44 scored between 150 and 200 spm,
> 28 scored between 200 and 250 spm,
> 5 scored between 250 and 300 spm,
> 1 read at a rate of 334 spm.

Met preset standards?

Table 10.15 summarizes the results.

Table 10.15. Spanish Test: Met preset standards?

Participants per community:	Declined to take the test (too hard)	Did not meet standards	Met standards	Total part.
Camisea	2	11	35	48
Camaná	2	12	8	22
Chokoriari	0	3	7	10
Mayapo	3	2	4	9
Pto. Huallana	7	8	9	24
Segakiato	2	6	2	10
Shivankoreni	1	3	4	8
Total participants	17	45	69	131

Seventeen advanced readers declined to take the Spanish Test, feeling it was too hard for them—four men, nine women, and four students (one in grade 5, two in grade 6, and one in First Year Secondary). Interestingly, many of these felt quite able to read the material aloud, giving us to understand that Spanish is considered easier to read than Machiguenga, but they knew that they would not understand it.

Of the 114 who courageously took the test, forty-five were unable to meet all four preset minimum standards. Of these, thirty were adults—thirteen men and seventeen women. The remaining fifteen were students—one in grade 5, five in grade 6, three in First Year of secondary, six in Second Year of secondary. Failing scores were distributed as follows:

Accuracy	Fluency	Comprehension	Rate
27	3	32	2

Those who did meet the standards numbered sixty-nine, which is 60.52 percent of the Spanish Test takers and 22.77 percent of the entire population surveyed. Of these, forty-nine were adults—twenty-seven men and twenty-two women. The remaining twenty were students—two in grade 6, four in First Year of secondary, twelve in Second Year of secondary, one in Third Year of secondary, and one in Fourth Year of secondary.

Community Literacy Levels

To answer the question, "Are reading levels uniform among communities?" the scores were standardized and averaged to yield the following profile. Participants fell into four groups: nonliterate, semiliterate, functionally literate, and fully literate.

Table 10.16. Community Literacy Levels

Community	Non-literate		Semi-literate		Functional		Fully literate		Total literates	
	N	%	N	%	N	%	N	%	N	%
Camisea	2	1.7	26	22.0	51	43.2	39	33.0	90	76.3
Camaná	4	11.8	6	17.6	9	26.5	15	44.1	24	70.6
Chokoriari	1	5.3	6	31.6	0	0.0	12	63.1	12	63.1
Mayapo	1	4.8	8	38.1	5	23.8	12	33.3	12	57.1
Pto. Huallana	0	0.0	9	25.0	10	27.8	17	47.2	27	75.0
Segakiato	2	5.1	24	61.5	12	30.8	1	2.6	13	33.3
Shivankoreni	3	8.6	15	42.8	14	40.0	3	8.6	17	48.6

Thus, the literacy levels of the communities studied varied from 76.3 percent in Camisea to 33.3 percent in Segakiato. Three communities, two of them isolated, had literacy rates of over 70 percent. Teacher competence appeared to be the major factor contributing to the differences.

A Summary of the Results

The standardized and averaged scores yielded the following summary, which is comparatively high for an ethnolinguistic group of Amazonia. Again, the participants fell into four groups: nonliterate, semiliterate, functionally literate, and fully literate.

A Summary of the Results

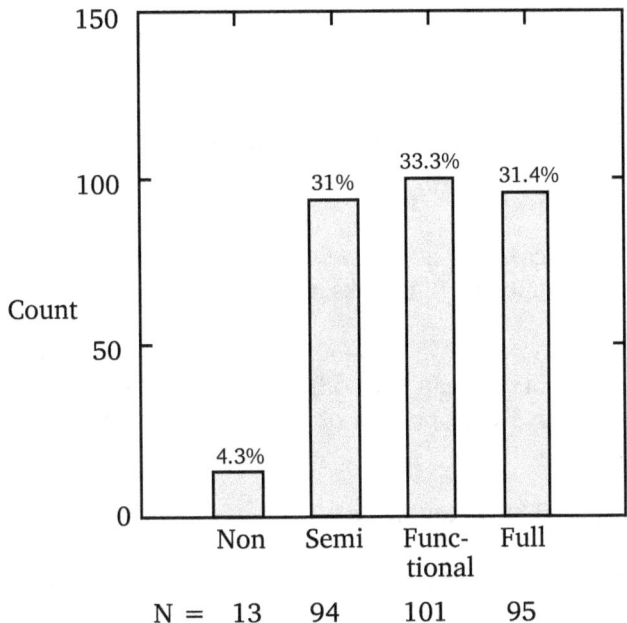

Figure 10.18. Literacy level—Machiguenga communities.

Nonliterate adults—Of the population surveyed 4.3 percent had never had literacy instruction of any kind and did not know how to read or write.

Semiliterates—Of the population surveyed 31 percent—twenty-two primary school children and seventy-two adults—were semiliterate.

The *children* (seven enrolled in grade 3, seven in grade 4, six in grade 5, and two in grade 6) were in the process of learning how to read but had not yet acquired sufficient skills to meet the preset minimum standards for the Basic level test which was administered as part of the reading survey. They composed 23.4 percent of the semiliterate category.

The semiliterate *adults* subdivided into three groups: (1) Thirty-two (34 percent of the semiliterate total) who had not attended school but had enrolled in adult literacy classes. Most of these participants had acquired a few skills, but no one from the adult literacy classes had become an independent reader. (2) Twenty-seven adults who had attended school but were unable to meet standards on the Basic Test. (3) Thirteen adults who had attended school before 1980 for varying amounts of time and later as adults had also attended adult literacy classes. Although they averaged 15.7 months each of adult literacy instruction, they had not developed sufficient skill to meet the requirements of the Basic reading test.

Functional literates, formed a category composed of readers from three different levels:

1. Those who met the preset standards for the Basic Test.
2. Those who were able to take the Intermediate Test.
3. Those who attempted, but failed, to meet all of the standards of the Advanced Test.

These 101 participants—33.3 percent of the population surveyed—can handle most common reading tasks, given enough time and, occasionally, some help.

Full literates were those who met all of the criteria for the Advanced Test and were able to read very difficult material with comprehension. Ninety-five adults—31.4 percent of the population surveyed—qualified for this category.

Literates by UNESCO standards

According to the UNESCO (1983) definition, a literate is "a person who can with understanding both read and write a short, simple text on his everyday life" (p.3). By that definition, I estimate that at least twenty-eight more individuals from my sampling would have classified as functional literates. I did not test writing for Basic readers, but the assumption among the Machiguenga is that whatever one can read, one can write (although, at Basic level, writing may be slow and spelling is not guaranteed). By these criteria, the literacy graph would then be as follows:

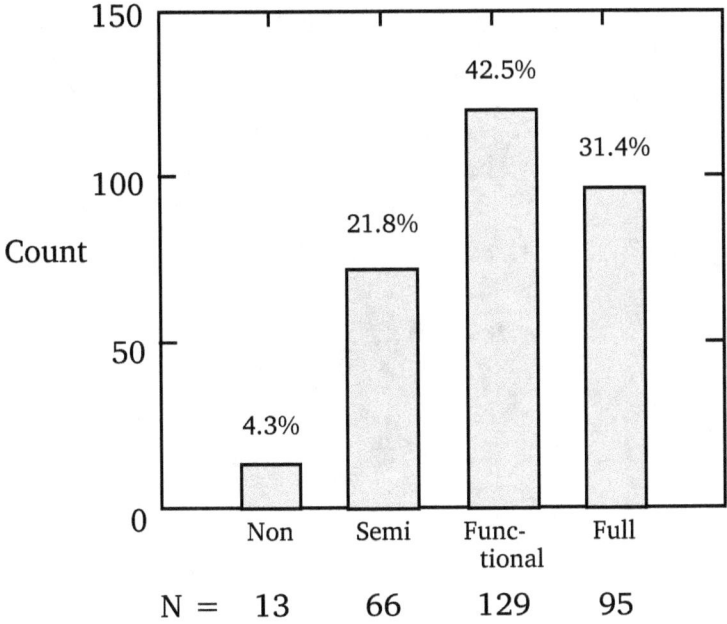

Figure 10.19. Literacy level—by UNESCO standards.

Thus, 224 individuals out of 303 would have classified as literates—that is a literacy rate of 73.9 percent.

Chapter Summary

This chapter presents the results of the reading tests. In a sampling of 303 individuals in seven communities, the literacy rates ranged from 33.3 percent in Segakiato to 76.3 percent in Camisea. Overall, thirteen (4.3 percent) of the population surveyed were found to be totally nonliterate; ninety-four (31 percent) were semiliterate; 101 (33.3 percent) were functionally literate, and ninety-five (31.4 percent) were fully literate, able to read the most difficult material available in their language and still meet preset standards for accuracy, fluency, comprehension and rate. This is a literacy rate of 64.7 percent. By more generous UNESCO standards, the literacy rate could be considered to be 73.9 percent.

Above: Parents in Mantara Chico cooperate in constructing the school building.

Below: Camaná students line up for morning exercises—flag raising, health inspection, announcements. (P. Davis photos)

11

Interpreting the Findings

Before I entered school, I could not read; neither could my father. But when the school came and brought books, I was able to attend. Now I am learning. That is good. School is good for learning Machiguenga and for learning Spanish. It is good for knowing things, for being able to read and answer letters, for holding community office...
— Father, House 6, Camaná

Introduction

During the testing we gained many interesting insights from the test results, but we also learned about the tests themselves. The main body of this chapter discusses significant items gleaned from our statistical findings. A final section comments on the procedural questions of the study: whether preset standards were appropriate; whether the instruments developed did in fact access the core data in culturally appropriate ways, and whether assessment procedures proved feasible under village conditions.

Met Standards—All Tests

Of the 303 people included in the survey, sixty-six were given the Basic level test, eighteen were given the Intermediate Test, and 143 were given the Advanced Test. One hundred fourteen of the Advanced readers also took a test in Spanish reading. The overall statistical summary is shown in table 11.1.

Table 11.1. Overall summary

Total observations: 303   Nonliterate adults: 13

Tests	Accuracy	Fluency	Comprehension	Rate	Met preset standards?	Syllables correct	Disqualified	Miscellaneous
Basic Test	BA	BF	BC	BR	BMet?	BSyll	Disqu.	Misc.
No. of cases	54.0	54.0	54.0	54.0	25.0	53.0	12.0	6.0 (Disabled)
Minimum	79.1	0.0	0.0	38.6		0.0		
Maximum	98.4	11.0	12.0	204.3		10.0		
Range	19.3	11.0	12.0	165.7		10.0	53.0 (Declined*)	
Mean	93.3	4.7	5.8	110.3		6.3		
Standard dev.	3.6	2.6	3.6	45.0		2.5		

Basic Test Total: 125

Intermediate Test	IA	IF	IC	IR	IMet?	Disqu.	Misc.
No. of cases	15.0	15.0	15.0	15.0	7.0	3.0	2.0 (Disabled)
Minimum	90.3	0.0	0.0	64.7			
Maximum	99.0	12.0	9.0	316.5			
Range	8.7	12.0	9.0	251.8			
Mean	95.4	5.9	4.1	173.3			
Standard dev.	2.4	3.7	2.7	71.6			

Intermediate Test Total: 20

Advanced Test	AA	AF	AC	AR	AMet?	Disqu.	Misc.
No. of cases	139.0	139.0	140.0	139.0	95.0	3.0	1.0 (Disabled)
Minimum	87.4	3.0	0.0	72.2			
Maximum	100.0	12.5	12.0	492.2			
Range	12.6	9.5	12.0	420.0			1.0 (Official)
Mean	96.4	8.8	6.4	211.3			
Standard dev.	2.2	2.9	3.5	69.1			

Advanced Test Total: 145

Spanish Test**	SA	SF	SC	SR	SMet?	Disqu.	
No. of cases	114.0	114.0	114.0	114.0	69.0	17.0 (Declined)*	
Minimum	81.0	0.0	0.0	50.1			
Maximum	100.0	12.0	12.0	334.0			
Range	19.0	12.0	12.0	283.9			
Mean	94.0	7.9	6.4	176.0			
Standard dev.	3.8	2.7	3.7	49.9			

Spanish Test Total: 131

* Declined: These participants declined to take the test because they felt unable to do the required tasks.
** The same individuals took both the Advanced Test and the Spanish Test.

This summary shows a mean for the Basic reading test of 93.3 percent accuracy, 4.7 fluency (equivalent to 2+ on my scale of 1 to 5), 5.8 comprehension (equivalent to 3 on my scale of 1 to 5), and a rate of 110 syllables per minute—scores above the preset minimums. However, the mean for the Basic Test "Met preset standards?" column reflects the fact that comparatively few of the beginning readers who took the Basic Test met all four preset minimums. The means for the Intermediate and Advanced Test improved over the Basic Test scores in all categories except Intermediate comprehension, which dropped a point below the preset standard, chiefly because six grade 5 students who took the Intermediate Test found it too hard. (They should have been given a Basic Test.) I interpret the general improvement on the more difficult tests as a sign of greater reading maturity.

Means for the Spanish Test dropped below the Advanced Test levels in four of the five categories, as can be expected for second-language material, but accuracy, fluency, comprehension, and rate still remained well above the preset minimum standards.

Critiquing the Scores

What did the test scores really indicate? A more detailed summary of the scores is shown in table 11.2.

Table 11.2. Detailed summary

Basic Test

Accuracy levels in percent	No. of participants	Met all standards	Reason, if standards were not met:*				
			Low accuracy	Low fluency	Low comprehension	Low Rate	Low syllables
99–100%	0	—					
95–98%	22	14	0	3	7	4	
92–94%	15	10	0	0	3	2	3
90–92%	10	0	9	2	4	4	2
79.1–90%	7	0	7	3	2	4	5
Totals	54	24	16	8	16	14	10

Intermediate Test

99–100%	1	1					
95–98%	11	5	0	2	5	1	
92–94%	1	1					
90–92%	0	0					
90.3–92%	2	0	2	1	1	1	
Totals	15	7	2	3	6	2	

Advanced Test

99–100%	12	11	0	0	1	0	
95–98%	102	76	0	0	25	0	
92–94%	21	7	0	0	11	1	
90–92%	3	0	3	0	2	0	
87.4–90%	1	0	1	0	0	0	
Totals	139	94	4	0	39	1	

* Since some participants had low scores in more than one domain, the sum of the low scores surpasses the number of participants.

The accuracy scores

To reach an accuracy score, the number of syllables for each text was counted and recorded. After the reading, deviations from the written text (omissions, insertions, substitutions, corrections attempted, and corrections achieved) were coded, and counted (by syllables) to arrive at an error total. This procedure was tedious but possible to accomplish with a fairly high degree of precision as demonstrated by a high consensus between raters. The error total was then divided by the total number of syllables and multiplied by 100 to arrive at a calculation of the percentage of syllables read accurately.

Of equal concern, however, was the question as to whether the minimum standards for accuracy were correctly set. I also wondered if low accuracy might correspond to low comprehension. Analysis of the scores is revealed in table 11.3.

Table 11.3. Basic Test—Low accuracy compared with low comprehension

Accuracy levels in percent	No. of participants	Met all standards	Low accuracy	Low comprehension
99–100%	0	—		
95–98%	22	14	0	7
92–94%	15	10	0	3
90–92%	10	0	9	4
79.1–90%	7	0	7	2
Totals	54	24	16	16

Of the thirty who did not meet standards on the Basic Test, sixteen evidenced low comprehension. Nine of these participants read at rates below 80 spm; three read over 200 spm, suggesting that extremely slow and extremely fast reading can affect understanding. Only six of the seventeen who read below 92 percent accuracy evidenced lack of comprehension, however. Low accuracy occurred simultaneously with low comprehension in only five cases.

The Basic Test readers who fell below the 92 percent accuracy mark demonstrated much of the reading behavior characteristic of semiliterates—slow rate, often syllable-by-syllable or word-by-word production without natural phrase and clause breaks, sighs, frequent repetitions, and many attempted corrections.

The sampling size for the Intermediate Test was too small to be definitive, but six of the eight participants who failed to meet the preset standards experienced difficulty with comprehension. Of these, one read at a very slow rate; two others read over 200 spm. The extremes of speed may have affected the comprehension of these three participants. Low accuracy occurred simultaneously with low comprehension in only one case.

Of the two readers who fell below the 92 percent accuracy level, one met the preset comprehension standard; the other did not.

Table 11.4. Intermediate Test—Low accuracy compared with low comprehension

Accuracy levels in percent	No. of participants	Met all standards	Low accuracy	Low comprehension
99–100%	1	1		
95–98%	11	5	0	5
92–94%	1	1		
90–92%	2	0	2	1
Totals	15	7	2	6

Forty-five of the participants who took the Advanced Test did not meet the four preset standards. At this level, speeds above 200 spm may have influenced the thirteen participants who did not meet comprehension standards. However, it is hard to know who was affected since forty-six comprehending readers read at 200 spm or above. Of the four who fell below the 92 percent accuracy level, lack of comprehension was evident in only two cases.

Table 11.5. Advanced Test—Low accuracy compared with low comprehension

Accuracy levels in percent	No. of participants	Met all standards	Low accuracy	Low comprehension
99–100%	12	11	0	1
95–98%	102	76	0	25
92–94%	21	7	0	11
90–92%	3	0	3	2
87.4–90%	1	0	1	0
Totals	139	94	4	39

Eleven percent of Basic readers and 33 percent of Intermediate and Advanced readers who achieved accuracy scores higher than the minimum still had difficulty with comprehension. As noted previously, I judge that anxiety, shyness, rate extremes, and—perhaps occasionally—lack of understanding of the task skewed the comprehension scores. However, many of these individuals belonged within the levels labeled questionable and instructional by Ekwall and Shanker (1988); at these levels reading maturity is not yet fully developed.

Thus, although accuracy scores could be plotted, they appeared to reflect an approximate area of ability rather than a precise level. For example, one adult (Mother, House 11, Camisea) who scored 91.3 percent in accuracy, and therefore by my standards had to be classified as a semi-literate, achieved very satisfactory ratings on all other measures (4+ in fluency, 3+ in comprehension, and 98.2 syllables per minute in rate). With her, as with several other readers, the 92 percent dividing line seemed arbitrary. Further testing might have permitted a finer-tuned assessment.

Composite accuracy scores presented a maturation profile such as one would expect. For Basic Test takers the mean was 93.3 percent; for Intermediate Test takers, 95.4 percent, and for Advanced Test takers, 96.4 percent. This improvement in accuracy scores occurred even though the difficulty level of each test increased, evidence of developing reading skill. The mean accuracy level for the Spanish Test given to advanced-level readers dipped to 94 percent; however, this is not surprising for second-language material. The salient mistake accounting for a large proportion of the errors in the Spanish readings was the omission of the letter *s* in word-final position. The letter *s* does not occur word-finally in Machiguenga, and thus is hard to pronounce. The omission of word-final *n* (also foreign to Machiguenga) accounted for another large segment of the errors. Had these two errors been counted only once per reading instead of each time they occurred, the accuracy scores would have been considerably higher.

The fluency scores

Fluency was rated on a scale of one to five (which in order to include plus and minus values was expanded for the purposes of statistical computation from 0 to 12.5). The elements—syllable by syllable, word by word, phrase by phrase, punctuation observance, and natural, communicative expression—were not mutually exclusive. Rather, the rater sought to determine the degree to which all of the components were harmoniously blended. The task was complicated by the fact that rather than one level of fluency, two or three levels were frequently in evidence. Readers usually began with ease, having practiced and memorized the beginning part of the passage. Upon reaching less familiar material, many began to stumble, sound out words, and repeat, dropping back to characteristic behaviors of less experienced readers. Their lack of skill became increasingly evident as the reading progressed, the material became even less familiar, and minds tired under the stress of production.

Under these circumstances, it was difficult to assign one fluency score, but a serious attempt was made to give a rating which best represented the reading as a whole. The scores should be considered somewhat subjective, even though interrater comparison showed a satisfactory level of agreement.

As in the case of accuracy, fluency scores improved with increased reading maturity, even though the difficulty of the text increased. On a scale of 1 to 5, means for the Basic Test were 2+ (4.7 on the numerical scale), for the Intermediate Test almost 3 (5.9 on the numerical scale), for the Advanced Test 4− (8.8 on the numerical scale). The mean for the Spanish Test was almost 4− (7.9 on the numerical scale).

The comprehension scores

Comprehension scores were the most difficult to assign and—as reading specialists warn (May and Eliot 1978:144; Bond et al. 1989:118)—are at best imprecise. Many readers who did not meet minimum standards on the comprehension test simply did not respond due to nervousness or shyness; others whose excellent mechanical skills indicated that they were well able to understand the reading could not recall the passage because they had concentrated on speed instead of on meaning. Other recounts were so different from the text that they were hard to assess, and still other readers appeared to draw more on general knowledge than on passage content once they had recognized the topic.

Means for comprehension scores (on a scale of 0 to 12.5) began at 3 (6 on the numerical scale) for Basic Test takers, dropped to 2+ (4.1 on the numerical scale) for Intermediate Test takers, rose to 3 (6.4 on the numerical scale) for Advanced Test takers, and remained at 3 (6.4) for Spanish Test takers. The drop in score for Intermediate Test takers reflects the fact that several grade 5 students were given Intermediate Tests which were too hard for them, when they should have had Basic Tests instead. They would have undoubtedly met standards on an easier test.

Over all, my conclusion has been that many of the comprehension scores suggest capabilities lower than those actually possessed by readers. Perhaps our instructions should have stated more emphatically that comprehension was more important than speed; but under the strain of the test situation I noticed that some readers still read too fast, even after being warned. Under non-test conditions I would expect that understanding would, in a number of cases, be higher than the level indicated by these scores.

Critiquing the Scores

The rate scores

With a stop watch, rate could be easily and precisely recorded. The major difficulty encountered was the tendency of some participants to concentrate on speed rather than on meaning. We sought to prevent this problem by explaining that speed was not the goal and that we would request a recount of the passage—a procedure I recommend. Under the pressure of the test situation, however, not everyone seemed able to understand and act upon this instruction. The following displays show how rate related to comprehension:

Table 11.6. Basic Test—Rate related to comprehension

Accuracy levels in percent	No. of participants	Met all standards	Low comprehension	Low Rate
99–100%	0	—		
95–98%	22	14	7	4
92–94%	15	10	3	2
90–92%	10	0	4	4
79.1–90%	7	0	2	4
Totals	54	24	16	14

Table 11.7. Intermediate Test—Rate related to comprehension

Accuracy levels in percent	No. of participants	Met all standards	Low comprehension	Low Rate
99–100%	1	1		
95–98%	11	5	5	1
92–94%	1	1		
90–92%	2	0	1	1
Totals	15	7	6	2

Table 11.8. Advanced Test—Rate related to comprehension

Accuracy levels in percent	No. of participants	Met all standards	Low comprehension	Low Rate
99–100%	12	11	1	0
95–98%	102	76	25	0
92–94%	21	7	11	1
90–92%	3	0	2	0
87.4–90%	1	0	0	0
Totals	139	94	39	1

Here we see that on the Basic Test the number of low comprehension scores and low rate scores are nearly equal (sixteen and fourteen, respectively). The proportion decreased on the Intermediate Test—six low comprehension scores to two low rate scores. On the Advanced Test, the effect of low rate was negligible—thirty-nine low comprehension scores and only one low rate score. These figures suggest that low rate may be most closely related to low comprehension at beginning levels, but not at some advanced levels.

Rate increased notably with reading maturity. Note table 11.9.

Table 11.9. Summary of rate and comprehension

	Mean rate in spm	Range of rate for comprehending readers
Basic Test	110.0 spm	66.0–202.3 spm
Intermediate Test	173.2 spm	64.7–259.8 spm
Advanced Test	211.2 spm	72.2–385.5 spm
Spanish Test	176.0 spm	80.0–334.0 spm

The decrease in mean for the Spanish Test reflected the increased difficulty of second-language material.

Syllable recognition

I hoped to discover if ability to read syllables (especially closed syllables, which are the most difficult and most of which are learned last) might be a predictor of reading success. To this end, the syllable list included six (out of ten) closed syllables. Regression analysis showed the following correlation:

$N = 53$ Coefficients: Constant $= -1.609$
$r = 0.733$ Slope $= 0.154$

A T-test for the significance of the correlation yielded:
$T = 7.6947$ $df = 51$ $p = 0.0000$

These results provide strong evidence that ability to read isolated syllables correlates highly with ability to read whole passages. They supported my intuition that knowledge of closed syllables is important to Machiguenga readers and that it is necessary for teachers to complete the teaching of the third primer in order for students to be successful with unrestricted reading material.

Camisea versus the Other Communities

Because the community of Camisea comprised approximately 40 percent of the sample (a larger representation than for any other community), it was necessary to determine if the scores in Camisea resembled those of the other villages or might have distorted the overall sample. A number of statistical tests were run in order to determine (a) whether variation between communities was significant and (b) whether scores in Camisea could be considered representative of the entire Machiguenga community.

Table 11.10. Distribution of measured fluency and comprehension skills among the Machiguenga community

	ANOVA Within the entire group is there variation?			T-tests (inclusive) Camisea compared to the entire sample, Camisea included			T-tests (exclusive) Camisea compared to the other communities as a set		
Basic Test									
	F	df	p	T	df	p	T	df	p
Fluency	0.424	5, 48	0.8297	0.805	76	0.432	1.302	52	0.1987
Comprehension	2.299	5, 48	0.0595	0.388	76	0.699	0.585	52	0.5590
Advanced Test									
	F	df	p	T	df	p	T	df	p
Fluency	3.079	6, 132	.00747	1.737	192	.0839	2.602	137	.002
Comprehension	3.398	6, 132	.00377	.293	193	.7698	0.420	137	.652
Spanish Test									
	F	df	p	T	df	p	T	df	p
Fluency	5.800	6, 107	.0000	2.983	155	.0033	4.747	112	.00000
Comprehension	2.374	6, 107	.0342	1.761	158	.0802	2.712	112	.00774

Table 11.10 contains the results of an investigation of two educational outcomes seen in Camisea when compared to those of the entire Machiguenga population included in our sample. The variables fluency and comprehension were selected as being proxies for the full set of educational variables included in the study.

Three different statistical measures were examined in order to refine our insight into the distribution of these skills. First, an ANOVA was done for each variable separately in order to assess the level of difference between each of the test communities for the distribution of fluency and of comprehension. Second, a T-test was done comparing the village of Camisea to the entire sample in order to assess the similarity of this one village to the entire sample. Third, another T-test was done comparing Camisea to the Machiguenga sample, with the data for Camisea removed. This second comparison was done to accentuate any areas of contrast between Camisea and the other villages.

An examination of the chart reveals considerable variation in the distribution of educational skills in the Machiguenga community. In the Basic Test, for example, there were no statistically significant differences between any of the communities. This suggests a high level of homogeneity among all communities in terms of the basic educational skills being developed in students at the early primary level. Of particular interest is the fact that the village of Camisea is not significantly different from the other communities sampled.

When we move to the Advanced and Spanish Tests, however, the picture changes. An ANOVA comparison of all the communities indicates statistically significant differences in performance on both the Advanced and Spanish Tests. Subsequent sections of this chapter will further clarify the source of this variation.

Comparisons (by means of T-tests) done when Camisea is included or not in the full sample indicate that Camisea does contrast with the remainder of the Machiguenga population at several points. On the response variable of Fluency, we note a move from nonsignificance ($p = .0839$) to significance ($p = .002$) when the Camisea scores are compared to the remainder of the population with Camisea excluded. The same, however, does not occur on the variable of comprehension. These data suggest that the skills leading to fluency are being better taught in Camisea than elsewhere. The variable of comprehension, however, varies little between Camisea and other communities.

The pattern is similar, but slightly more marked, in the case of the Spanish Test. As observed elsewhere, this seems to reflect the fact that Camisea is an educational and economic center where Spanish is more important than in other communities. The placement of Spanish-speaking high school teachers in the community generates more need for daily use of the language on the part of villagers.

Apart from the data on the Spanish Test, the data suggest that Camisea is/was a reasonably good representative of the entire Machiguenga population and did **not** unduly distort or perturb the profile which emerges of literacy among the Machiguenga.

Distribution of Literacy Skills

Not all who took the tests met the preset standards, but the ratios between individuals in Camisea who did meet the standards as compared with those in other villages who also met the standards are displayed in table 11.11. The percentages shown have been calculated on the basis of the number who met standards on each test. For example, of the twenty-five participants from all villages who met standards on the Basic Test, the ten individuals from Camisea represented 40 percent.

Table 11.11. Met standards—Camisea versus other communities

Test	No. who met st.	Camisea No	Camisea Percent	Other villages No	Other villages Percent
Basic	25	10	40.00	15	60.00
Intermediate	7	6	85.70	1	14.30
Advanced	95	39	41.05	56	58.95
Spanish	69	35	50.70	34	49.30
Test totals	196	90	45.90	106	54.10

Of the eighteen Intermediate Tests administered, fifteen were given in Camisea and only three in other villages. Reflecting this disparity, of the seven test takers who met all four preset standards, six (85.7 percent) were from Camisea and one (14.3 percent of the total) was from a more isolated village.

A slightly higher ratio of Spanish Test takers met standards in Camisea—50.7 percent versus 49.3 percent in other villages. However, chi-square goodness of fit calculations (tables 11.13–11.15) failed to show a significant variation for Camisea scores as compared with the other communities, some of which also had a number of capable Spanish speakers. Since a number of participants declined to take the Spanish Test, it is possible that only those took the test who felt they had a good chance of doing it well, and this factor has affected the final figures. A small number of tests in three communities and the absence of some of the secondary school students may have also influenced results in the remote villages.

Analyzing the tests from a within-group perspective, the results were as follows:

Table 11.12. Met standards—within group

	Camisea		Other villages		All villages	
	Took	Met	Took	Met	Took	Met
Test	test	standards	test	standards	test	standards
Basic	25	10	41	15	66	25
Intermediate	15	6	3	1	18	7
Advanced	57	39	87	56	144	95
Spanish	46	35	68	34	114	69
Totals	143	90	199	106	342	196
	% of 143: 62.9		% of 199: 53.3		% of 342: 57.3	

Chi-square goodness of fit calculations were next done to ascertain whether the performance in Camisea was comparable to the performance of the general population.

Table 11.13. Camisea

Test	Observed	Expected	
Basic	10	11.484	$df = 3$
Intermediate	6	3.213	$x^2 = 3.447$
Advanced	39	43.623	$x^2\ .05 = 7.815$
Spanish	35	31.680	This result is not significant.
	90		

Table 11.14. The remote communities

Test	Observed	Expected	
Basic	15	13.53	$df = 3$
Intermediate	1	3.784	$x^2 = 2.918$
Advanced	56	51.378	$x^2\ .05 = 7.815$
Spanish	34	37.312	No significance. The remote
	106		communities, as a group, are
			not significantly different
			from the overall population.

Table 11.15. Spanish Test—Camisea versus remote communities

	Observed	Expected	
Camisea	35	31.68	$df = 1$
Others	34	37.32	$x^2 = 0.64$
	69		$x^2\ .05 = 3.84$

These results show figures which fail to reach statistical significance at the .05 level. From this we infer that Camisea scores have not varied significantly from those of the other communities.

Distribution by Literacy Levels

Hoping to understand more completely the overall profile of literacy levels in each village and the variance among them, chi-square goodness of fit tests were calculated as seen in table 11.16.

According to these results, Camisea, Camaná, Chokoriari, Segakiato and Shivankoreni vary significantly. Comparing these villages, Camisea varies the least. Mayapo, where the chi-square variance is less than one, is the most representative of the total population; the greatest variation occurs in Segakiato where scores were lowest. The total chi-square variance is highly significant, but less because of Camisea than because of variance in other communities. Since my goal in choosing the sampling was to represent the range of variances with one middle-of-the-road community from the main river and then the outliers, it appears that the objective was accomplished reasonably well.

Table 11.16. Calculations for chi-square goodness of fit tests

No. entire sample	Camisea Observed	Camisea Expected	Camaná Observed	Camaná Expected	Chokoriari Observed	Chokoriari Expected
13 Nonliterate	2*	5.06	4*	1.46	1*	0.82
94 Semilit.	26	36.6	6	10.55	6	5.89
101 Funct.	51	39.33	9	11.33	0*	6.33
95 Full	39	37.0	15	10.66	12	5.96
$N =$	118		34.00		19	
	$x^2 = 8.49$		$x^2 = 8.64$		$x^2 = 12.50$	
	$x^2\ .05 = 7.815$					

No. entire sample	Mayapo Observed	Mayapo Expected	Puerto Huallana Observed	Puerto Huallana Expected	Segakiato Observed	Segakiato Expected
13 Nonliterate	1*	0.9	0*	1.54	2*	1.67
94 Semilit.	8	6.51	9	11.17	24	12.1
101 Basic	5	7.0	10	12.0	13	13.0
95 Full	7	6.59	17	11.29	1*	12.23
$N =$	21		36		39	
	$x^2 = .95$		$x^2 = 5.19$		$x^2 = 22.16$	

No. entire sample	Shivankoreni Observed	Shivankoreni Expected		
13 Nonliterate	3*	1.5	All $x^2 = 67.27$	
94 Semilit.	15	10.86	$df = 18$	
101 Basic	14	11.67	$x^2\ .05 = 28.869$	
95 Full	3*	10.97		
$N =$	35			
	$x^2 = 9.34$			

* Note: Chi-square reliability breaks down at quantities of less than five.

Generalization of the Results

The average results for the seven communities surveyed—4.3 percent illiteracy, 31 percent semiliteracy, 33.3 percent functional literacy, and 31.4 percent full literacy—can, perhaps, be generalized to the other Machiguenga bilingual school communities not included in the survey, although I am not sure it is wise to do so. Two of the main river villages not surveyed have academic advantages: Nueva Luz has hosted the Machiguenga-Piro secondary school since 1984, and Nuevo Mundo has hosted the Machiguenga Bible Institute since 1976. They also have mixed-language populations—Piro (in Nueva Luz) and Asháninka (in Nuevo Mundo). The joint population of these villages is reported to be 725, and their educational opportunities are estimated to have raised the literacy level to at least that of Camisea. In contrast, a large village still gathering in 1992 (Montetoni, reported population 346), was composed nearly entirely of nonliterates. Further research would be needed to ascertain how literacy levels in other communities compare with those of the seven villages studied.[13]

Procedural Questions

In addition to the educational questions raised by this study, I wished to evaluate the effectiveness of the methods chosen. The following brief discussion summarizes my informal conclusions to the questions I asked myself.

Were the preset minimum reading standards appropriate?

Rather to my surprise, the preset standards—despite their potential for subjectivity and lack of testing in languages other than English—appeared appropriate in their application to Machiguenga and to Spanish.

I had hypothesized that Machiguenga readers could not attain less than 92 percent accuracy and still comprehend the meaning of the text, although Betts (1946, 1954) set frustration level at 90 percent accuracy. Although the results were uneven, at 92 percent accuracy the readers I observed were stumbling, repeating, guessing, sighing, and in general evidencing much tension and frustration. Thirty-nine percent of the time, their comprehension suffered as well.

I had hypothesized that readers must achieve a fluency score of at least 2 (word-by-word reading) to glean the meaning of the text. In general, this appeared to be true, although low fluency often combined with confounding factors—i.e., low scores in accuracy and/or rate.

I had hypothesized that readers must achieve a comprehension score of at least 3 − (scanty recount of the main idea) to give evidence of having understood the passage. The evidence supported this hypothesis, since recounts with lesser scores mentioned only scattered ideas without indicating how they were connected or what purpose they served in the text as a whole.

---

[13]Subsequent linguistic analysis has established that the inhabitants of Montetoni speak a language which is related to Machiguenga but which requires separate school materials. They should no longer be included in computations of Machiguenga literacy levels.

I had hypothesized that readers must read at least at a rate of 80 syllables per minute in order to comprehend the text. In general this appeared to be true. However, lack of accuracy and fluency often combined with low rate and served as confounding factors.

Cross-cultural testing is fraught with hazards, as are Informal Reading Inventories. One can scarcely overestimate the possibilities for skewing when these two factors converge. Nevertheless, my impression from listening to the tests was that the preset standards were reasonable for beginners. They may have been somewhat low for mature readers, since many of the advanced readers of our survey far surpassed the minimum requirements. I was interested to find that the reading characteristics displayed by Machiguenga readers do in general match descriptions of behaviors described by English-language reading specialists for readers who fall at equivalent levels of skill. These findings support Goodman's (1982b:67) hypothesis that basic reading processes are universal.

Were the assessment instruments appropriate?

As described in chapter 7, concerted effort was expended to make the test instruments and our visit as culturally acceptable as possible. During the testing and interviews the effectiveness of the instruments continued to be evaluated. Insofar as I could determine, the instruments were culturally appropriate, and did access the core data adequately.

Reflecting...

I feel the methods employed in this study can be utilized by anyone, anywhere, with any number of speakers. Although easiest to apply in a small population, the procedures are simple enough to be used with large numbers as well. Mother-tongue speakers of the language, when trained, are able to collect the data, code, and evaluate it with more ease and accuracy than can nonnative speakers; thus the method is appropriate for use by local supervisors.

Were the research procedures feasible under village conditions?

Many of the highly technical procedures commonly used to collect data in developed nations have proved unmanageable under isolated village conditions, where there is no electricity and equipment is removed from temperature and humidity control. My research, dependent on a solar-powered computer and printer and battery-powered tape recorders, might likewise have succumbed to the rigors of distance, the rainy season, or the overturning of a canoe had it not been for a superb backup team, skillful Machiguenga boatmen who brought us safely into port, and the willing help of the Machiguenga villagers. With the generous cooperation of all concerned, the logistics proved possible under village conditions.

In particular, testing in the homes by family groups produced less tension for the Machiguenga than would have been the case had individuals been isolated in a room in front of a test team and tape recorder. Fear was mitigated because individuals had the protection of other family members, and suspicions were allayed as the proceedings were carried out on open porches in view of all observers. Professor Barrientos' presence also served to reduce anxiety.

Reflecting...

To reach the communities required great effort, and transcription of the data was time-consuming and costly, but I know of no other methods which would have achieved equally satisfactory results. Until better techniques are available, I will recommend these for shy, group-oriented, non-Western societies, where no standardized reading tests exist.

Chapter Summary

This chapter discusses the test results and presents an overall statistical survey. It also describes some of the researcher's challenges and concerns as testing was initiated. The chapter closes with a discussion of the evaluation instruments and research procedures. Despite limitations, they are deemed to be the most appropriate currently available.

Above: Extra reading and number practice is now frequently provided by logos on imported T-shirts, or by those written on by the Machiguenga. (Rosemary Clayton photo, Mayapo, 1992)

Below: A traditional dance is presented as part of the closing exercises of the 1992 school year. (Woody Clayton photo, Puerto Huallana, 1992)

12

Gender, Time in School, and Literacy Retention

> *Women should have the same opportunity as men—learn to read, write, attend high school...the only problem is money.*
> -Father, House 17, Camisea

Introduction

The following section discusses the findings having to do with gender equality and the amount of instructional time the participants required to reach each literacy level. It also reports on the rate of literacy retention among Machiguenga adults who participated in the survey.

Gender

World-wide, women are offered fewer educational opportunities than men (Bhola 1989:62). In contrast, in the Machiguenga sampling, the proportion of literate females actually surpassed the number of literate males. Table 12.1 shows the proportion of literates by gender and community.

Table 12.1. Gender of participants

Community:	Camisea		Camaná		Chokoriari		Mayapo	
Literacy level	Fem.	Masc.	Fem.	Masc.	Fem.	Masc.	Fem.	Masc.
Nonliterate	0	2	2	2	1	0	0	1
Semiliterate	17	9	4	2	4	2	6	2
Functional	24	27	6	3	0	0	4	1
Fully literate	20	19	10	5	6	6	3	4
Subtotals	61	57	22	12	11	8	13	8
Totals	118		34		19		21	

Community:	Nueva Luz	Pto. Huallana		Segakiato		Shivankoreni		Totals	
Literacy level	Masc.	Fem.	Masc.	Fem.	Masc.	Fem.	Masc.	Fem.	Masc.
Nonliterate		0	0	2	0	2	1	7	6
Semiliterate		6	3	12	12	6	9	55	39
Functional		6	4	8	4	10	4	58	43
Fully literate	1	7	10	0	1	0	3	46	49
Subtotals	1	19	17	22	17	18	17	166	137
Totals	1	36		39		35		303	

Note, however, that more females than males ranked in the lower level of skill (functional, rather than full literates), as shown in table 12.2.

Table 12.2. Literate ranking of females versus males

Number of literates	Female	Male	Total
Functional	58	43	101
Fully literate	46	49	95
Total	104	92	196

Hoping to find whether there were significant differences within and among the villages, chi-square tests were calculated. First, a chi-square goodness of fit was done to test the distribution of literacy levels with respect to each of the genders separately. A chi-square test of independence then tested for any interaction effects between gender and the literacy levels.

Table 12.3. Goodness of fit—Camisea

No.–entire sample Literacy levels	Female Observed	Female Expected	Male Observed	Male Expected
13 Nonliterate	0	2.62	2	2.44
94 Semiliterate	17	18.92	9	17.68
101 Functional	24	20.33	27	19.0
95 Fully literate	20	19.12	19	17.87
$N =$	61		57	
	$x^2 = 3.518$		$x^2 = 7.78$	
	$df = 3.0$		$df = 3.0$	
	$p = 0.315$		$p = 0.051$	

A chi-square independence test for the interaction of the variables gender and literacy levels for Camisea revealed that the two variables were not interacting ($x^2 = 4.533$; $df = 3$; $p = 0.209$). This meant that males and females had a similar pattern of distribution into the four literacy levels.

Table 12.4. Goodness of fit—Camaná

No.–entire sample Literacy levels	Female Observed	Female Expected	Male Observed	Male Expected
13 Nonliterate	2	0.94	2	0.51
94 Semiliterate	4	6.82	2	3.72
101 Functional	6	7.33	3	4.0
95 Fully literate	10	6.90	5	3.76
$N =$	22		12	
	$x^2 = 3.995$		$x^2 = 5.81$	
	$df = 3.0$		$df = 3.0$	
	$p = 0.262$		$p = 0.121$	

A chi-square independence test for the interaction of the variables gender and literacy levels in Camaná showed no significant interaction between the two ($x^2 = 0.429$; $df = 3$; $p = 0.93$). A similar pattern of distribution of male and females into the four literacy levels is thus indicated.

Table 12.5. Goodness of fit—All communities

No.–entire sample Literacy levels	No.-in percent	Female Observed	Female Expected	Male Observed	Male Expected
13 Nonliterate	4.29	7	7.12	6	5.88
94 Semiliterate	31.02	55	51.5	39	42.5
101 Functional	33.33	58	55.33	43	45.66
95 Fully literate	31.35	46	52.04	49	42.95
N =		166		137	
Female:	$x^2 = 1.07$ $df = 3$ $p = 0.784$	Male:	$x^2 = 1.3$ $df = 3$ $p = 0.729$		

A chi-square independence test for the interaction of the variables gender and literacy levels in all communities revealed no significant interaction between these variables ($x^2 = 2.369$; $df = 3$; $p = 0.499$). This result indicated that males and females had a similar pattern of distribution into the four literacy levels.

Since none of the chi-square tests reached levels of significance, we conclude that they reveal no significant inequalities in the distribution of literacy with respect to gender.

Equal opportunity is a factor in the female literacy rate, however. I attribute educational equality among the Machiguenga to the following circumstances:

1. Traditionally, Machiguenga women have been accorded more respect and autonomy than in some ethnolinguistic groups (Rosengren 1987:106). Johnson (1978) notes, "male/female cooperative work [is] based on complementary tasks that establish interdependence and reciprocal relations between husbands and wives" (p. 71). As well, women maintain intra-female activity, establish exchange relations outside the domestic unit, and consequently maintain some independent social and economic networks (p. 71).

2. It is not a peasant or a landless society. Peasants and the landless tend to need all hands for all available time simply to eke out a living. The Machiguenga still have some discretionary time.

3. From the start, school and adult education classes have been open to all.

4. Class locations have been within walking distance of almost all students.

5. Parents have become convinced of the need to educate both boys and girls.

6. The role modeling of women seen in teaching and administrative positions, may have had some effect on the Machiguenga concept of women's roles. In recent years a number of women teachers have been named, church women have been trained as Sunday school teachers and deaconesses, and in 1992, educated women were beginning to be elected to community public office.

Despite educational opportunities and a nearly equal distribution of men and women who were advanced readers, women still formed the larger number of functional literates (fifty-eight females compared to forty-three males). This may be due to the fact that some women seem to find little need for reading so do not maintain their skills as well as men, who tend more often to find themselves in situations which require literacy.

Instruction Time Required for Participants to Reach Each Level of Skill

In the early days of the Machiguenga schools, no one cared much how long students took to learn. Now, however, a key concern of educators is not only that students should learn quickly but also that they reach a level of skill which will assure maintenance of their ability to read. Gray (1961:26) asserts that four to seven years in school is necessary for a student to acquire adult reading skills. I was interested, then, to discover how much time Machiguenga students had invested to become basic and advanced readers. Analysis revealed the following.

Basic Test

Of the twenty-five participants who met the preset standards for the Basic Test, ten were primary school children, mostly in grades 3 and 4. Years of schooling for the fifteen adults who met the preset standards ranged from two to fourteen years, with the mode falling at six years. The median length of school attendance for the entire group was 4.7 years.

Intermediate Test

Of the fifteen who took the Intermediate Test, seven met the preset minimum standards. One was an adult with five years of schooling. The other six were elementary school children who had just finished the 1992 school year. Of these, one had completed grade 4, one had completed grade 5, and four had completed grade 6. The median length of schooling for the entire group was 5.42 years.

Advanced Test—adults

Of the sixty-nine individuals who met the preset minimum standards for the Advanced Test, forty were adult men. Three of these men were teachers whose education far surpassed that of their peers, ranging from the completion of Secondary school to the completion of Pedagogical Institute teacher training. In order to clarify the situation among the majority of the villagers, the teachers' years of schooling were omitted from this calculation. The schooling of the remaining thirty-seven men ranged from five to 9.5 years, with a mean of 6.62 years.

Adult women numbered thirty-three, but one of these was also a teacher with Pedagogical Institute training, so her years of schooling were omitted from this computation. Years of schooling for the rest of the women ranged from six to eleven years, with a mean of 6.53 years.

The mean length of schooling for the adults (with the exception of the teachers) was 6.57 years.

Advanced Test—students

Students who met the preset minimum standards for the Advanced Test numbered twenty-one, as shown in the following chart.

Gr. 5 Primary		Gr. 6 Primary		1st Year Secondary		2nd Year Secondary		3rd Year Secondary		4th Year Secondary	
M	F	M	F	M	F	M	F	M	F	M	F
0	1	2	4	1	1	5	5	0	1	1	0

The mean years of schooling for the students was 6.76 years, with the distribution ranging from fifth grade primary to fourth year secondary.

Spanish Test

Sixty-nine readers met all four preset standards for the Spanish Test—forty-nine adults, and twenty students. The twenty-seven men of this group averaged 7.81 years of schooling each, while the twenty-two women averaged 7.72 years of schooling. The students—two in grade 6, four in First Year of secondary, twelve in Second Year of secondary, one in Third Year of secondary, and one in Fourth Year of secondary—averaged

7.75 years of schooling apiece. As a group, the sixty-nine participants averaged 7.76 years of schooling per person.

Reflecting...

These data indicate that, on the average, 4.7 years of schooling were required for participants in this study to acquire basic (functional) literacy skills, and 6.5 to 6.7 years of school were required for them to become fully skilled readers of Machiguenga. Seven to eight years were necessary for them to become comprehending readers of Spanish. Remember, however, that most of the adult test takers were first generation readers, who needed more time to acquire basic concepts than those already oriented to a literate environment. They also studied in an era in which there was little pressure on teachers or students to hurry; learning well was a more important criterion.

The figures explain in part why adult literacy classes, with their much shorter time investment, have not been able to bring enrollees to independent reading.

Extent to which Basic Literacy Has Been Maintained

Our sampling of 303 cases in seven communities identified a total of thirteen nonliterates and ninety-four semiliterates—35.3 percent of the entire population surveyed—who fell within the range of nonliterate and semiliterate. The remaining 64.7 percent of the population surveyed performed tasks which identified them as literate at the basic level or above. Indeed, including those adults who were in school, ninety-five—i.e., 31.4 percent of the population surveyed—met preset standards for the Advanced Test.

Adults who met preset standards

Our concern was not with the school children, since, for the most part, they were learning to read. We did, however, wish to know how many adults had retained literacy skills. By separating the adults who had left school from the students still enrolled in school, the number who had retained their literacy skills over time were identified by location and sex as follows.

Table 12.6. Adults who met preset standards

Community	Basic Test			Intermediate Test			Advanced Test		
	M	F	Total	M	F	Total	M	F	Total
Camisea	2	2	4	1	0	1	14	15	29
Camaná	0	0	0	0	0	0	5	7	12
Chokoriari	0	0	0	0	0	0	6	6	12
Mayapo	1	0	1	0	0	0	2	2	4
Puerto Huallana	0	1	1	0	0	0	8	5	13
Segakiato	1	1	2	0	0	0	1	0	1
Shivankoreni	1	6	7	0	0	0	2	1	3
Total	5	10	15	1	0	1	38	36	74

The distribution of these individuals was then plotted with relation to how many years they had attended school and how long it had been since they had left school. The results were as follows.

Table 12.7. Adults who met preset standards for the Basic and Intermediate Tests

Years in school:	2	3	4	5	6	7	8	14	Total
Year left school									
1959	1								1
1965–1969		1	1	1	2				5
1975–1979		1		1	1	1	1		5
1980–1984		1	1						2
1985–1989			1		1			1	3
Total	1	3	3	2	4	1	1	1	16

Of these, fifeen adults had met preset standards on the Basic Test, and one had met the standards on the Intermediate Test. All of these adults had attended school for three or more years, with the exception of one person who had left school in 1959 after only two years of school. This father was faithful in the church and not only had maintained his literacy skills through Bible reading but said that his reading had improved. The group as a whole had been out of school for periods ranging from four to thirty-four years. Fourteen of the seventeen had been out of school eight years or longer.

Adults who met preset standards for the Advanced Test included one who had not attended school but had taught himself to read in about 1984. The distribution for the remaining seventy-three adults who had attended school is shown in table 12.8.

Table 12.8. Adults who met preset standards for the Advanced Test

Years in school:	3	4	5	6	7	8	9	11	14+	Total
Year left school										
1960–1964				1						1
1965–1969				2	1					3
1970–1974				1			5			6
1975–1979		1	2	3	2	4	3		1	16
1980–1984	1	1	5	6			2			15
1985–1989	1	1	4	9	1	2	1	1		20
1990–1992			2	1	2	1		3	3	12
Total	2	3	13	22	7	7	11	4	4	73

These seventy-three adults had been out of school for periods ranging from 1963 to 1992 (the count includes one drop-out from the 1992 school year). Forty-one had been out of school from eight to thirty-two years. All of the adults who met preset standards on the Advanced Test had attended school three or more years.

The Spanish Test was not included in this computation since, except for one, all of the individuals who took the Spanish Test had already taken the Advanced Test and had been counted as meeting the standards for literacy. One adult who could read Spanish but could not meet standards for Machiguenga literacy was counted as literate in the data base but was not included in the above scoring.

Adults who had not maintained literacy skills

Adults who had not maintained their literacy skills numbered forty-four (14.52 percent of the survey population). Table 12.9 indicates the distribution of these adults by location and sex.

Table 12.9. Adults unable to meet preset standards

Community	Basic Test			Intermediate Test			Advanced Test		
	M	F	Total	M	F	Total	M	F	Total
Camisea	3	4	7	0	3	3	2	6	8
Camaná	0	0	0	0	0	0	1	4	5
Mayapo	0	0	0	0	0	0	0	2	2
Puerto Huallana	0	0	0	0	0	0	2	3	5
Segakiato	3	3	6	0	0	0	1	1	2
Shivankoreni	2	2	4	0	0	0	0	2	2
Total	8	9	17	0	3	3	6	18	24

According to these figures, fourteen men and thirty women were unable to meet preset standards. The higher proportion of women may be due to the fact that women are busy with home and child-rearing responsibilities, have less contact with the outside, and in general have fewer reasons to read than do men, many of whom now have considerable contact with activities which require literacy.

Of those adults who could not meet the Basic Test requirements, twenty-seven had attended school. Some of these had dropped out before learning to read well; some may have been too nervous to perform well on the test; others were able to meet three out of four criteria on the Basic Test and were very close to being independent readers. Several in this group, however, told us they had left off reading and had forgotten how. Based on that information, it appears to be possible for individuals who have attended school for as many as nine years to lose their skills through disuse. Table 12.10 displays the numbers of adults who had attended school but who failed to meet the preset standards for the Basic Test.

Table 12.10. Adults who attended school but did not meet standards on the Basic Test

Years in school:	1	2	3	4	5	6	7	8	9	Total
Year left school										
1956–1959		1								1
1960–1964										0
1965–1969						1		2	1	4
1970–1974				1					1	2
1975–1979		1	1	2					2	6
1980–1984	2			1	2	1				6
1985–1989			1		1	3			1	6
1990–1991			1			1				2
Total	2	2	3	4	3	6	0	2	5	27

Seventy percent (nineteen) of these twenty-seven adults had been out of school for eight years or longer. They averaged 5.3 years of schooling per person. The eleven individuals who attended school from one to four years may never have established their literacy skill securely. It appears, however, that the sixteen participants who attended school from five to nine years and who should have been independent readers had either lost their skill through lack of practice or the skill had become so rusty that the individual could not access it quickly at test time.

A second group composed of thirteen adults had attended school before 1980 and had later attended adult literacy classes. Their strong desire to learn is evidenced by the fact that among them this group averaged 15.7 months each of adult literacy instruction. Nevertheless, they had not developed sufficient skill to meet the requirements of the Basic reading test. Table 12.11 presents the profile of these individuals.

Table 12.11. Adults who attended both school and adult literacy classes but who could not meet standards on the Basic Test

Years of school: Year left school	1	2	3–7	8	9
1956–1959	1 + 24 mo. 1 + 18 mo.				
1969-1964	1 + 18 mo.	1 + 9 mo. 1 + 18 mo.			
1965-1969	1 + 18 mo.			1 + 9 mo.	
1970-1974		1 + 9 mo. 1 + 12 mo. 1 + 18 mo.			1 + 24 mo.
1975-1980	1 + 9 mo. 1 + 18 mo.				
Total	6	5	0	1	1

Eleven of these thirteen adults had attended school for only one or two years, insufficient time, apparently, for literacy skill to be well established.

Results from Adult Literacy Classes

Thirty-two adults did not attend school but had enrolled in adult literacy classes for the following periods of time (as best could be calculated):

Adult classes:	1 year	2 years	3 years	4 years	Total
Enrolled:	18	9	2	3	32

Participants in the adult literacy classes acquired a varied array of skills. Depending on the length of time they had attended, they might recognize a few letters and words, perhaps print their name, or read from the first or second primer. However, no one from the adult literacy classes had become an independent reader, even at a basic level. Consequently, many expressed sharp disappointment that, after exerting all the effort, they had not made more progress. On inquiry we learned that most of the adult literacy teachers had had little training and also that each year adult classes had started over from the beginning instead of carrying readers on from where they had left off. The finding that those who met standards on the Basic Test had attended an average of 4.7 years of school, supported my further intuition that adult classes had not been continued for a sufficient length of time to produce independent readers.

In summary, when test results were computed separating out the adults, the following picture emerged.

Table 12.12. Literacy retention—Adult test takers

Test	Retained literacy skills		Classification
	Met standards	Out of school 8 yrs. or more	
Basic	15	12	Functional readers
Intermediate	1	1	Functional readers
Advanced	73 + 1	41 + 1	Advanced readers
Total	90	55	

Test	Did not maintain skills		Classification
	Did not meet standards	Out of school 8 yrs. or more	
Basic	17		Semiliterate
Intermediate	3	32 all together	Functional readers
Advanced	24		Functional readers
Total	44	32	

This table shows that 67 percent (90 / 134 × 100) of the adult readers tested passed the minimum standards. Of those who passed, 61 percent (55 / 90 × 100) had retained literacy skills for eight years or longer. Calculating in relation to the total number of adults tested, 41 percent (55 / 134 × 100) had retained literacy skills for eight years or longer. More had retained their literacy skills than had lost them (fifty-four versus thirty-two).

Chapter Summary

Although female literates slightly outnumbered males (103 to 93), more females than males ranked as functional (rather than full) literates.

The median length of school attendance for Basic readers was 4.7 years, for Intermediate readers, 5.42 years, and for adult Advanced readers, 6.57 years.

Sixteen adults (5.28 percent of the total number surveyed) had retained Basic literacy skills, and seventy-four (24.42 percent) had retained Advanced literacy skills, after having left school over a span of time ranging from one to thirty-two years.

Forty-four adults (14.52 percent of the survey population) were not able to meet preset standards on the test they were given; seventeen had to be classed as semiliterates. Twenty-seven of the forty-four had attended school from one to nine years, averaging 5.3 years per person. The span of time since they had left school ranged from 1959 to 1991. A second group of thirteen adults had both attended school (before 1980) and, later, adult literacy classes but had not reached the stage of independent reading. Thirty-two adults had attended adult literacy classes only; none of these could read independently. For this latter group, lack of adequate class time and failure of literacy teachers to carry them far enough appear to be contributing factors.

Chapter Summary

Boys, girls, adults, and young mothers study together in Machiguenga classrooms. (P. Davis photos. c. 1972)

13

Lessons and Implications

When I attended [high school] in Nueva Luz, people said to me, "Stay, settle here." But I replied, "Long ago when I entered school I was told, 'Enter and then come back to your community to live'." Thus it is that I have returned to my community. I am not going to go away. I will live here.   - Father, House 6, Camaná

This chapter discusses the strengths and limitations of the study and compares the literacy rate of the Machiguengas to that of other minority language groups. It further lists the lessons learned from the study, makes recommendations for policy makers and educators, and suggests directions for future research. It concludes with an expression of gratitude to the Machiguenga.

Strengths and Limitations of the Study

Few studies in minority language communities have the advantage of forty years of documentation or the willing cooperation of hundreds of individuals who have been participant-observers over the entire period. Even fewer benefit from the aid of research colleagues as skilled as Professor Barrientos. The fact that I was known to the people and spoke the language was also important among the shy Machiguenga. These combined factors permitted access to more information than is ordinarily possible. An attempt has been made to report this information objectively; still, the argument can be made that those involved in programs are more apt to be optimistic about them than are outsiders.

Striving for accuracy, I have constantly checked the information received against evidence accumulated in years past, yet realize that to some extent participants anxious to help may report what they think the questioner wants to hear, while on another occasion with a different questioner the data may be reported quite differently. As regards reading evaluation, the Informal Reading Inventory—one of the few methods available for analyzing oral reading in the absence of standardized tests—is recognized to be imprecise, suffering from the problem of process versus content control and from the subjective criteria used in determining "increasing difficulty" and "frustration level." To achieve more precision, several tests would have had to be administered to each individual. Limitations of time and expense did not allow that luxury; however, statistically, the 303 cases are sufficient to give a composite picture of literacy levels which matches reality fairly closely, judging from my observations. Under more relaxed conditions, comprehension should have been somewhat higher for readers who suffered from test anxiety during my data gathering and, therefore, actual literacy levels may well be somewhat higher than our test scores indicate.

Results from the testing may possibly be generalized, with caution, to the villages not included in the survey, but because of their great diversity, this has not been done.

The Literacy Rate Compared

The 64.7 percent literacy rate found amongst the Machiguenga compares favorably with UNESCO (Bhola 1989:63) literacy rates for adults fifteen years of age and above in Asia (63.7 percent) and Africa (46.0 percent). Moreover, the Machiguenga rating is much higher than for most minority language groups.

A 1993 world-wide survey of 1,539 minority-group languages showed that in this sample literacy rates—judged as the ability to read in some language, not necessarily in one's mother tongue—averaged approximately 40 percent. The same survey showed mother-tongue literacy rates of 5 percent or less for more than 1,000 of the languages with an average rate of 11 percent when adjusted for the size of the population. Only slightly over 100 languages were considered to have a mother-tongue literacy rate of above 60 percent (International Literacy Coordinator, SIL International, Dallas, TX, 1993).

Where educational programs have been initiated, as is the case among certain minority groups of Latin America, the estimated literacy rates for adults fifteen years of age and above are typically higher than the average for minority groups worldwide but can still vary widely. The following examples are representative:

Table 13.1. Literacy rates among certain minority groups in Latin America

Group	Per cent of literacy		Language of education
	Any language	Vernacular literacy	
Central Quiché, Guatemala	15–25%	1%	Mainly Spanish
Quechua of Ayacucho, Peru	25–50%	5–10%	Mainly Spanish
Aguaruna, Peru	50–75%	60–100%	Mainly mother tongue
Páez, Colombia	25–50%	10–30%	Mainly Spanish
Piro, Peru	50–75%	30–60%	Mainly mother tongue

(SIL International Literacy Coordinator files, 1993)

With the exception of the Piro, these language groups are all larger than the Machiguenga, which makes it more difficult to extend education to all, but they have had educational programs for a much longer period of time—centuries of majority-language schooling in the case of the Quiché and Quechua. The Quiché have also had bilingual education opportunities since 1980, while two experimental bilingual education programs have been sponsored among the Quechua of Ayacucho. Social pressures, however, have led to rejection of the mother tongue by Quiché and Quechua speakers, and among them literacy has not flourished in any language.

Nazarene missionaries began a school (Spanish-speaking) among the Aguaruna of Peru some twenty-five years before the government bilingual school program was founded. Under the leadership of dynamic Aguaruna supervisors, the Aguaruna bilingual schools have expanded and today are very strong, as is indicated by the 60–100 percent literacy rate.

The Páez of Colombia, numbering 67,000 in the 1990 census, have had Spanish-speaking government schools for many years but now are also served by three full-time and thirteen part-time literacy workers who teach some six hundred students per year (personal conversation with field linguists M. Slocum and F. Gerdel, September, 1994). As a result, literacy rates are improving rapidly but still are estimated to have reached only 25–50 percent.

These comparisons provide a measure by which to judge the accomplishments of the Machiguenga literacy program.

Lessons and Implications

From the very beginning, curriculum developers for the Machiguenga made as many cultural adaptations as possible within Ministry of Education guidelines. Children were allowed to wear traditional attire and to speak their own language in school. Machiguenga teachers presented beginning lessons in the mother tongue, with culturally-appropriate examples—unconsciously, very often—from the standpoint of the Machiguenga worldview. The concepts and assumptions underlying subject material were pointed out and explained, especially those recognized as new, or different from those held by the traditional society. Beginning reading material was culturally based, as were all the primer illustrations. Special teaching methods were devised for especially difficult concepts, such as that of invariant quantity for each number symbol, and the breakdown of words into syllables. Teachers were encouraged to observe traditional behavior in the classroom insofar as possible—allowing toddlers to accompany mothers to class, soliciting choral (rather than individual) responses, teaching native arts and crafts in the curriculum. The first grades were programmed slowly in order to allow students sufficient time to internalize new ideas. Spanish was taught with second-language methodology, along with explanations of Hispanic culture. A strong community development program accompanied the literacy program.

These efforts appear to have met with a measure of success. The following comments are typical: "[The school has brought] teachers, reading, math, history, all the subjects, knowledge about how to live well, [has taught] children to work and help their parents....[Kindergarten and high school] are needed; I want my daughter to finish them all" (Father, House 38, Shivankoreni). "If it had not been for the school, I would not have been able to talk for people who need help [i.e., interpret] or write letters for them" (Father, House 17, Camaná).

1. The foremost finding of this research project, then, is that a well-implemented mother-tongue educational program can produce sound and enduring educational outcomes, despite the difficulty of the circumstances or the remoteness of the location. However, numerous other sociological and educational lessons can also be learned, all of which are useful to those working in preliterate contexts.

2. Successful literacy acquisition requires a considerable array of enabling factors ranging from laws to supportive educational conditions. Isolation protected the Machiguenga from the extreme subjugation suffered by some other indigenous groups. Favorable laws have included authorization for the use of their mother tongue in education, government sponsorship of the bilingual schools, the training of Machiguenga teachers and supervisors, and

the provision of textbooks. Time has also been an important factor, for time is required for new concepts to be internalized. The years of preparation before heavy contact with the outside world began have helped the people learn under less pressured conditions and have helped avoid demoralization. Subjects taught in the bilingual schools—reading, writing, math, Spanish, knowledge about the outside world (geography, history, civic organization, and the national legal system)—have alleviated feelings of helplessness and provided some options for problem resolution. The emergence of educated leaders has permitted the Machiguenga to represent themselves in the outside world. Experience in managing the schools, church, agricultural cooperative, and community organizations not only has provided reinforcement for literacy skills but also has given the group experience in shared leadership and a sense of being in charge of their own affairs. I believe that in isolated minority groups, literacy programs will be more sustainable and produce the most constructive results if those involved take pains to see that all of these elements are incorporated.

3. A strong community development program created many uses for literacy. The training of many people in various skills which have required reading and writing on a continuing basis has contributed to popularizing literacy use. The development of management structures and income-generating projects to pay for books has strongly influenced literacy maintenance and retention.

4. Subsequent to the introduction of literacy the Machiguenga have developed their own set of institutions (for example, community organizations, parents' associations, and mothers' clubs) and group customs (such as posting signs, letter writing, and labeling clothing) which require reading and writing. This cultural institutionalization of literacy has been an important factor in literacy retention.

5. The favorable attitudes developed towards literacy are predictive of literacy maintenance, barring major changes. This salient impression overshadowed all others: the Machiguenga love to learn. They learn, not just for pragmatic reasons but for the joy of learning. "Why do you say reading is good?," we would ask, and time and again the answer came back, "It is good for knowing things." In the villages, any time a new skill is demonstrated, or a new idea is presented, an interested crowd gathers. As we interviewed, someone in almost every village expressed an interest in continuing adult education, and many adults lamented both their lack of opportunities to study and the shortage of post-school reading materials. The majority of those interviewed (85.4 percent) expected to continue reading and writing in Machiguenga and 68.7 percent expected to continue in Spanish as well.

6. Another important effect of literacy is that the people's self-esteem and ability to cope with the outside world has been significantly enhanced and shows itself in their bearing. J. Henrich, an anthropologist who returned in November 1994 from research among the Machiguenga of the Lower Urubamba, commented that in contrast with some other villages, the Machiguenga of the bilingual school communities he visited, "were in charge, and knew themselves to be" (personal conversation). The organizations they have formed—the Machiguenga *Central* and community organizations—enable them to manage both the internal and external affairs over which they have jurisdiction and to relate officially to outside entities whereas previously they had neither a united voice nor channels for communication.

7. The program has resulted in the protection of human rights. According to field linguist Wayne Snell, with the advent of education and community development, the clandestine slave trade, which was still going on in the area as late as the 1950s, was broken. Machiguenga parents had other ways to acquire the goods they needed without selling their children. By living in communities they could help protect each other. Through education they have also learned to make themselves understood in Spanish, to manage the documents required when filing applications, petitions, and claims, to count money, and to calculate prices. All of these measures combine to reduce exploitation.

8. Despite the isolation of the area, nearly one quarter of the participants in this reading survey met the rather demanding standards of the Spanish Test. This level of Spanish acquisition is largely attributable to the teaching provided by the bilingual schools and is an important factor in providing individuals better individual and group communication with outsiders as well as giving them access to more written material. Because Spanish acquisition has been an additive, not a subtractive measure, the mother tongue continues to be valued by virtually all of the individuals surveyed.

9. Adult education is not successful unless adequate time is dedicated to study and lessons are carefully sequenced to carry learners on to mastery. Machiguenga adult literacy classes tended to repeat the same content every session; as a result, learners who have spent considerable time in class have not studied the upper-level books of the basic primer series or learned all of the skills necessary to become independent readers. Many adults, however, are still anxious to learn, and many who have learned to read are requesting opportunity for continuing education. If teachers and students could give time until the primer series is fully taught, adults should be able to master literacy skills. Continuing education lectures on health, agriculture, current events, and science would also be greatly appreciated.

10. Although the assessment model developed for this study was a pioneer endeavor (no cases were found in the literature describing reading tests or setting standards for reading in non-Indo-European languages), it proved manageable and useful in the village setting. Cultural adaptations included interviewing and testing by family groups, the use of native-authored, culturally familiar readings for beginning and intermediate levels, and administration of the tests in the mother tongue by the Machiguenga school supervisor. Use of Informal Reading Inventories provided a way to test reading where no standardized tests exist. Standards for accuracy, fluency, comprehension, and rate based upon a modified Betts model, while not entirely precise, allowed a more accurate measure than is otherwise available. Until better techniques are developed, this model might be useful as a starting point for other studies of reading where standardized tests are not available.

11. The research and the program studied demonstrate that under moderately supportive conditions—favorable policies, adequate training, technical support, and encouragement—indigenous people are able to adapt to and manage their own complex (for them) technological programs such as cooperatives and educational systems. They do so with creativity and cultural sensitivity. Although, significant teaching, training, and mentoring are required initially, ultimately such programs do not need to be controlled by outsiders.

Unfortunately, this concept runs counter to much of the prevailing thought in South America, where, historically, indigenous peoples have been exploited by European colonial rule. An indigenous group which seeks to become self-sufficient often meets opposition at several levels. Conceptually, the majority society is not convinced of their ability; economically, their self-sufficiency may threaten the profits of those who formerly benefitted from their labor or their purchases. Territorially, they may hold land desired by colonists. Administratively, their legitimate needs, formerly neglected, now compete for attention and create new pressures for officials, for example, in the areas of budgeting and planning. If, in addition, the group is poor and without political clout, it is extremely difficult for them to overcome the obstacles. What the Machiguenga have achieved is due not only to their hard work and the program developed among them but to courageous and sympathetic officials at national and regional levels who have extended facilities and allowed them to succeed.

Recommendations

Based on the Machiguenga experience and the present research certain recommendations can be made. Some of these may be applicable in other situations which are similar:

Recommendations for policy makers

Marginalized people like the Machiguenga, who wish to be self-sufficient and self-governed, are willing to take responsibility for their own affairs and are able to support themselves as productive, contributing citizens. It is in the interest of a nation to see these aspirations realized. However, self-sufficiency is only possible if enabling laws and policies exist which make the goals attainable. Without central governmental support and also the support of local officials, native peoples—especially where majority societies depreciate indigenous populations—tend to find themselves trapped in no-win situations. Among the most important enablers are the following.

Policies which permit self-government

1. Protection of native land. Because the jungle is fragile ecologically—large areas are infertile, and the thin soil is easily damaged—minority peoples of Amazonia need relatively large extensions of land in order to sustain supplies of animals, fish, and building materials, and to allow for farm rotation. Peruvian authorities have been sensitive to this need, but unless land reservations continue to be protected, the very existence of the Machiguenga, and other ethnolinguistic groups of the jungle, will be jeopardized. This is a threat authorities need to take very seriously, especially in light of increased colonization of the jungle. When land rights are secure, agricultural pursuits, which are the basis of economic prosperity in any nation, can prosper, and the people can be self-sustaining. Without secure land, self-sufficiency is difficult to achieve. My recommendation is that governments, regional authorities, and field workers alike give high priority to the allocation of land titles for minority peoples.

2. Protection of native rights. Minority groups—just as much as majority society groups—need budget apportionment for the development of infrastructures (such as medical services), justice in the courts, and opportunities for work and education. Native peoples also need to be included in decisions which concern them. For example, in 1994 and again in 2000 agreements between the Peruvian government and oil industry representatives have

permitted petroleum exploration and extraction of natural gas from the Machiguenga heartland. In such cases, governments need to take energetic initiatives to safeguard the ecology and native rights, even as they encourage industry and development. The United Nations (1993) Draft Document of the Declaration of Human Rights for Indigenous Peoples provides useful recommendations.

3. Infrastructures which facilitate income-generating projects within the ability of the minority group—e.g., feeder roads, transportation to market, fair prices for agricultural produce. It is very difficult for rural people to be successful financially (and therefore self-supporting) unless supportive economic policies are in place. These policies must be passed and implemented by central and regional officials. Officials also need to be active in the regulation of wages and working conditions and provision of benefits whenever private landholders and large companies hire indigenous people as laborers. Thus far, the oil companies have been generous in their dealings with the Machiguenga, but continuing government oversight is needed for all similar situations.

4. Recognition of native authorities. Leaders elected by native communities know the needs of their region and, better than anyone else, understand their people and work in culturally appropriate ways. If oriented to the national life, they can provide important liaison between government officials and the minority language community. It is not wise to substitute these leaders with others from the majority society.

5. A hearing for petitions. Unfortunately, legitimate requests from minority peoples are often ignored, as the Machiguengas have complained, or are assigned low priority. This prevents the group from doing what needs to be done and may even result in irreparable harm. Officials who receive requests from native peoples of the jungle need to be aware that it has cost the group great effort in time and money just to travel to the city to present the request. They seldom make the attempt unless the matter is urgent. Their Spanish may be limited, but once their concern is understood, it may indeed require immediate action.[14]

Policies which promote rural indigenous education

Minority people like the Machiguenga need educational provision. Among the most important factors are the following.

1. Authorization for the writing of the local language and at least sufficient language analysis to permit the development of a workable alphabet.

---

[14]In all cases, administrators would be well advised, however, to ascertain that the petitioner does indeed represent all his people, rather than seeking personal power or benefits for a favored few.

2. Authorization for the use of the local language in education. In isolated language groups much of the success of the school depends upon the use of the mother tongue in the beginning years.

3. Stability in the educational system. Sweeping changes aimed at more general national goals also affect remote areas. In the case of the Educational Reform in Peru, we found that massive change disoriented teachers, invalidated textbooks, and made the system too difficult and expensive for minority groups to continue without considerable aid. In my experience, small changes implemented in small increments are more successful than are large changes.

4. Educational budget. Minority peoples living in remote areas need the same kind of budget apportionment assigned to other rural school systems for school building and office maintenance, teachers' salaries, and supervision. Because of the distance, supervisors also desperately need travel allowances. The Machiguenga school supervisors, who have received no budget for travel, have rarely been able to visit the schools under their jurisdiction. Unfortunately, these needs are easily forgotten in the city when district budgets are made up.

5. Educational training. Provision must be made for teacher and supervisor training and updating. Summer courses such as those established by the Peruvian Ministry of Education for the bilingual school program provide a good model (see Shell 1981). Machiguenga teachers have paid all their own travel and living expenses at such courses, as well as paying for materials and textbooks. Under normal conditions they were able to do this; in the last years, due to massive devaluation and low prices for agricultural products, they have had great difficulty in paying for the summer courses and have much need of scholarships so that they may complete their education. A 1994 law, however, requires teachers to hold a Pedagogical Institute degree, rather than only a high school certificate as formerly. The Coordinator of Education for the Machiguenga area (personal correspondence, August 1994, in author's files) reported that under the new law mestizo teachers are being assigned to the Machiguenga schools, displacing the Machiguenga teachers. Unless authorities are willing to make an exception until the Machiguenga teachers in the process of completing their Pedagogical Institute training can graduate, bilingual classrooms will become monolingual Spanish classrooms. Here is a case which illustrates the dependency of bilingual education upon favorable laws and their implementation at local level. It is also one which merits intervention from educational authorities.

Policies which allow time for adaptation

We have learned that change can be introduced effectively only at the pace at which the majority of the people are able to accept it. Beginning from the creation of the bilingual schools, I estimate three generations for the Machiguenga society as a whole to become comfortable with and to control the skills and understandings needed to interact with the outside world to their satisfaction. Individuals, however, may make the transition in less time, if conditions are favorable. Pushing faster than the people can adapt may harm both them and the program.

Recommendations for educators and field workers

The following recommendations for educators and field workers are born of the experience represented in this report.

1. If at all possible, begin education in the mother tongue. This fundamental principle makes possible clear concept formation, builds self-esteem, and lays a firm foundation for the learning of a second language. Mother-tongue education is indicated when beginning students do not speak the majority language and the mother tongue lacks prestige (Dutcher 1982). Bilingual education programs which begin in the mother tongue and teach the majority language with second-language acquisition methodology are more costly in terms of time, and materials, but—as can be seen in the case of the Machiguenga—can produce effective long-term results. In contrast, immersion programs like those of the Quechua and Quiché, in which monolingual children are plunged into majority language classrooms, suffer from student demoralization and high drop-out rates. In these cases, the money spent on education has not been effectively used.[15]

2. If possible, begin with adults to avoid creating a generation gap and disrupting lines of authority.

3. Be very careful to consult the people, to respond to their desires, to respect their customs, values, and goals. Encourage and work together with local leadership. Attitudes of superiority harm program implementation.

4. Adapt the materials and methods to the language and culture.

5. Train native teachers and supervisors carefully. They understand the culture and are able to communicate knowledge more effectively than any outsider, but many training courses are too short for maximum effectiveness.

6. Provide adequate supervision, with mechanisms for replacing teachers who, after a reasonable training time, are unable to improve. Many of the

---

[15]Thomas and Collier (1997) provide convincing research evidence as to the cognitive and academic superiority of well-implemented bilingual education programs.

problems experienced by schools can be avoided if supervision is frequent and if inefficient teachers can be replaced.

7. Supply a large amount of interesting post-primer literature. Reading skill is established by reading, and this study has highlighted the importance of continued practice. (See example (7) on page 275.)

8. Generate many reasons for many people to use literacy. From this study it appears that skills which are not used are not well retained. Large community development programs may not be needed if services are already established in the area. However, reading clubs, continuing education, letter writing, authors' workshops, recording of legends, and discussion groups based on a text are other ways that literacy can be promoted.

9. Make self-administration (not dependence) the end goal. Work towards this goal from the beginning.

10. Encourage income-generating projects to help finance books and supplies. Bean fields cleared by the parents and planted and harvested by the school children with their teachers provided school supplies for each Machiguenga community until financial chaos engulfed the nation in the late 1980s. In 1992, after the crash, students in some remote communities were found to be up to two years behind in reading for lack of books, and parents lamented that they had no money with which to purchase school texts or notebooks.

11. Especially in groups unused to community living, allow the people much freedom to adapt innovations to the culture and as much time as possible to internalize the new concepts being introduced.

12. Provide training for adult education teachers beyond the use of the first book. They need to be able to carry their students through the primer series and on to post-primer and independent reading.

Recommendations for future studies

Future studies could profitably test the methods devised for this study in other languages and cultures. It may be possible to refine evaluation criteria further. If the residents are willing, reading tests could be conducted in the Machiguenga villages not included in the survey. The reading material collected cries for miscue analysis—a procedure beyond the scope of this study and one which would need to be approached with caution and the help of a well-oriented native speaker of Machiguenga. Because changes inevitably occur both in social systems and school systems, a subsequent study could continue to trace developments among the Machiguenga, increasing our understanding of longitudinal change.

(7) Example from a post-primer reader—a book of folk tales

Ikanti:

—Sa nagakerityo, ¿ario tyari nagakeri? Nokitsatakeri okapatsatakera.

Ikantaigi tovairi:

—Teratyo, kañotari chapi tera onkapatsavetempa piatake pagakiti, naroegi nokitsakitsageigavetaka tera ario nagaige.

Ipiriniventaiganakerityo samanityo itimagevetanaka kantankicha avisanakeri ishinkiro ikavakavavetanaka pairotyo yogitaiganakeri.

Impogini ikanti:

—Inti noneake kagantageri tonoanto ipegakena isari pairatama atsantsatsempokirika. Noaigake nokitsavageigakera itatsempokigemata imonteakaro pairatamatake ariotserarika itsera.

Ikematigiri otsapiku tsotagn:

—Viroratyo kavegantatsirira.

Ikavakavaiganake:

—Ejeje, ejeje.

Because research should benefit the participants as well as the researcher and the academic community, future studies should be made available to the Machiguenga. The results of the present reading survey have already been placed at the disposal of the Machiguenga school supervisor to aid him in his work; a summary of the study has been distributed to the Machiguenga teachers; chapters 4 and 5 of this book have been published as a separate history book for the Machiguenga; and the entire book will be published in Spanish to provide a base line record for the Machiguenga and for the Peruvian public.

Predictions and Concerns for the Future

Looking ahead, the following predictions and concerns are cautiously offered: The institutionalization of literacy and the many uses developed for it in Machiguenga society auger well for the continuance of reading and writing, given stable conditions. Fluency in Spanish will tend to increase as contact with the outside world increases and Machiguenga students continue secondary education. The leadership structures and confidence developed to this point provide tools for meeting coming change and for finding solutions to new challenges, although success cannot be guaranteed. The extent to which Machiguenga teachers and educational supervisors have been trained will allow them to continue to operate their own school system, given a supportive administration.

Isolated though they are, literacy is a moving target for the Machiguenga, and literacy expectations are rising as contacts with the majority society increase. Whereas once only the most basic of literacy functions sufficed for almost everyone, now secondary and tertiary school students must compete with native speakers of Spanish for mastery of technical academic subjects, and leaders must control the vocabulary and composition skills needed for official documents.

The replacement of Machiguenga-speaking teachers with Spanish-speaking teachers and the extraction of natural gas in the Machiguenga area, with an influx of laborers and colonists and far-reaching effects on the ecology, are matters for serious concern. They deserve attention from all levels of government.

Each of these events will produce heavy stresses; so it is still too early to assume that the Machiguenga will escape destabilization as they undergo cultural change. We have reason to believe, however, that by availing themselves of the coping tools offered, they have thus far avoided mass demoralization. At present, the group is maintaining its identity and autonomy;

however, in the future, the Machiguenga will need the sympathetic help of policy makers and local officials if they are to be successful in their journey toward self sufficiency and self administration.

A Tribute

In conclusion, appreciation must go to the Machiguenga for their admirable accomplishments in the face of great difficulties, and for their willingness to allow information about themselves to be placed at the service of educators. Their desire, and mine, is that this experience contribute to the design of ever-more appropriate educational programs for minority peoples. Although the task is difficult, through cooperation and knowledge sharing, it becomes possible. I am continually heartened by the memory of a secondary school student who chased after me one day on a remote, hand-hewed airstrip to express a concept for which formerly the Machiguenga had no words, "Thank you for bringing me education!" It was obvious from the look on his face that he really meant it.

Chapter Summary

Few studies in minority language communities have the advantage of forty years of documentation or the willing cooperation of hundreds of individuals who have been participant-observers over the entire period. To compensate for the recognized imprecision of the Informal Reading Inventory used to test reading, the study included a higher than normal sampling—ten percent of the reported accessible population of the bilingual school communities of the Lower Urubamba area. The 64.7 percent mother-tongue literacy rate found among the Machiguenga falls in the top six percent of the literacy rates recorded for 1,539 minority-group languages world wide.

This chapter reviews the sociological and educational conditions which promoted the success of literacy among the Machiguenga, and notes that among the results one can observe institutionalization of literacy, enhanced personal self-esteem, protection of human rights, and increased acquisition of Spanish.

Policy makers are urged to support policies which permit self-government, protect native rights, facilitate income-generating projects, and to recognize native authorities and their petitions. Educational administrators are urged to support the use of the mother tongue, especially in primary education; to adapt materials to the language and culture, to assign budgets commensurate with the high cost of transport to remote communities, to assign Machiguenga teachers to the Machiguenga schools, and to facilitate high-quality teacher preparation and in-service training. Self-administration (not dependence) must be the goal; to this end, income-generating projects will be necessary. Change can be introduced effectively only at the pace at which the majority are able to accept it; pushing faster than the people can adapt may harm both them and the program.

Future studies may refine the evaluation procedures devised for this study or test them in other languages and cultures. As for the Machiguenga, increased impingement from the outside world will continue to tax their resilience. To be successful long-term, they will need the sympathetic support of policy makers and local officials.

Once again, I wish to express my appreciation to the Machiguenga for their admirable accomplishments and their willingness to allow information about themselves to be placed at the service of educators.

Chapter Summary

Above:
Tucked away in the rafters, one school boy has found a quiet place to read his book.

Right:
The school horn continues to blow at 7:00 a.m. in Machiguenga villages.
(P. Davis photos. c. 1972)

Appendix A
Interview Form

Identity:_____ Masc._____ Fem._____
Community:_____ Age:_____
Years of schooling:_____ Last yr. of study_____
                                          Last yr. of study_____
Positions held: _____   Year_____
                   _____   Year_____
                   _____   Year_____

I. Uses of Reading and Writing

a. Do you read?_____   a. Do you write?_____

b. What do you read?   b. What do you write?
   Letters_____ Books_____   Letters_____ Accounts_____
   Bus.ltrs_____ Pamphlets_____   Bus.ltrs_____ Minutes_____
   Bible_____   Newspapers___   Bible verses_____
   Textbks (Gr. 1-3)_____   Homework (Gr. 1-3)_____
   Textbks (Gr. 4-6)_____   Homework (Gr. 4-6)_____
   Textbks (High School)_____   Homework (High School)_____
   Other_____   Other_____
   _____   _____

c. How often do you read?   c. How often do you write?
   Every day_____   Every day_____
   Several times a day_____   Several times a day_____
   Once in a while_____   Once in a while_____
   Hardly ever_____   Hardly ever_____
   Never_____   Never_____
   Other_____   Other_____
   _____   _____

d. For how much time?   d. For how much time?
   Short_____Long_____periods.   Short_____Long_____periods.
   Other_____   Other_____

Interview Form

II. Self Evaluation

a. What is reading?

_____
_____

b. How do you know if someone can read?

_____
_____

c. How can you tell the people who can read from those who cannot?

_____
_____

d. How did you learn to read?
  Teacher_____
  Adult lit. teacher_____
  Other_____

e. Do you feel you read well?
  Yes____ Fair____ No____
  Other_____

f. Would being able to read better help you in any way?_____

  How?_____

  _____
  Why might it not be useful?
  _____
  Do you want to read better?
  _____
  _____

a. What is writing?

_____
_____

b. ...that someone can write?

_____
_____

c. How can you tell the people who can write from those who cannot?

_____
_____

d. How did you learn to write?
  Teacher_____
  Adult lit. teacher_____
  Other_____

e. Do you feel you write well?
  Yes____ Fair____ No____
  Other_____

f. Would being able to write better help you in any way?_____

  How?_____

  _____
  Why might it not be useful?
  _____
  Do you want to write better?
  _____
  _____

g. Do you read better now than
   when Pat was here before?
   Yes____ No____ Other____

g. Do you write better now than
   when Pat was here before?
   Yes____ No____ Other____

III. Attitudes towards Reading and Writing

a. Do your parents know
   how to read?
   Yes_____ No_____

a. Do your parents know
   how to write?
   Yes_____ No_____

b. Have things changed since
   people learned how to read?
   Yes_____ No_____
   If so, how?
   _____
   _____

b. Have things changed since
   people learned how to write?
   Yes_____ No_____
   If so, how?
   _____
   _____

c. Is it good to read?
   Yes_____ No_____
   If so, what is it good for?
   _____
   _____

c. Is it good to write?
   Yes_____ No_____
   If so, what is it good for?
   _____
   _____

d. Do you expect to continue
   reading?
   Yes_____ No_____

d. Will you continue writing?
   Yes_____ No_____

e. Will you read a lot or a little?
   A lot_____ A little_____

e. Will you write a lot or a little?
   A lot_____ A little_____

f. In which language will you
   read?
   Machi____ Spanish____ Both____

f. In which language will you
   write?
   Machi____ Spanish____ Both____

g. Who needs to read?
   Masc.__ Fem.__ Everyone__

g. Who needs to write?
   Masc.__ Fem.__ Everyone__

Interview Form

h. Can elected officials function if they do not know how to read?

   Yes_____ No_____

i. If a man can't read, does it cause him problems?

   Yes_____ No_____

j. If a woman can't read, does it cause her problems?

   Yes_____ No_____

k. What hopes have you for your children? Do they need to know how to read?

   Yes_____ No_____

   Should surpass you?_____

_____

l. Do you connect any problems with reading?

   Yes_____ No_____

_____

h. Can elected officials function if they do not know how to write?

   Yes_____ No_____

i. If a man can't write, does it cause him problems?

   Yes_____ No_____

j. If a woman can't write, does it cause her problems?

   Yes_____ No_____

k. What hopes have you for your children? Do they need to know how to write?

   Yes_____ No_____

   Should surpass you?_____

_____

l. Do you connect any problems with writing?

   Yes_____ No_____

_____

ll. What good things has the school brought?

_____
_____
_____

What bad things has the school brought?

_____
_____
_____

IV. Knowledge of Numbers

a. Can you sell your____(name of item)_____?

   Yes_____ No_____

   Other_____

b. Can you count money?
   Yes_____   No_____
   Other_____

Appendix B
Examples of the Reading Tests

Example of a Basic Test - Conocimientos Básicos No.1

PRUEBA DE LECTURA

SILABAS:

a	yam	tsim	pun	she
tyon	je	su	kim	ran

LECTURA No. 1

YOYARIVE

Ikemakotagani pairani itimi paniro matsigenka ipaita Yoyarive. Pairotyo ikisanti, aikiro inti mashitsari. Ikisavintsavagetakerotyo itsinanetsite. Yagavagetirika imichatapitsavagetakarotyo kara.
 Tatarika yagavageti irirori tera impero ijina onkotakera, inti kotapaatsi. Yagatakera isekatakara ipakotanakero itsinanete iani osekatakempara irorori, ario ikañotiro maika. Agaka...

LECTURA NO. 2

TSAME VETSIKAIGAKERA TSIGARINTSI

Antari ovetsikaganira tsigarintsi oketyo asapeagani kamonatonki, tirotitonki, ontirika aikiro segatonki osatyo aikiro tsigarotonki impogini opietonkitunkani. Onkotashitagani konori intirika kapi inkovaanakerika iroveatanakemparika yoguitagani ashi tiritonkitakerora ontsotenkakemparika opiatunkani kapiropiku ashi itsigataganira tsimeripage...

Example of an Intermediate Test - Conocimientos Intermedios No. 3

PRUEBA DE LECTURA

LECTURA No. 1   TSOMIRI (A)

Maika nonkenkitsateri tsomiri. Itimi pairani matsigenka paniro itimi ontiri itsinanetsite itimavageti anta parikoti tera intentagantempa aikiro tera inkoge ineaigakerira ishaninkaegi.

Impogini iatake matsigenka iranuivagetera anta inkenishiku iavagetake samani ikentake osheto, ipigaa ivankoku yamakeri osheto ineapaakero ijina, onkotavakeri iposatanakera isekatavageigaka. Okutagitetanai ikanti: —Noateta inkenishiku nonkamosovagetakitera osheto. Iroro iatanakera, oga ijina oneiri ikenapaake tsomiri kañotaka matsigenka inkametivageteratyo kara, icharianisanotyo inake ikantiro...

LECTURA No. 2

"Shiriagarini isuretakotaaganira Cesar Vallejo ontiri oneavakagakara pitetipage kipatsi"

Kamisea, 24 de junio de 1992

Sankevanti otsirinkakara No. 01-EEMB-No.64443-c.92
- Tinkamitarorira escuela No.64443.
- Nokaemakagantanakempi ashi imagempiitaigakera ananekiegi gititsiku intiri akotsiku.

Notsirinkanakempi oka sankevanti ashi nonkamantakempira viro, aka naroegi gotagantaigatsirira aka Kamiseakunirira, napatoitaigaka visanankitsirira tomingo ashi nonkaemakagantaigakempiniri pimpokaigakera aka imagempiitaigakera ananekiegi gititsiku intiri akotsiku. Ontsititantanakempa kutagiteri 03 irashi julio imagempitantaigarira komunidad irinanakera shavini...

The print shown is the size actually used, but due to lack of space, the readings illustrated are incomplete.

Example of an Advanced Test

Paniro Tasorintsi
yagaveakagasanotakai gotasanoigakera

[13] Aiñorika kara gotatsirira isuretara kantetyo inegintevagetakempara, aikiro inkavintsaantavagetakera, kantankicha gara yaventakotaro kameti iokotagantakempaniri arisano opaitaka yogovagetakera. [14] Kantankicha pinkisasanotakeririka pitovaire pinkogakera pavisaigakerira, aikiro vikiirorika suretakotaachane, garatyo pitsoega pinkantakera: "Nogovageti". [15] Teranika Iriro gotagempirone Tasorintsi pinkañotakempara maika, tsikyatatyo pisuretakaro viro, ariotari ikantaigari matsigenkaegi, aikiro inti suretagakempiro kamagarini. [16] Nonkantaigakempi tyarikara itimaigake kisantasanoigatsirira, aikiro ikiiro suretakotaacha, omirinka ikisavakagaigaka, aikiro yovetsikagisevageigake posantepage terira onkametite. [17] Kantankicha yogari yogotagasanotakerira Tasorintsi kametikya itimi, tenige inkisantavagete, aikiro isuretakotantavageta. Tyanirika niakeri ikemisantasanotakeri. Itsarogakagantavageta, aikiro ikavintsaantavageti, itsatagasanogetiro ikantakerira, tera iramatavitantumate. [18] Yogaegiri gametigantaigatsirira ganiri ikisavakagaiga kametikya itimaigake, ariompatari ineginteiganakari.

Example of a Spanish Test

Conocimientos Avanzados – Castellano No. 16

5 de mayo de 1986

Oficio No. 05-SSE-22-NL-86

Señor: Director de la escuela No. 64443-B, Camisea

Asunto: Cursillo sobre Promoción Comunal

 Es grato dirigirme a Ud., para comunicarle que a partir del 2 al 6 de junio del año en curso se llevará un Cursillo de Promoción Comunal en la sede de la Supervisión, comunidad nativa de Nueva Luz. Este Cursillo es de carácter obligatorio, debiendo asistir todos los profesores y alfabetizadores, como también los líderes de las comunidades.

 En este cursillo todos los participantes se harán acreedor de un Certificado de Participación. Los exponentes serán funcionarios del Ministerio de Educación, del INIPA, y de Vecinos Mundiales.

Examples of the Reading Tests   293

The print shown is close to the size actually used; the type is slightly smaller. The information, however, is complete.

Appendix C
Reading Score Chart

Identity _____
Masc. _____ Fem. _____
Community _____   Age _____
Studies completed _____   Year _____
               _____   **Year** _____
               _____   Year _____

Machiguenga	**Spanish**
Passage: _____	Passage: _____
Total no. of syllables read	
Time required:	
Rate (syllables per minute):	
No of syllables correct: __ (Basic reading only)	
Accuracy: Omissions	
Insertions	
Substitutions	
Corrections Attempted	
Corrections Achieved	
Fluency (scale of 1 to 5): Syllable Word Phrase Punctuation Expression 1 2 3 4 5	1 2 3 4 5
Comprehension (scale of 1 to 5): None Poor Fair Good Excellent 1 2 3 4 5	1 2 3 4 5
GLOBAL STANDARDIZED SCORE	

Reading Score Chart

Example of the coding system used when scoring the reading tests

PRUEBA DE LECTURA

SILABAS:

a	yam	tsim	pun	she°
tyo(n)	je	su	kim	ran

7 out of 10

LECTURA No. 1   YOYARIVE

Ikemakotagani pairani itimi paniro m̄atsigenka ipaita
Yoyarive. Pairo(tyo) ikisanti, aikiro inti∧mashitsari.
(*omission*) (*tari - addition*)

Ikisavintsavagetakerotyo itsinanetsite. Yagavagetirika
(imichatapitsavagetakarotyo) kara.
  aid given

Tatarika yagavageti irirori tera impero ijina
Tatoita - substitution

onkotakera, inti kotapaatsi.

Yagatakera isekatakara ipakota(na)kero itsinanete iani
           A———————— ri - *attempted correction*

osekatakempara irorori, ario...
——C———— - *successful correction*

LECTURA No. 2

TSAME VETSIKAIGAKERA TSIGARINTSI

Antari [1]ovetsikaganira tsigarintsi oketyo asapeagani
[3]kamonatonki, [5]tirotitonki, ontirika aikiro [5]segatonki
osatyo aikiro [4]tsigarotonki impogini opietonkitunkani.
[7]Onkotashitagani konori intirika kapi inkovaanakerika
iroveatanakemparika yoguitagani [2]ashi tiritonkitakerora
ontsotenkakemparika opiatunkani kapiropiku ashi
itsigataganira tsimeripage.

Superscript numbers indicate items included in the person's recount of the story.

Appendix D
Example of the Comprehension Scale

Conocimientos Avanzados No. 3 - Castellano

CONGRESO DE LAS COMUNIDADES NATIVAS DEL BAJO URUBAMBA
Congress   of   the Native Communities   of the Lower Urubamba

    Fecha: 1 al 6 de agosto de 1991
    Date: 1 to 6 of August, 1991.

COMISIÓN 2.   Tema: SALUD
Committee 2.   Theme: Health.

Problemas: Problems:

1. Falta de medicamentos en las comunidades.
   Medicine is lacking in the communities.

2. Falta de equipamiento de las postas.
   The health posts lack equipment.

3. Las comunidades de Nueva Vida, Mayapo, Camaná,
   The communities of Nueva Vida, Mayapo, Camaná,

       Shivankoreni, y Campo Verde carecen de sanitarios.
       Shivankoreni, and Campo Verde lack health workers.

Alternativas: Alternatives:

1. Solicitar a las instituciones públicas y privadas
   Request   institutions public and private

       un mayor apoyo para el suministro de medicamentos.
       for more support for the provision of medications.

2. Solicitar a nuestro Representante su apoyo para
   Request of our Representative his support in

       exigir el equipamiento de las postas.
       insisting upon the equipping of the health posts.

3. Gestionar ante las instituciones la capacitación
   Pursue with institutions training

       de los promotores del Bajo Urubamba.
       for the health workers of the Lower Urubamba.

Example of the Comprehension Scale

Comprehension Examples—Scale of 1–5

Level 1   - No response.   (House 41, Camaná, Da #3)

Level 2   - Poor. Scattered thoughts but not the main idea.
- "Medicines are lacking."
- "In Nueva Vida, Mayapo, Camaná, Campo Verde."
                                     (House 6, Camaná, Son)

Level 3   -Fair. The main idea.
- Topic -"medicines for the communities".
- "Camaná and Shivankoreni need medicines."
- "More help will be requested - donations of medicines."
                                     (House 24, Camaná, Father)

Level 4   - Good. The main idea plus supporting information.
- Topic - "medicines."
- "We need medicines."
- "Here there are none; the communities are short."
- "They are needed in Mayapo, Camaná, Campo Verde."
- "The leaders will request medicines."
                                     (House 16, Camaná, Father)

Level 5   - Excellent. Most of the ideas of the text. (No Level 5 example from this reading occurred in my data, but this is what I would have expected.)
- "The Congress of Native Communities met in August 1991."
- Problems:
    - "The communities lack medicines."
    - "The health posts lack equipment."
    - "Nueva Vida, Mayapo, Camaná, Shivankoreni and Campo Verde lack health workers."
- Alternatives:
    - "Ask public and private institutions for greater support in providing medicines."
    - "Request our representative to insist on equipment for the health posts."
    - "Request training for health promotors for the Lower Urubamba."

References

Alegría, J., and J. Morales 1991. Segmental analysis and reading acquisition. In L. Rieben and C. A. Perfetti, 135–148.

Anderson, R. C., Hiebert, E. H., Scott, J. A., and I. A. G. Wilkinson. 1985. *Becoming a nation of readers: The report of the commission on reading.* Washington, D.C.: The National Institute of Education, U.S. Department of Education.

Anthony, R. J., T. D. Johnson, N. I. Mickelson, and A. Preece. 1991. *Evaluating literacy: A perspective for change.* Portsmouth, N.H.: Heinnemann.

Anzalone, S., and S. McLaughlin. 1983. *Making literacy work: The specific approach.* Amhurst: Center for International Education, University of Massachusetts.

Ardery, J. Fall/Winter 1988. Measuring illiteracy: "Functional Competency" and the realms of gold. *Texas Journal of Ideas, History and Culture,* 58–61.

Au, K. H., and J. A. Kawakami 1986. The influence of the social organization of instruction on children's text comprehension ability: A Vygotskian perspective. In T. E. Raphael (ed.), *The contexts of school-based literacy,* 370–394. New York: Teachers College Press.

Aulls, M. W. 1978. *Developmental and remedial reading in the middle grades.* Boston: Allyn and Bacon.

Aulls, M. W. 1982. *Developing readers in today's elementary school.* Boston: Allyn and Bacon.

Baker, Colin. 1997. *Foundations of bilingual education and bilingualism.* Philadelphia, Penn.: Multilingual Matters.

Baksh, G. M. 1984. *Cultural ecology and change of the Machiguenga Indians of the Peruvian Amazon.* Ph.D. dissertation. University of California, Los Angeles. Ann Arbor, Mich.: University Microfilms.

Barr, R., and Johnson, B. 1991. *Teaching reading in elementary classrooms.* New York: Longman.

Barr, R., M. L. Kamil, P. B. Mosenthal, and P. D. Pearson, eds. 1991. *Handbook of reading research,* Vol. 2. New York: Longman.

Barr, R., M. Sadow, and C. Blachowicz. 1990. *Reading diagnosis for teachers: An instructional approach.* New York: Longman.

Barton, D. 1994. *Literacy: an introduction to the ecology of written language.* Cambridge, Mass.: Blackwell Publishers.

Betts. Emmet A. 1946. *Foundations of reading instruction,* New York: American Book Co.

Betts, Emmet A. 1954. *Foundations of reading instruction,* revised edition. New York: American Book Co.

Bhola, H. S., J. Muller, and P. Dijkstra. 1983. *The promise of literacy.* Baden-Baden, Germany: Nomos Verlagsgesellschaft.

Bhola, H. S. 1989a. The right to learn. *1985 International Conference on Adult Education.* Paris: UNESCO.

Bhola, H. S. 1989b. International literacy year: A summons to action for universal literacy by the year 2000. *Educational Horizons,* 62–67.

Bhola, H. S. 1990a. *Evaluating "literacy for development" projects, programs and campaigns.* Hamburg, Germany: UNESCO Institute for Education and German Foundation for International Development.

Bhola, H. S. 1990b. Literature on adult literacy: New directions. *Comparative Education Review* 34(1):139–144.

Bloomfield, L., and C. L. Barnhart. 1961. *Let's read: A linguistic approach.* Detroit, Mich.: Wayne State University Press.

Bond, G. L., M. A. Tinker, B. B. Wasson, and J. B. Wasson. 1989. *Reading difficulties, their diagnosis and correction,* sixth edition. Englewood Cliffs, N.J.: Prentice-Hall.

Brown, M., and E. Fernández. 1991. *War of shadows: The struggle for Utopia in the Peruvian Amazon.* Berkeley and Los Angeles: University of California Press.

Bruner, J. S., R. R. Olver, and P. J. Greenfield. 1966. *Studies in cognitive growth; A collaboration at the center for cognitive studies.* New York: Wiley.

Bull, W. 1955. The use of vernacular languages in education. *International Journal of American Linguistics* 21:228–294.

Burns, N. 1984. Functors and discourse analysis in Quechua primer design. *Notes on Literacy* 42:11–14.

Cairns, J. December 1985. *World literacy—an overview.* Keynote address presented at the World Literacy and International Cooperation Seminar, Gananoque, Ontario, Canada. In author's files.

Calfee, R., and E. Hiebert. 1991. Classroom assessment of reading. In R. Barr, M. L. Kamil, P. B. Mosenthal, and P. D. Pearson, 281–309.

Carpenter, P. A., and M. A. Just. 1977. Reading comprehension as eyes see it. In P. A. Carpenter and M. A. Just (eds.), *Cognitive processes in comprehension,* 109–139. Hillsdale, N.J.: Lawrence Erlbaum.

Chall, J. S. 1967. *Learning to read: The great debate.* New York: McGraw-Hill.

Chall, J. S. 1983. *Stages of reading development.* New York: McGraw-Hill.

Clammer, J. R. 1976. *Literacy and social change. A case study of Fiji.* Leiden, The Netherlands: E. J. Brill.

Cook-Gumperz, J. 1986. *The social construction of literacy.* Cambridge: Cambridge University Press.

Cook-Gumperz, J., and D. Keller-Cohen. 1993. Alternative literacies in school and beyond. *Anthropology and Education Quarterly* 24(4):283–287.

Couvert, Roger. 1979. *The evaluation of literacy programmes.* Paris: UNESCO.

Cowan, G. 1986. Scripture use among Machiguenga and Ashaninca Campa of Peru. *Notes on Scripture in Use* 10:3–23.

Cressey, D. 1983. The environment for literacy: Accomplishment and context in seventeenth-century England and New England. In D. Resnick (ed.), *Literacy in historical perspective,* 23–42. Washington, D.C.: Library of Congress.

Cummins, J. 1979. Linguistic interdependence and the educational development of bilingual children. *Review of Educational Research* 49(2):222–251.

Daneman, M. (1991). Individual differences in reading skills. In R. Barr, M. L. Kamil, P. B. Mosenthal, and P. D. Pearson, 512–538.

Davis, P. M. 1973a. Confeccionando cartillas. *Comunidades y Culturas Peruanas,* 1:19–36. Yarinacocha, Peru: Instituto Lingüístico de Verano.

Davis, P. M. 1973b. Informe sobre el viaje de los profesores bilingües a Quillabamba y Cuzco. (Microfiche. Información de Campo No. 123) Yarinacocha, Peru: Instituto Lingüístico de Verano.

Davis, P. M. 1981a. The program and the community. In Larson and Davis, 199–207.

Davis, P. M. 1981b. The village schools: Goals and their implementation. In Larson and Davis, 109–148.

Davis, P. M. 1981c. The challenges of primer making. In Larson and Davis, 265–281.

Davis, P. M. 1988. Literacy amongst the Machiguenga: A case study. *Notes on Literacy* 55:51–58.

Davis, P.M. 1991. *Cognition and learning: A review of the literature with reference to ethnolinguistic minorities.* Dallas: Summer Institute of Linguistics.

Davis, P.M. 1992. How numeracy came to the Machiguenga. Manuscript.

Davis, P. M., S. Parker, and C Noordam Eilander. 1990. La cultura autóctona y algunas sugerencias para el aula bilingüe. In A. Bergli (ed.), *Educación intercultural*, 91–100. Comunidades y Culturas Peruanas 23. Yarinacocha, Peru: Instituto Lingüístico de Verano.

Davis, P. M., W. W. Snell, and Betty A Snell. 1992. Leaping into the space age: Community development among the Machiguenga. Paper presented to the Conference on Inter Cultural Community Work, Dallas, Tex., May 1992.

de Castell, S., A. Luke, and K. Egan, eds. 1986. *Literacy, society, and schooling: A reader.* Cambridge: Cambridge University Press.

de Castell, S., A. Luke, and D. MacLennan. 1986. On defining literacy. In S. de Castell, and A. Luke, K. Egan, 3–14.

Dirección General de la Educación Bilingüe. 1989. *Política nacional de la educación bilingüe intercultural.* Lima, Peru: Ministerio de Educación.

Dorsey, B. J. 1989. Educational development and reform in Zimbabwe. *Comparative Education Review* 33(1):40–58.

Dowhower, S. L. 1987. Effects of repeated reading on second-grade transitional readers' fluency and comprehension. *Reading Research Quarterly* 22:389–406.

Dowhower, S. L. 1991. Speaking of prosody: Fluency's unattended bedfellow. *Theory into practice* 30(3):165–175.

Downing, J., and C. K. Leong. 1982. *Psychology of Reading.* New York: Macmillan.

Dutcher, N. 1982. *The use of first and second languages in primary education: Selected case studies.* World Bank Staff Working Paper, No. 504. Washington, D.C.: The World Bank.

Dutcher, N. 1995. *The use of first and second languages in education: A review of international experience.* Pacific Islands Discussion Paper, No. 1. Washington, D.C.: The World Bank.

Education Commission of the States. 1972. *Reading rate and comprehension, 1970–71 assessment.* National Assessment of Educational Progress (Report 02-R-09). Washington, D.C.: U.S. Government Printing Office.

Ekwall, E. E., and J. L. Shanker. 1988. *Diagnosis and remediation of the disabled reader.* Boston: Allyn and Bacon.

Ekwall, E. E. 1989. *Locating and correcting reading difficulties.* Colombus, Ohio: Merrill.

Farr, R., and R. F. Carey. 1986. *Reading: What can be measured?* Newark, Del.: International Reading Association.

Ferguson, C. 1987. Literacy in a hunting-gathering society: The case of the Diyari. *Journal of Anthropological Research* 43(3):223–237.

Flinn, J. 1992. Transmitting traditional values in new schools: Elementary education of Pulap Atoll. *Anthropology and Education Quarterly* 23(1):44–58.

Foley, D. 1990. *Learning capitalist culture: Deep in the heart of Tejas.* Philadelphia: University of Pennsylvania Press.

Foley, D. 1991. Reconsidering anthropological explanations of ethnic school failure. *Anthropology and Education Quarterly* 22(1):60–86.

Fordham, S. 1993. "Those loud black girls": (Black) women and gender "passing" in the academy. *Anthropology and Education Quarterly* 24(1):3–32.

Foster, George M. 1973. *Traditional societies and technological change.* New York: Harper and Row.

Foster, P., and A Purves. 1991. Literacy and society with particular reference to the non-Western world. In R. Barr, M. L. Kamil, P. B. Mosenthal, and P. David Pearson, 26–45.

Fried, M. 1967. *The evolution of political society.* New York: Random House.

Freire, P., and D. Macedo. 1987. *Literacy: Reading the word and the world.* South Hadley, Mass.: Bergin and Garvey.

Galtung, J. 1976. Literacy, education and schooling—for what? In L. Bataille, *A turning point for literacy,* 93–105. New York and Oxford: Pergamon.

Gibson, M. 1988. *Accommodation without assimilation: Sikh immigrants in an American high school.* New York: Cornell University Press.

Giesecke, M., and G. Elwert 1982. Adult literacy in a context of cultural revolution: Structural parallels of the literacy process in sixteenth century Germany and present day Benin. Paper presented at Tenth World Congress of Sociology, Subsection 9, Mexico City, Mexico.

Gillette, A. 1977. The Experimental World Literacy Programme: Taking stock. In *Teaching reading and writing to adults: A sourcebook.* Tehran, Iran: International Institute for Adult Literacy Methods.

Gillette, A. and J. Ryan. 1983. Eleven issues in literacy for the 1990s. In P. E. Mandi (ed.), *Assignment children: Literacy, health, nutrition and income,* 19–44. Geneva: UNICEF.

Giroux, H. 1983. *Theory and resistance in education.* London: Heinemann Education Books.

Gleitman, L. R., and P. Rozin. 1977. Reading 1: Language structure. In A. S. Reber and D. L. Scarborough, *Towards a psychology of reading:*

The proceedings of the CUNY Conference 48–50. Hillsdale, N.J.: Lawrence Erlbaum.

Goodman, K. S. 1969. Analysis of oral reading miscues: Applied psycholinguistics. *Reading Research Quarterly* 5:9–30.

Goodman, K. S. 1981. Letter to the editors. *Reading Research Quarterly,* 16(3):477–478.

Goodman, K. 1982a. Orthography in a theory of reading instruction. In F. V. Gollasch (ed.), *The selected writings of Kenneth S. Goodman, II,* 90–95. London: Kegan Paul.

Goodman, K. 1982b. Psycholinguistic universals in the reading process. In F. V. Gollasch (ed.), *The selected writings of Kenneth S. Goodman, II,* 64–69. London: Kegan Paul.

Goodman, K. 1986. *What's whole in whole language?* Portsmouth, N.H.: Heineman.

Goodman, K. S., Y. Goodman, and B. Flores. 1978. Literacy in a multilingual world. In *Reading in the bilingual classroom: Literacy and biliteracy,* 5–10 (second edition, 1984). Rosslyn, Va.: Inter America Research Associates, Inc., National Association for Bilingual Education.

Goodman, Y. M., and C. L. Burke. 1972. *Reading miscue inventory manual: Procedure for diagnosis and evaluation.* New York: Macmillan.

Goody, J., ed. 1968. *Literacy in traditional societies.* Cambridge: Cambridge University Press.

Goody, J. 1977. *The domestication of the savage mind.* Cambridge: Cambridge University Press.

Goody, J. 1986. *The logic of writing and the organization of society.* Cambridge: Cambridge University Press.

Gough, K. 1968. Literacy in Kerala. In J. Goody, 133–160.

Gough, P. B. 1972. One second of reading. In J. F. Kavanagh, and I. G. Mattingly (eds.), *Language by ear and by eye,* 331–358. Cambridge, Mass.: MIT Press.

Gough, P. B., and C. Juel. 1991. The first stages of word recognition. In L. Rieben and C. A. Perfetti, 47–56.

Graff, H. J. 1986. The legacies of literacy: Continuities and contradictions in western society and culture. In S. de Castell, A. Luke, and K. Egan (eds.), 61–86.

Gram Vikas and Pradan. 1990. Communal rights vs. private profit. *The Ecologist* 20(3):105–107.

Gray, W. S. 1956. *The teaching of reading and writing.* Chicago: Scott Foresman.

Gray, W. S. 1961. *The teaching of reading and writing.* Monographs on fundamental education 10, second edition. Paris: UNESCO.

Gray, W. S. 1984. *Reading: A research retrospective, 1881–1941.* Newark, Del.: International Reading Association.

Greaney, V., and S. Neuman. 1990. The functions of reading: A cross-cultural perspective. *Reading Research Quarterly* 25(3):172–195.

Gudschinsky, S. C. 1973. *A manual of literacy for preliterate peoples.* Ukarumpa, Papua New Guinea: Summer Institute of Linguistics.

Guiora, A. 1984. The dialect of language acquisition. *Language Learning* 35:3–12.

Guszak, F. J. 1985. *Diagnostic reading instruction in the elementary school.* New York: Harper and Row.

Harris, R. 1981. *The language machine.* Ithaca, N.Y.: Cornell University Press.

Harris, R. 1986. *The origin of writing.* La Salle, Ill.: Open Court.

Harris, S. 1982. Traditional Aboriginal education strategies and their possible place in a modern bicultural school. In J. Sherwood (ed.), *Aboriginal education: Issues and innovations.* Perspectives in Multicultural Education II, 127–139. Perth, Australia: Creative Research.

Heath, S. B. 1982. What no bedtime story means: Narrative skills at home and school. *Language in Society* 11:49–75.

Heath, S. B. 1983. *Ways with words.* Cambridge: Cambridge University Press.

Heath, S. B. 1984. Oral and literate traditions. *Sociolinguistic theory and research* 36(1):41–57. Paris: UNESCO.

Heath, S. B. 1986a. Critical factors in literacy development. In S. de Castell, A. Luke, and K. Egan, 209–230.

Heath, S. B. 1986b. The functions and uses of literacy. In S. de Castell, A. Luke, and K. Egan (eds.), 15–26.

Heath, S. B. July 1987. Some very tentative principles of literacy retention. Paper presented at the meeting of the Vernacular Literacy Conference, Stanford University, Stanford, Calif.

Heath, S. B. 1991. The sense of being literate: Historical and cross-cultural features. In R. Barr, M. Kamil, P. B. Mosenthal, and P. D. Pearson, 3–25.

Henderson, L. 1984. Writing systems and reading processes. In L. Henderson (ed.), *Orthographies and Reading,* 11–24. Hillsdale, N. J.: Lawrence Erlbaum.

Henne, M. G. 1985. *Why mother tongue literature failed to take root among the Maya Quiche: A study in the sociology of language in a field program of the Summer Institute of Linguistics, 1955–1982, Guatemala, Central America.* M.A. thesis. University of Texas at Arlington.

Henze, R, and L. Vanett. 1993. To walk in two worlds—or more? Challenging a common metaphor of native education. *Anthropology and Education Quarterly* 24(2):116–134.

Herriman, M. L. 1986. Metalinguistic awareness and the growth of literacy. In de Castell, Luke, and Egan (eds.), 159–174.

Hittleman, D. R. 1988. *Developmental Reading, K-8: Teaching from a whole language perspective.* Columbus, Ohio: Merrill.

Hoffman, J. V., and M. E. Isaacs. 1991. Developing fluency through restructuring the task of guided oral reading. *Theory into Practice,* 30(3):185–194.

Hornberger, N. H. April, 1981. Bilingual education projects in the southern Peruvian sierra, 1. Research report presented at the 1981 Annual Meeting of the Southern Anthropological Society, Fort Worth, Texas.

Huebner, T. 1987. A socio-historical approach to literacy development: A comparative case study from the Pacific. In Langer, 178–196.

Huey, E. B. 1968. *The psychology and pedagogy of reading* (first edition 1908). Cambridge, Mass.: The MIT Press.

ICE (International Conference on Education). September 1992. *Draft final report. International Conference on Education.* Forty-third Session. Geneva: Author.

Inkeles, A., and D. H. Smith 1974. *Becoming modern.* Cambridge, Mass.: Harvard University Press.

International Reading Association. 1986. *How to prepare materials for new literates.* Newark, Del: International Reading Association.

International Reading Association. April/May 2001. Association issues position statement on second-language literacy instruction. *Reading Today,* 6. Newark, Del.: International Reading Association.

Johnson, O. R. 1978. *Interpersonal relations and domestic authority among the Machiguenga of the Peruvian Amazon.* Ann Arbor, Mich.: University Microfilms.

Johnson, P. L. 1993. Education and the "new" inequality in Papua New Guinea. *Anthropology and Education Quarterly,* 24(3):183–204.

Juel, C. 1991. Beginning reading. In R. Barr, M. L. Kamil, P. B. Mosenthal, and P. D. Pearson, 759–788.

Kashoki, M. E. 1989. On the notions and implications of the concept of mother tongue in literacy education in a multilingual context: The case of Zambia. In E. Zuanelli Sonino (ed.), *Literacy in school and society: Multidisciplinary perspectives,* 3–14. New York: Plenum.

Keller-Cohen, D. 1993. Rethinking literacy: Comparing colonial and contemporary America. *Anthropology and Education Quarterly,* 24(4):288–307.

Kelman, Herbert. 1971. Language as an aid and barrier to involvement in the national system. In J. Rubin and B. Jernudd (eds.), *Can language be planned?,* 21–51. Honolulu: University Press of Hawaii.
Kennedy, E. C. 1981. *Methods in teaching developmental reading.* Itasca, Ill.: P. E. Peacock Publishers.
Killgallon, P. A. 1942. *A study of relationships among certain pupil adjustments in language situations.* Doctoral. Pennsylvania State University.
Klein, M. L., S. Peterson, and L Simington. 1991. *Teaching reading in the elementary grades,* Annotated instructor's edition. Boston, Mass.: Allyn and Bacon.
Klich, L. Z., and G. R. Davidson. 1984. Australian Aboriginal competence in cognitive functions. In J. R. Kirby (ed.), *Cognitive strategies and educational performance,* 155–202. Orlando, Fl.: Academic Press.
LaBerge, D., and S. Samuels. 1974. Toward a theory of automatic information processing in reading. *Cognitive Psychology* 6:293–323.
LaBerge, D., and V. Brown. 1986. Variations in the size of the visual field in which targets are presented: An attentional range effect. *Perception and Psychometrics* 40:188–200.
Lambert, W. 1978. Some cognitive and sociocultural implications of being bilingual. In J. E. Atlatis (ed.), *International dimensions of bilingualism,* 214–229. Georgetown University Round Table on Language and Linguistics. Washington, D.C.: Georgetown University Press.
Langer, J. A. 1987. A sociocognitive perspective on literacy. In J. A. Langer (ed.), *Language, Literacy and culture: Issues of society and schooling,* 1–20. Norwood, N. J.: Ablex.
Lapp, D., and J. Flood 1992. *Teaching reading to every child.* New York: Macmillan.
Larson, M. L., and P. M. Davis, eds. 1981. *Bilingual education: An experience in Peruvian Amazonia.* Washington, D.C.: Center for Applied Linguistics and Dallas, Tex: Summer Institute of Linguistics.
Laubach, F. C. 1951. The each one teach one method. 1950 supplement to *Teaching the world to read.* New York: Committee on World Literacy and Christian Literature.
Leap, W. L. 1991. Pathways and barriers to Indian language literacy-building on the Northern Ute reservation. *Anthropology and Education Quarterly* 22(1):21–41.
Lewis, E. Glynn. 1982. Movements and agencies of language spread: Wales and the Soviet Union compared. In Robert L. Cooper (ed.), *Language spread: Studies in diffusion and social change,* 214–259. Washington, D.C.: Center for Applied Linguistics.
Liberman, Isabelle Y., and Donald Shankweller. 1991. Phonology and beginning reading. A tutorial. In l. Rieben and C.A. Perfetti, 3–18.

Lingenfelter, J., and C. Gray. 1981. The importance of learning styles in literacy. *Notes on Literacy* 36:11–17.

Lipka, J. 1991. Toward a culturally-based pedagogy: A case study of one Yup'ik Eskimo Teacher. *Anthropology and Education Quarterly* 22(3):203–223.

Malone, D. 1994. "Dear Nolly..." *Notes on Literacy* 20(2):35–58.

Mangubhai, F. 1987. Literacy in the South Pacific: Some multilingual and multiethnic issues. In D. A. Wagner, 186–206.

Matshazi, M. J. 1987. Mother tongue literacy: The importance of learning to read and write in one's mother tongue. In M. Gayfer (ed.), *Literacy in industrialized countries: A focus on practice*, 50–53. *Convergence* 20:3–4. Toronto: International Council for Adult Education.

May, F. B., and S. B. Eliot. 1978. *To help children read* (first edition, 1973). Columbus, Ohio: Merrill.

McCracken, R. 1967. The informal reading inventory as a means of improving instruction. In T. Barrett (ed.), *The evaluation of children's reading achievement* 79–96. Newark, Del.: International Reading Association.

Mehan, H., L. Hubbard., and I. Villanueva. 1994. Forming academic identities: Accommodation without assimilation among involuntary minorities. *Anthropology and Education Quarterly* 25(2):91–117.

Mendoza, J. 1981. Resolution authorizing bilingual education in the Peruvian jungle (appendix A). In Larson and Davis, 393–394.

Mikulecky, L. and R. Drew. 1991. Basic literacy skills in the workplace. In. R. Barr, M. L. Kamil, P. B. Mosenthal, and P. Davis Pearson, 669–689.

Miller, G. A. 1956. Human memory and the storage of information. *IRE Transactions on information theory* IT-2(3):129–137.

Miller, G. A. 1967. The magical number seven, plus or minus two: Some limits on our capacity for processing information. In *The psychology of communication: Seven essays [by] George A. Miller*, 14–44. New York: Basic Books.

Miller, G. A. September 9, 1988. The challenge of universal literacy. *Science Magazine*, 1293–1299.

Miller, W. H. 1978. *Reading diagnosis kit*, second edition. West Nyack, N.Y.: The Center for Applied Research in Education.

Ministerio de Educación. July 2, 1957. *El Peruano* (official government newspaper). Lima, Peru.

Ministerio de Educación. 1972. *Política Nacional de Educación Bilingüe*, 10, "Objetivos". Lima: Ministerio de Educación.

Modiano, N. 1968. National or mother tongue language in beginning reading: A comparative study. *Research in the teaching of English* 2:32–43.

Modiano, N. 1973. *Indian education in the Chiapas highlands.* New York: Holt, Rinehart, and Winston.

Monroe, M. 1932. *Children who cannot read: The analysis of reading disabilities and the use of diagnostic tests in the instruction of retarded readers.* Chicago: University of Chicago Press.

Morris, D. 1992. Concept of word: A pivotal understanding in the learning process. In S. Templeton and D. R. Bear (eds.), *Development of orthographic knowledge and the foundations of literacy,* 53–77. Hillsdale, N.J.: Lawrence Erlbaum.

Murdock, G. P. 1946. The common denominator of culture. In Ralph Linton (ed.), *The science of man in world crisis,* 123–142. New York: Columbia University Press.

Murdock, G. P. 1960. *Social structure.* New York: Macmillan.

Nathan, R. G., and K. E. Stanovich. 1991. The causes and consequences of differences in reading fluency. *Theory into Practice* 30(3):176–184.

Neijs, K. 1961. *Literacy primers: Construction, evaluation, and use.* Manuals on adult and youth education, 2. Paris: UNESCO.

Nida, E. A. 1949. Approaching reading through the native language. *Language Learning* 2:16–20.

Nida, E. A. 1954. *Customs and cultures,* 245–247. New York: Harper.

Nkemnji, J. 1989. Education in Cameroon: National and colonial elements for children in a new nation. *Kappa Delta Pi Record* 25(4):99–103.

Official Report. August, 1991. Nueva Luz, Cusco, Peru: Congreso de Comunidades Nativas del Bajo Urubamba.

Ogbu, J. 1978. *Minority education and caste: The American system in cross-cultural perspective.* New York: Academic Press.

Ogbu, J. 1987. Variability in minority school performance: A problem in search of an explanation. *Anthropology and Education Quarterly* 18(4):312–334.

Ogbu, J. 1991. Immigrant and involuntary minorities in comparative perspective. In M. Gibson and J. Ogbu, *Minority status and schooling,* 3–37. New York: Garland Publishing.

Olson, D. R., N. Torrance, and A. Hilyard, eds. 1985. *Literacy, language, and Learning: The nature and consequences of reading and writing.* Cambridge: Cambridge University Press.

Ong, W. 1982. *Orality and literacy: The technologizing of the word.* New York: Methuen.

Ouane, A. 1989. *Handbook on learning strategies for post-literacy and continuing education.* UIE studies on post-literacy and continuing education 7. Hamburg: UNESCO Institute for Education.

Paulston, C. B. 1980. *Bilingual education: Theories and issues.* Rowley, Mass.: Newbury House.

Pearson, P. D., and L. Fielding. 1991. Comprehension instruction. In R. Barr, M. L. Kamil, P. B. Mosenthal, and P. D. Pearson, 815–860.

Pearson, P. David, L. R. Roehler, J. A. Dole, and G. G. Duffy. 1992. Developing expertise in reading comprehension. In S. Jay Samuels and Alan E. Farstrup (eds.), *What research has to say about reading instruction*, 145–199. Newark, Del.: International Reading Association.

Perez-Crespo, C. A. 1986. *Agricultural cooperatives: Perspectives from the Aymara and the Bolivian state.* Ph.D. dissertation. State University of New York, Binghamton.

Perfetti, C. A. 1985. *Reading ability.* New York: Oxford University Press.

Pierce, J. E. c. 1960. *A frequency count of Turkish words.* A report of a study by the staff of the Georgetown University Language Program Ankara, Turkey, under the chairmanship of Joe E. Pierce. Ankara, Turkey: Ministry of Education, Directorate of Publications, Printed Education Materials Development Center.

Purves, A. C. 1987. Literacy, culture and community. In D. A. Wagner (ed.), *The future of literacy in a changing world,* 216–232. Elmsford, N.Y.: Pergamon.

Rae, G., and T. C. Potter. 1981. *Informal reading diagnosis: A practical guide for the classroom teacher.* Englewood Cliffs, N.J.: Prentice-Hall.

Ramírez III, M., and A. Castañeda. 1974. *Cultural democracy, bicognitive development, and education.* New York: Academic Press.

Rao, S. V. 1985. *Education and rural development.* New Delhi: Sage.

Rayner, K. 1981. Eye movements and the perceptual span in reading. In F. J. Pirozzolo and M. C. Wittrock, *Neuropsychological and cognitive processes in reading,* 145–165. New York: Academic Press.

Rayner, K., and G. G. McConkie. 1977. Perceptual processes in reading: The perceptual spans. In A. Reber and D. Scarborough, 183–205.

Rayner, K., and A. Pollatsek. 1989. *The psychology of reading.* Englewood Cliffs, N.J.: Prentice Hall.

Reber, A. S., and D. L. Scarborough, eds. 1977. *Toward a psychology of reading: The proceedings of the CUNY Conference.* Hillsdale, N.J.: Lawrence Erlbaum.

Richards, A. I. 1935. The village census in the study of culture contact. *Africa* 8:20–23.

Rieben, L., and C. A. Perfetti, eds. 1991. *Learning to read: Basic research and its implications.* Hillsdale, N.J.: Lawrence Erlbaum.

Rogers, Alan. 1992. *Adults learning for development.* New York: Cassell Educational Limited.

Rosenblatt, L. M. 1989. Writing and reading: The transactional theory. In J. A. Mason (ed.), *Reading and writing connections,* 153–176. Boston: Allyn and Bacon.

References

Rosengren, D. 1987. *In the eyes of the beholder: Leadership and the social construction of power and dominance among the Matsigenka of the Peruvian Amazon.* Etnologiska Sudier 39, Goetborg, Sweden: Goteborgs Etnografiska Museum.

Ross, J. A. 1979. Language and the mobilization of ethnic identity. In Howard Giles and Bernard Saint-Jacques (eds.), *Language and ethnic relations,* 1–13. New York: Pergamon Press.

Rummenhoeller, K., and Lazarte Velarde. 1990. Comunidades indígenas de Madre de Dios (Perú): Un enfoque de la realidad educativa. *América Indígena* 50(4):159–192.

Samuels, S. J., and D. LaBerge. 1983. A critique of a theory of automaticity in reading. Looking back: A retrospective analysis of the LaBerge-Samuels reading model. In L. Gentile, M. Kamil, and J. Blanchard (eds.), *Reading research revisited,* 39–55. Westerville, Ohio: Merrill.

Samuels, S. Jay, N. Schermer, and D Reinking. 1992. Reading fluency; Techniques for making decoding automatic. In S. Jay Samuels and Alan E. Farstrup (eds.), *What research has to say about reading instruction,* 124–144. Newark, Del.: International Reading Association.

Sanford, A.J., and S. C. Garrod. 1981. *Understanding written language: Explorations of comprehension beyond the sentence.* New York: John Wiley and Sons.

Santeusanio, R. P. 1983. *A practical approach to content area reading.* Reading, Mass.: Addison-Wesley.

Schallert, D. L., and S. C. Vaughan. 1979. Author and reading: The communication connection. In J. L. Vaughan, Jr. and P. L. Anders (eds.), *Research on reading in secondary schools 4,* 49–56. Tucson: University of Arizona.

Schieffelin, B. and M. Cochran-Smith. 1984. Learning to read culturally: Literacy before schooling. In H. Geolman, A. Oberg, and F. Smith (eds.), *Awakening to literacy,* 3–23. Exeter, N.H.: Heinemann.

Schieffelin, B., and P. Gilmore, eds. 1986. *The acquisition of literacy: Ethnographic perspectives.* Advances in Discourse Processes 21. Norwood, N.J.: Ablex.

Scribner, S. 1988. Literacy in three metaphors. In E. R. Kintgen, B. M. Kroll, and M. Rose (eds.), *Perspectives on literacy,* 71–81. Carbondale: Southern Illinois University Press.

Scribner, S., and M. Cole. 1981. *The psychology of literacy.* Cambridge, Mass.: Harvard University Press.

Sebastián Santoval, Juan. 1983. [School report.] Unpublished raw data. In author's files.

Shell, O. A. 1981. The training of bilingual teachers. In Larson and Davis, 87–108.

Smalley, W.A. 1963. How shall I write this language? In W. A. Smalley (ed.), *Orthography studies,* 31–52. Amsterdam: North-Holland Publishing Company.

Smith, E. C. 1950. *The story of our names.* New York: Harper.

Smith, F. 1975. *Comprehension and learning: A conceptual framework for teachers.* New York: Holt, Rinehart, and Winston.

Snell, W. W. 1964. *Kinship relations in Machiguenga.* Masters thesis. The Hartford Seminary Foundation, Hartford, Conn.

Soifer, R., M. Irwin, B. Crumrine, E. Honzaki, B. Simmons, and D. Young. 1990. In D. Strickland and C. Genishi (eds.), *The complete theory-to-practice handbook of adult literacy: Curriculum design and teaching approaches,* 11 Language and Literacy Series. Columbia University, New York: Teachers College Press.

Solomon, R. P. 1992. *Black resistance in school: Forging a separatist culture.* Albany: State University of New York Press.

Spindler, G. D, and L. Spindler. 1971. *Dreamers without power: The Menomini Indians.* New York: Holt, Rinehart, and Winston.

Spolsky, B., G. Engelbrecht, and L. Ortiz. 1983. Religious, political and educational factors in the development of biliteracy in the Kingdom of Tonga. *Journal of Multilingual and Multicultural Development* 4:459–469.

Spolsky, B., ed. 1986. *Language and education in multilingual settings.* Avon, England: Multilingual Matters.

Stahl, S. A., and P. D. Miller. 1989. Whole language and language experience approaches for reading: A quantitative research synthesis. *Review of Educational Research* 59(1):87–116.

Stanovich, K. E. 1980. Toward an interactive-compensatory model of individual differences in the development of reading fluency. *Reading Research Quarterly* 16:32–71.

Stanovich, K. E. 1986. Matthew effects in reading: Some consequences of individual differences in the acquisition of literacy. *Reading Research Quarterly* 21:360–407.

Stanovich, K. E. 1991a. Word recognition: Changing perspectives. In R. Barr, M. L. Kamil, P. B. Mosenthal, and P. D. Pearson, Vol. 2, 418–452.

Stanovich, K. E. 1991b. Changing models of reading and reading acquisition. In L. Rieben and C. A. Perfetti, 19–32.

Stayter, F. Z., and R. L. Allington. 1991. Fluency and the understanding of texts. *Theory into Practice* 30(3):143–148.

Sticht, T. 1991. *The intergenerational issues: Transfer of cognitive skill, Vol. 1.* J. Orasanu (ed.), Programs, policies, and research. Norwood, N.J.: Ablex.

Sticht, T. G., and Barbara A. McDonald. 1992. In S. Jay Samuels and Alan E. Farstrup (eds.), *What research has to say about reading instruction,* 314–334. Newark, Del.: International Reading Association.

Street, B. V. 1984. *Literacy in theory and practice.* Cambridge: Cambridge University Press.

Street, B. V. 1987. Literacy and social change: The significance of social context in the development of literacy programmes. In D. A. Wagner, 48–64.

Street, B. V., ed. 1993. *Cross-cultural approaches to literacy.* Cambridge: Cambridge University Press.

Stringer, M., and N. Faraclas. 1987. *Working together for literacy: A guidebook for local language literacy programs.* Wewak, Papua New Guinea: Christian Books Melanesia.

Stromquist, Nellie P. 1989. Determinants of educational participation and achievement of women in the Third World: A review of the evidence and a theoretical critique. *Review of Educational Research* 59(2):143–183.

Stromquist, N. P. 1990. Women and illiteracy: The interplay of gender subordination and poverty. *Comparative Education Review* 34(1):95–111.

Stubbs, M. 1980. The state of the art and some definitions. *Language and literacy: The sociolinguistics of reading and writing,* 3–18. London: Routledge and Kegan Paul.

Taylor, B., L. A. Harris, and P. D. Pearson. 1988. *Reading difficulties: Instruction and assessment.* New York: Random House.

Taylor, Maurice C., and James A. Draper. 1989. *Adult literacy perspectives.* Toronto, Ont.: Culture Concepts.

Thomas, D. M. 1990. Why the 'Gudschinsky Method'? *Notes on Literacy* 63:55–59.

Thomas, H. 1974. Literacy without formal education: A case study in Pakistan. *Economic Development and Cultural Change* 22:489–495.

Thomas, Wayne P., and Virginia Collier. 1997. *School effectiveness for language minority students.* NCBE Resource Collection Series. Washington, D.C.: National Clearing House for Bilingual Education.

Thorndike, E. L. 1917. Reading as reasoning: A study of mistakes in paragraph reading. *Journal of Educational Psychology* 8:323–332.

Tierney, R. J., and P. D. Pearson 1981. Learning to learn from text: a framework for improving classroom practice. (ERIC Document Reproduction Service No. ED 205 917.)

Tippett, A. 1987. *Introduction to missiology.* Pasadena, Calif.: William Carey Library.

Trudell, B. 1993. *Beyond the bilingual classroom: Literacy acquisition among Peruvian Amazon communities.* Summer Institute of Linguistics and the University of Texas at Arlington Publications in Linguistics 117. Dallas.

Turner, Charles V. 1966. Culture change and the Sinasina church. *Practical Anthropology* 13:103–106.

UNESCO. 1953a. African languages and English in education. *Education Studies and Documents* 11. Paris: UNESCO.

UNESCO. 1953b. *Progress of literacy in various countries.* Paris: UNESCO.

UNESCO. 1957. *World illiteracy at mid-century.* Paris: UNESCO.

UNESCO. 1963a. *Simple reading material for adults: Its preparation and use.* Paris: UNESCO.

UNESCO. 1963b. *World Campaign for universal literacy.* UNESCO document E/3771. New York: UNESCO.

UNESCO. 1965. *World conference of Ministers of Education on the eradication of illiteracy. Final report.* Paris: UNESCO.

UNESCO. 1971. *Statistical yearbook.* Paris: UNESCO.

UNESCO. 1976. *The experimental world literacy programme: A critical assessment.* Paris: UNESCO.

UNESCO. June 1983. *Qu'est-ce que: l'alphabetisation.* Paris: UNESCO.

UNESCO. March 5–9 1990. *World declaration on education for all and Framework for action to meet basic learning needs,* Jomtien, Thailand, World Conference on Education for All. Paris: UNESCO.

UNESCO. 1993a. *Education for all: Status and trends.* Paris: UNESCO.

UNESCO. December 1993b. *Education for all.* EFA 2000, Special Bulletin. Focus: Education for all summit, 13–16 December 1993, New Delhi: Paris: UNESCO.

UNESCO. January–March 1994. *Targeting the poor.* EFA Bulletin No. 14, 7–10. Paris: UNESCO.

U.S. Office of Education. 1977. *Final report: the adult performance level study.* Washington, D.C.: Department of Health, Education, and Welfare.

Varese, S. 1985. Cultural development in ethnic groups: Anthropological explorations in education. *International Social Science Journal* 37:201–216.

Venezky, R. L. 1990. Definitions of literacy. In R. L. Venezky, D. A. Wagner, and B. S. Ciliberti (eds.), *Toward defining literacy,* 2–16. Newark, Del.: International Reading Association.

Vygotsky, L. S. 1962. *Thought and language.* Cambridge, Mass.: MIT Press.

Vygotsky, L. S. 1978. *Mind in society: The development of higher psychological processes.* M. Cole, V. John-Steiner, S. Scribner, and E. Souberman (eds. and trans.). Cambridge: Harvard University Press.

Wagner, D. A. 1986. When literacy isn't reading (and vice versa). In M. E. Wrolstad and D. F. Fisher (eds.), *Toward a new understanding of literacy,* 319–331. New York: Praeger.

Wagner, D. A., ed. 1987. *The future of literacy in a changing world.* Elmsford, N.Y.: Pergamon.

Wagner, D. A. 1993. *Literacy, Culture, and Development: Becoming literate in Morocco.* Cambridge: Cambridge University Press.

Walker, Roland. 1987. *Towards a model for predicting the acceptance of vernacular literacy by minority-language groups.* Doctoral dissertation. University of California at Los Angeles.

Walker, W. 1981. Native American writing systems. In C. A. Ferguson and S. B. Heath (eds.), *Language in the USA,* 145–174 Cambridge: Cambridge University Press.

Wallace, A. F. C. 1956. Revitalization movements. *American Anthropologist* 58:264–281.

Watters, J. 1990. Mass literacy programs. *Notes on Literacy* 61:49–54.

Weaver, W. W. 1977. The word as the unit of language. In A. J. Kingston (ed.), *Toward a psychology of reading and language: Selected writings of Wendell W. Weaver,* 34–40. Athens: The University of Georgia Press.

Weber, Diana. October 1994. Mother-tongue education for speakers of Quechua. In P. Cole, G. Hermon, and M. D. Martin (eds.), *Language in the Andes,* 90–115. Newark, Del.: Latin American Studies Department, University of Delaware.

Weiderholt, J. L., and B. R. Bryant 1987. *Assessing the reading abilities and instructional needs of students.* Austin, Tex.: Pro-Ed.

Wendell, M. M. 1982. *Bootstrap literature: Preliterate societies do it themselves.* Newark, Del.: International Reading Association.

Winchester, I. 1990. The standard picture of literacy and its critics. *Comparative Education Review* 34(1):21–40.

Wise, M. R., and Riggle, E. 1981. Mathematical terminology and instruction in basic mathematical concepts among ethnic groups of the Peruvian Amazon. *Revista Peruana de Lenguas Indoamericanas* 1(1):21–38.

Wise, M. R., and A. Shanks. 1977. *Bibliografía del Instituto Lingüístico de Verano en el Perú, 1946–1976* and *Bibliografía del Instituto Lingüístico de Verano Suplemento: enero de 1977 a agosto de 1981.* Yarinacocha, Peru: Instituto Lingüístico de Verano.

Zarzar, A. 1985. The political dimension of intertribal relations: An ethno-historical approach. In J. Hemming (ed.), *Change in the Amazon*

Basin, Volume II: The frontier after a decade of colonization, 216–227. Manchester: Manchester University Press.

Zutell, J., and T. V. Rasinski. 1991. Training teachers to attend to their students' oral reading fluency. *Theory into Practice* 30(3):211–227.

SIL International
Publications in Language Use and Education

2. "And I, in My Turn, Will Pass It On": Knowledge Transmission among the Kayopó, by Isabel I. Murphy, 2004.
3. *Namel Manmeri* 'The In-Between People': Language and Culture Maintenance and Mother-Tongue Education in the Highlands of Papua New Guinea, by Dennis L. Malone, forthcoming in 2004.
4. **Language Contact and Composite Structures in New Ireland,** by Rebecca Sue Jenkins, forthcoming in 2004.

Publications in Sociolinguistics

8. **Borrowing Versus Code-Switching in West Tarangan (Indonesia),** by Richard J. Nivens, 2002.
7. **The Dynamics of Sango Language Spread,** by Mark E. Karan, 2001.
6. **K'iche': A Study in the Sociology of Language,** by M. Paul Lweis, 2001.
5. **The Same but Different: Language Use and Attitudes in Four Communities of Burkina Faso,** by Stuart Showalter, 2000.
4. **Ashéninka Stories of Change,** by Ronald James Anderson, 2000.
3. **Assessing Ethnolinguistic Vitality: Theory and Practice,** M. Paul Lewis and Gloria Kindell, eds., 1999.
2. **The Early Days of Sociolinguistics: Memories and Reflections,** Christina Bratt Paulston and G. Richard Tucker, eds., 1997.
1. **North Sulawesi Language Survey,** Scott Merrifield and Martinus Selsa, 1996.

For further information or a full listing of SIL publications contact:

International Academic Bookstore
SIL International
7500 W. Camp Wisdom Road
Dallas, TX 75236-5699

Voice: 972-708-7404
Fax: 972-708-7363
Email: academic.books@sil.org
Internet: http://www.ethnologue.com

www.ingramcontent.com/pod-product-compliance
Lightning Source LLC
Chambersburg PA
CBHW052145300426
44115CB00011B/1521